Anorexia Nervosa and Family Therapy in a Chinese Context

Joyce L. C. Ma

The Chinese University Press

Anorexia Nervosa and Family Therapy in a Chinese Context
by Joyce L. C. Ma

© **The Chinese University of Hong Kong** 2011

ISBN 978-962-996-460-3

The Chinese University Press
The Chinese University of Hong Kong
Sha Tin, N.T., Hong Kong
Fax: +852 2603 6692
    +852 2603 7355
E-mail: cup@cuhk.edu.hk
Web-site: www.chineseupress.com

Printed in Hong Kong

Text layout by Tony Tang, Twin Age Limited
e-mail: twinage@netvigator.com

TABLE OF CONTENTS

Acknowledgments

Over the past 10 years, I have carried out cross-disciplinary practice research titled "Evaluation of the Effectiveness of Structural Family Therapy for Chinese Patients Suffering from Anorexia Nervosa in Hong Kong" together with two colleagues, Prof. K. Lai and Prof. S. Lee, both of the Department of Psychiatry of The Chinese University of Hong Kong. I thank the Hong Kong Research Grants Council for financial support (CUHK: 4090/99H).

I have felt an increasing urge to share my clinical experiences in working with young people suffering from anorexia nervosa with mental health professionals, both in my homeland and abroad. This book would not have been possible without the contributions of my two collaborators, Prof. K. Lai and Prof. S. Lee, who have referred most of the patients and their families for family treatment and provided psychiatric treatment.

I am indebted to Prof. K. Lai for contributing chapter 2. This important chapter gives readers an overview of the diagnostic criteria, symptoms, etiologies, and management of anorexia nervosa.

I also thank the mental health care team of the Department of Child Psychiatry, Tai Po Ho Mui Ling Nethersole Hospital. They have given me professional support and timely access to their service when patients were in urgent need of hospitalization. I am grateful to helping professionals in the community for their referrals, especially Miss Wong Chi Kan and Mr. Tse Sui Kwong, supervisors of the Community Social Work Service of Caritas–Hong Kong.

Gratitude goes to the emaciated young people and families who have participated actively in treatment and research. I am privileged to have had the opportunity to help them and to witness their recovery. I appreciate their perseverance, courage, and resilience, as they struggle through the pain and suffering and subsequently recover. I have learned immensely from them.

Thank to the two anonymous reviewers of The Chinese University Press and also my best friend, Miss Lily Yau; they have helped me in reading and giving me invaluable comments on the first, second, and the final drafts of this book. My three postgraduate students, Dr. Zenobia Chan, Dr. Long Di, and Miss Erica Wan, have been cotherapists as well as the members of our observation team during treatment. We had fruitful discussions at the end of each treatment session, and they provided me with alternative lenses to understand the young persons and their families. Zenobia also helped to conduct the pre- and posttreatment interviews. I am also grateful to a team of master's degree students in social work to help transcribe verbatim the pre- and posttreatment interviews.

I thank my husband, Lai Chi Man, for his endless support, occasional intellectual challenges, thoughtful arrangement of an overseas writing trip, and unconditional love and care. I want to thank my daughter and son, Lok Yin and Long Chung, whose company and achievement have filled my heart with grace and have helped me to concentrate on this demanding project.

Preface

When I started to work with young people diagnosed with anorexia nervosa (AN), I was absolutely aghast at their pain and suffering, their ambivalence toward change and recovery, the helplessness and hopelessness of their parents, and, frankly, the therapist's inability to help. A sense of professional incompetence was the force that propelled me onto the path of research over the past years. Driven by academic and professional curiosity, I decided to collaborate with two colleagues at the university, Prof. K. Lai and Prof. S. Lee of the Department of Psychiatry, to set up a family-based treatment and research project in December 1999. This project aims to develop a culturally specific, socially relevant, and clinically useful family treatment model for Chinese patients suffering from AN and to assess its applicability and helpfulness.

It is extremely important for a family therapist to look beyond the symptoms of the disorder, to understand the person and the interpersonal context in which the person is embedded. I have learned tremendously from the patients' journey of healing. From what I have learned, I have developed an urge to share their healing stories with mental health professionals including family therapists in my homeland and elsewhere. I do not wish for these professionals to repeat my past mistakes. I have learned to value and trust the ability of the patient and the family in utilizing their strengths to drive away the disorder. Ultimately the patients and their families suffer less when they meet a family therapist with genuine care and concern, professional competence, and confidence in helping.

Helping is like two travelers meeting each other at a crossroads in life. Although suffering is personal and highly subjective and a helper can be as helpless and impotent as the sufferer, any lonely traveler is consoled and supported by the presence and support of another. In family therapy, the therapist creates a therapeutic context in which family members gradually become the best companions and healers for the sufferer.

Chapter 1
Introduction

INTRODUCTION

Anorexia nervosa (AN) is a mental disorder predominantly afflicting females. Sufferers chose to engage in excessive dieting and excessive exercise even though they are extremely thin, with serious consequences on health, psychological well-being, schooling, and family and peer relationships. Gaining weight is a terrifying experience for the sufferers (Treasure, 1997), and resistance to change and recovery is great (Ward, Troop, Todd, & Treasure, 1996). The etiology of the disorder involves physical, psychological, and sociocultural factors. Without proper treatment, the mortality rate caused by heart problems or suicide is around 20% (American Psychiatric Association [APA], 2000).

Since its discovery, AN has been regarded as a complex disorder closely related to issues of growing up arising from the interplay between an individual child and the immediate social context. Unsurprisingly, drug treatment alone is ineffective. Although restoration of body weight through resumption of normal meals is fundamental to recovery, helping young people to deal with their developmental issue is extremely important.

AN is a family experience as well as an individual experience. Due to the significant contributions of master family therapists in the West, such as Selvini Palazzoli (1986) and Salvador Minuchin (Minuchin, Rosman, & Baker, 1978), dysfunctional family interaction and family dynamics are now known to be associated with the development and maintenance of the disorder. Nevertheless, the dysfunctional family context can be a consequence of the disorder rather than a cause (Eisler, 2005). The onset of AN inevitably induces a family crisis and demands the afflicted family to change in order to drive away the illness. The change can be functional or dysfunctional. A functional change will help the family to face challenges and difficulties of caring and ultimately will assist the young person in fighting the disorder, while a dysfunctional change will aggravate the existing stresses and hinder recovery. The family's success in coping with this crisis will depend heavily on family resilience, which comprises family belief systems, organizational patterns, and communication processes (Walsh, 1998).

Clinical experiences and the results of clinical research in the United Kingdom have shown that family therapy is effective for emaciated adolescents aged 18 or younger with an illness history of less than 3 years (Dare, Eisler, Russell, & Szmukler, 1990; Russell, Dare, Eisler, & Le Grange, 1992). Although family therapy has become a standardized care modality for emaciated young people in Western treatment centers such as the Maudsley Hospital in London, it is not a standard treatment protocol in Asia. Psychiatric service for children and adolescents in our homeland is still heavily based on the biomedical model, with the emphasis on diagnosis followed by prescription of medication. It remains unknown whether family therapy is applicable in helping the emaciated young people to recover or whether mental health professionals know, in the eyes of the afflicted and families, which aspects of treatment are therapeutic and facilitative to their healing and which components are not.

The diagnosis of AN has provided a universal tool and a scientific language for mental health professionals in symptom identification, in communication with patients, families, and significant others, and in the management and delineation of timely and appropriate care for the patients. While appreciating the contributions of the *DSM-IV* classification (APA, 1994) in psychiatric assessment and psychiatric management, mental health professionals including family therapists must not overlook its inadequacies in understanding the patients' subjective experience of the illness and their journey of recovery. Past Western studies (Beresin, Gordon, & Herzog, 1989; D'Abundo & Chally, 2004; Tozzi, Sullivan, Fear, McKenzie, & Bulik, 2003; Weaver, Wuest, & Ciliska, 2005) have shown the importance of listening to patients' accounts of their illness and understanding their subjective experience in recovery. Although AN has aroused academic and professional interest in recent years, there have been insufficient efforts to explore the interplay between the universality as well as the particularity, in this instance in terms of Chinese culture and of the sufferers' experiences of the disorder. In view of this knowledge gap, an attempt is made to unveil the mystery of AN by seeing the person and family behind the diagnosis and by contextualizing the disorder in a society where cultural forces collide and values are shifting quickly. The primary concerns are the interactions between the young person and her family and the linkage of the entangled relationships to the wider sociocultural context rather than the disorder itself.

This book describes the diversity and variability of the emaciated young people with whom the therapist has intensively worked. They have received the same diagnosis as their Western counterparts, but due to differences in their interpersonal contexts their subjective experiences in different stages of the disorder have idiosyncrasies and uniqueness. These young people and families told their stories and unveiled their family dramas, using their own language and perspectives. Readers will witness their battles with the disorder and their journeys of recovery in different case vignettes. Hopefully, in hearing their voices, mental health professionals and therapists will begin to appreciate them as individuals with different characteristics, facing varied stresses and tensions in a rapidly changing and transforming society.

SYSTEMIC UNDERSTANDING OF THE DISORDER

Different psychotherapy models that have evolved for AN are based on different explanatory models of the disorder (Eisler, 2005). The author's theoretical perspective has been strongly influenced by the ecological systemic theory proposed by Bronfenbrenner (1989) who views growth and development of human beings as a process of continued reciprocal and dynamic interaction of different systems at multiple levels: the microsystem (e.g., family, school, or peers), the mesosystem (e.g., interrelationship among the family, school, and peers), the exosystem (e.g., community facilities, health and social service provision), and the macrosystem (e.g., cultural values and beliefs, economic development of the society). The development and maintenance of AN is embedded in multiple systems ranging from the patient's physiological system to the family, the school, the mass media, and the standard of beauty prevalent in society (Churven, 2008). While recognizing an individual as an active being capable of shaping his or her environment, the social context has a tremendous impact on individual behaviors.

Like an onion with many layers, AN is not simply food refusal but is about the growing up of a young person and her entangled relationships in a constrained familial and sociocultural context. Nevertheless, professional assessment of the young person and her family situation is by no means objective and value free. It is impossible for the therapist to describe and understand the therapeutic situation without including himself or herself as part of the observing system (Elkaim, 1997). A therapist with his or her own personal history and professional training would select what to observe and how to observe it; hence, professional assessment is not a matter of truth but a discovery of the mutual construction of reality among the therapist, the patient, and her family.

CULTURE AND GENDER LENSES

Culture and gender perspectives, though originating from different academic disciplines, do share the same belief of contextualizing people's behaviors and experiences within the immediate sociocultural context. In light of the cultural perspective, a family therapist can go beyond the systemic framework to understand the cultural meaning of the seemingly bizarre and unintelligible beliefs and behaviors at multiple levels: individual, family, and society.

This project has prompted the author to research the standard of beauty and its changes through different dynastic periods in ancient China and to read widely on foot binding (Wang, 2000). The association between foot binding and AN is by no means a coincidence; both reflect the societal standard of beauty in a historical and social context.

In traditional Chinese society, a soft, tender young woman with a tiny waist and "three-inch lotus feet" was highly cherished and honored by the fetishistic emperors, feudal lords, the gentry, and rich merchants, which explains why the cruel Chinese mother would force her little daughter to bind her feet before adolescence (Ko, 2001). It also explains why women with tiny feet were so proud of their deformities despite great suffering in childhood and a permanent disability and handicap in life. When examined against the current norms of beauty and culture, the obsession of AN sufferers with dieting, vomiting, and excessive exercise has illuminated the same cultural heritage: The societal standard of beauty, which equates thinness and fragility with beauty, has become women's lifelong chain of suffering.

The gender perspective has supplemented the cultural perspective to deconstruct this cultural chain by examining the imbalance of power between men and women that is embedded in a patriarchal society (Luepnitz, 1988), the gendered division of labor in the family, the feminine mystique in society (Friedan, 1963), and a shift in societal expectations toward woman's roles and status in modern society (MacSween, 1993).

These two additional lenses have enlarged the therapist's professional horizon and enriched systems theory, the underlying theoretical framework of family therapy.

FAMILY THERAPY

Family is a significant socialization agent in society and is also a principal source of emotional support, nurturing, and care for young people. There is no reason to exclude the family in the care of the emaciated young person. Family therapy is an approach in treating human problems by bringing family members together to tap their resources for resolution of their difficulties (Nichols & Schwartz, 2007). It assumes that change in a family context and its larger systems can bring about changes to individual behaviors, which is in line with the philosophical assumptions of the ecological systems perspective.

Family therapy is not a unitary approach. Among various family treatment approaches in the West, the Maudsley approach has been increasingly adopted for use in Australia (Rhodes, 2003) and the United States (Lock, Le Grange, Agras, & Dare, 2001) because it is evidence based (Dare et al., 1990; Russell et al., 1992) and has already been manualized (Lock et al., 2001) for wider dissemination. The Maudsley approach was developed from Minuchin's model (Minuchin et al., 1978) with emphasis on a more collaborative process between the parents and the child in combating the externalized enemy, the anorexia.

While appreciating the significant contribution of the Maudsley approach in helping, the therapist's training and orientation have guided the selection of a treatment model developed by Micucci (1998). Fundamental to a helper is his or her degree of mastery of the helping approach and the use of the self in a creative and spontaneous manner. The strength of this model lies in directly dealing with family politics evolving from the disorder, which is so central in these families (Churven, 2008). Family therapists often fail to recognize the power and control issues between the young person and her parents, a prominent feature of family politics that has recurrently emerged from the young people's stories. Family politics has consumed much of the young person's and the family's energy and time and constrained their options and possibilities in coping.

Micucci trained at a structural family therapy school and practiced at the Philadelphia Child Guidance Clinic in the United States. He expanded Minuchin's model (Minuchin et al., 1978) by integrating the feminist's lens and incorporating the techniques developed by White (1983), such as externalization. In view of the characteristics of Chinese families, the therapist has modified the model by adopting three essential Chinese cultural concepts, namely, family (*jia*), face (*mianzi*), and filial piety (*xiao*), in family assessment and treatment; the details are discussed in chapter 4.

A few sufferers described in this book came from low-income families with multiple problems. The onset of the disorder has compounded their family distress. In order to respond to the multiple service needs of these families, the therapist has to join hands with community-based social workers to help resolve their difficulties, in addition to tackling problems and stresses rising directly from the disorder.

THERAPEUTIC RELATIONSHIP

As she was trained as a family therapist, the therapist's professional concern is primarily to help family members and the emaciated young person to combat the disorder, specifically to restore body weight and to continue to develop physically, psychologically, and socially. Contrary to expectations, the therapist's effort was met with repeated resistance, hostility, and rejection from the young person. Subsequently, a few patients dropped out from treatment, which led the therapist to critically review and examine her practice.

Individual work is an integral part of family treatment (Eisler, 1995; Fishman, 1996). The therapeutic relationship has been shown to be one of the common factors accounting for treatment success (Sprenkle & Blow, 2004). Recovery and healing are personal ordeals, and it would be futile to collaborate only with the parents, even if leading to superficial success, if the therapist failed to motivate and engage the young person to take care of her own health. The therapist faces the great challenge of having to win the trust of the young person, then working on her ambivalence toward change and recovery and successfully engaging her in treatment. The crux of the therapy is in effecting change, achieved through whichever therapeutic paths are possible at the individual, interpersonal, family, and societal levels. In view of the importance of developing rapport with the emaciated young person and motivating her to assume responsibility for recovery, two chapters (chapter 6 and part of chapter 7) in this book describe effective ways to develop therapeutic relationships with them and increase their level of motivation for treatment.

RISK ASSESSMENT AND CLINICAL MANAGEMENT

The life-threatening nature of AN is a huge challenge in clinical management. The sudden and drastic drop of body weight requires an efficient and effective professional decision to hospitalize the patient as soon as possible, often against the fierce resistance of the patient and her parents. A responsible therapist must have the courage and competence to deal with the health crisis and to take sensible and decisive action when needed to save the emaciated young person's life. Chapter 7 introduces a framework for risk assessment and clinical management.

USE OF LANGUAGE

Language is a medium to express a perception of reality and of the world. In this book, the pronoun *she* rather than *he* is consistently used to represent the emaciated young person because eating disorders affect adolescent girls and young adult women much more, with 90% to 95% of cases occurring in females (APA, 1994).

Although all of these young people and families gave written consent to participate in this project, it is our obligation to protect their privacy and confidentiality. All the names used in this book are pseudonyms; parts of the specifics of their family background and their personal information were modified without changing the essential elements.

CONTENTS OF THE BOOK

This book comprises 12 chapters, all written by the author, except for chapter 2, contributed by Prof. K. Lai. The book is divided into four parts.

Part I (chapter 2) presents the medical aspects of the disorder, including its nature, etiology, and overall management. Prof. Lai introduces an integrative perspective to account for the disorder and its management.

There are five chapters in Part II. Chapter 3 elaborates upon the four theoretical perspectives selected, namely the psychoanalytical perspective, the family perspective, the sociocultural perspective, and the feminist perspective. These four perspectives together provide the theoretical background to the treatment model, namely Micucci's (1998) model, which the therapist has adapted for use.

The family treatment model is described in chapters 4 and 5, with chapter 4 describing the characteristics of the treatment model and chapter 5 listing important tasks and roles undertaken by the therapist in different stages of treatment. Chapter 6 discusses the difficulties that the therapist has met in relating to the emaciated young people and proposes ways of developing rapport with them. In chapter 7, a risk assessment framework is proposed to deal with the health crisis arising from the sudden and drastic drop in body weight and the devastating effects on physical well-being.

Part III (chapters 8, 9, and 10) describes the therapeutic encounter and the journey of healing for three families. The three case vignettes shed light on treatment with families with different family shapes, family histories, and resources: an extended family, *jia*, a nuclear family, and a multiproblem family. Besides, each of these three families was chosen for a different reason. The case presented in chapter 9 illustrates the contribution of a family therapist to managing the disorder in a multidisciplinary team in a hospital, including psychiatrists, psychologists, social workers, psychiatric nurses, and a hospital-based teacher. The case presented in chapter 10 indicates the need of the family therapist to collaborate and cooperate with social workers in the community so that services are provided and resources mobilized to meet the service needs of a multiproblem family.

Part IV addresses the perceived treatment effectiveness and treatment efficacy of family therapy. Chapter 11 reports on the results of a qualitative posttreatment study on the perceived treatment effectiveness of family therapy in the perspective of the emaciated young people and their families, while in chapter 12 the views of the families and the therapist on treatment efficacy of family therapy are stated.

Last, if readers wish to learn more about the pain and sufferings of the emaciated Chinese young person and the family under the therapist's care, they can read appendices 1 and 2.

Part I

Anorexia Nervosa

Chapter 2
Medical Aspects of Anorexia Nervosa (written by K. Lai)

INTRODUCTION

Anorexia nervosa (AN) is a serious and protracted illness that is associated with high rates of morbidities and mortality. While typically affecting adolescent girls and young women, cases involving even younger children, including boys, are now drawing clinical attention (Fosson, Knibbs Bryant-Waugh, & Lask, 1987; Lask & Bryant-Waugh, 2000). Once thought to be culture bound, affecting only females from higher social classes in the West, AN has now been reported in non-Western societies, such as Hong Kong (Lai, 2000; Lee, Ho, & Hsu, 1993), Japan (Nakamura et al., 2000), India (Srinivasan, Suresh, & Jayaram, 1998), and the Middle East (Abou-Saleh, Younis, & Karim, 1998; Nobakht & Dezhkam, 2000). Patients across different socioeconomic strata are affected. The illness has therefore affected a much wider population and is of concern to health professionals in many parts of the world.

Conceptualizations of the cause of the disorder have, over the years, swung dramatically from the psychosocial to the biological. For a long time, AN was considered an illness with primarily a social and cultural etiology: an extreme manifestation of societies' obsessions with a slim body ideal. During the 1990s, gender issues emerged, with discussions about women's position in society and their struggles. The past decade, however, saw a shift in the pendulum, as genetic and family studies revealed convincingly an underlying genetic influence, renewing interest in research on the biological aspects of the illness.

The current understanding is that AN is a heterogeneous illness involving dynamic interactions between genetic and environmental influences. Because its onset typically peaks in adolescence and young adulthood, a developmental perspective needs to be considered. This chapter provides an overview of the medical aspects of the disorder, with a particular emphasis on children and adolescents, especially in the Chinese context, where data are available.

Diagnosis

According to two commonly used diagnostic systems—the fourth edition of the *Diagnostic and Statistical Manual of Mental Disorders* (*DSM-IV*; American Psychiatric Association, 1994), and the tenth edition of the *International Classification of Diseases* (*ICD-10*; World Health Organization, 1993)—the diagnosis is based on (a) a refusal to maintain a body weight at or above a minimally normal weight for age and height (which is suggested to be less than 85% of the expected weight according to *DSM-IV* and BMI less than 17.5 kg/m^2 in *ICD-10*), (b) a morbid fear of fatness, (c) disturbance in one's perception of body weight or shape or denial of the seriousness of one's current low body weight, and (d) secondary amenorrhoea. It is subtyped into (a) the restricting type and (b) the bingeing and purging type. In the former, weight loss is achieved primarily through dieting or excessive exercising; in the latter, the patient has regular binge eating and/or purging episodes through vomiting or laxative abuse.

Cardinal presentation of the illness is a severe and self-induced weight loss. Contrary to what the name suggests, patients do not suffer from a loss of appetite (anorexia), but they ignore their hunger and control their eating. Even at very low weights, they appear unconcerned, and some still consider themselves fat.

The patient's weight is primarily lost through severe dieting. The amount and range of food taken are drastically reduced, with an extreme avoidance of food considered by the patient to be "fattening," such as oil, carbohydrates, and meat. Food intake consists mainly of vegetables and fruits. Despite obvious weight loss, there may be additional weight-reducing behaviors such as excessive exercising, self-induced vomiting, laxative abuse, and excessive use of slimming agents. Yet they may also become preoccupied with food or with the preparation of elaborate meals that they will not eat. In a proportion of patients, bingeing episodes—defined as episodes of excessive intake, usually of carbohydrate-rich food—may be present. These are often secretive, associated with guilt and accompanied by vomiting or other purging behaviors. The result of these disturbed eating behaviors is a marked impairment in physical health. Hormonal balance is deranged, resulting in amenorrhoea in females, which is one of the diagnostic criteria. In some patients, menstruation stops before substantial weight is lost. There is a concomitant arrest in the development of secondary sexual characteristics.

The diagnosis also requires the presence of a distorted body image and an intense fear of fatness. Despite their low weight and emaciation, patients still perceive their overall body shape or parts of their body as "fat." They are very fearful of weight gain, sometimes checking their weight repeatedly and frequently, getting upset at tiny increases. They typically fail to grasp the severity of their problem and are not concerned about the consequences on their health.

Though these diagnostic criteria are widely accepted, their application is not without problems. First of all, the weight criterion poses particular problems for the younger age group. Because children are growing and developing, losing 15% or more of their weight or maintaining a weight that is below 85% of their ideal body weight is a much more serious situation than it is for young adults. The use of body mass index (BMI) can be equally misleading because BMIs change as children grow, and a BMI below 17.5 kg/m^2 may be within normal limits for certain ages (Hebebrand, Himmelmann, Heseker, Schäfer, & Remschmidt, 1996). Adhering strictly to this weight criterion may give a false picture of the situation. For this younger age group, the use of percentile charts for height, weight, and weight-for-height ratios may be more appropriate. Moreover, clinicians should also be alert to the possibility of AN when a child fails to gain weight (or height) and should not wait for the weight to drop substantially before confirming the diagnosis.

Second, the requirement of secondary amenorrhoea becomes irrelevant for boys and premenarcheal girls. Indeed, a delay in the onset of menstruation (or development of secondary sexual characteristics) may be a result of the eating problem and should cause concern in its own right.

Third, cross-cultural research has questioned the universality of "fear of fatness." Lee et al. (1993), in their examination of 70 Hong Kong adult Chinese women with the disorder in the 1980s, found that fewer than 50% reported a fear of fatness. Instead, reasons given for not eating included abdominal bloating, nausea, loss of appetite, and difficulty swallowing. On the other hand, in another case series reported by Lai (2000) of a group of 16 Hong Kong Chinese adolescents with the disorder in the 1990s, fear of fatness was present in 87%. Lai suggested that the difference between the two findings may be a reflection of the increased acceptance of the slim body ideal of the Western world among Chinese adolescents in the 1990s, so the pursuit of thinness became legitimized and presented as a justified reason for food refusal. Among younger children with AN, fear of fatness is also not universal (Fosson et al., 1987; Lask & Bryant-Waugh, 2000).

Epidemiology

Studies from Western countries have shown that about 10% of adolescents demonstrate disordered eating behaviors (Reijonen, Pratt, Patel, & Greydanus, 2003), and the prevalence of AN is estimated to be about 0.2% to 0.9% for young females (Hoek & van Hoeken, 2003). The incidence for males is a factor of 10 lower. The number of cases seen by medical professionals in the West has been on the rise (Hoek & van Hoeken, 2003), but whether this represents a genuine increase in the incidence rate is unclear. Studies in Hong Kong have also found that a desire to be thinner than one actually is is very common. In a survey of 357 adolescent female students between 15 and 21 years old, 85% wanted to weigh less, although only 4.8% were actually overweight (Fung & Yuen, 2003). To date, there has not been an epidemiological study to indicate the prevalence rate of the disorder in Hong Kong.

Physical Complications

The disordered eating behavior and the severe weight loss affect almost every body system. In the acute stage, patients look emaciated and dehydrated, their skin dry and sallow, their hair dry and thin. They are less tolerant of cold and often wear thick clothes even in hot weather. If their weight is very low, fine, downy lanugo hair may be present on their back and arms. Their palms and soles may have an orange discoloration, indicating some degree of liver dysfunction. Their hands and feet are cold and their pulse weak. Their heart rate and blood pressure may be dangerously low, and this may be associated with complaints of dizziness. Ankle swelling may be present. In severe cases, the heartbeat may become irregular, and heart failure and death may ensue. Muscle weakness may be evident, and patients may need substantial help in self-care and other daily tasks.

It is common for patients to complain of feeling bloated, even after eating a very small amount of food, to justify their inability to eat more. This bloating sensation is a result of delayed stomach emptying, which is a physiological response after a prolonged period of starvation. Resuming regular intake of a reasonable amount of food will gradually rectify the situation. Constipation is another common complaint and is partly the result of insufficient dietary intake. If there has been repeated vomiting, swelling of the parotid glands in the neck may be observed. Vomiting also runs the risk of esophageal tear, which may lead to severe bleeding and may prove fatal.

Laboratory investigations usually reveal a variety of abnormalities such as dehydration and electrolyte imbalance (noticeably low potassium level, low sodium level, and metabolic alkalosis due to repeated vomiting and purging), which can present with muscle weakness and seizures. Liver enzymes typically show some degree of derangement. Low blood sugar, mild iron-deficiency anemia, and low white blood cell count (and low immunity) are also common. Fortunately, many of these reverse with weight gain.

Hormonal disturbance includes a widespread suppression of the hypothalamic–pituitary–gonadal axis, leading to a derangement of sexual hormone balance and resulting in an arrest in secondary sexual development and amenorrhoea. Restoration of body weight does not immediately reverse the situation. The time when menses returns is variable but can be expected to occur only when weight and body composition have stabilized at their optimum levels. Serial pelvic ultrasound scans have been able to correlate the development of the ovaries with weight gain and predict the weight level at which menstruation is likely to return. Studies using this method found that attaining 95% or more of the "ideal body weight"—which is measured by the weight-for-height ratio in children and premorbid weight in adults—is associated with the return of menses (Key, Mason, Allan, & Lask, 2002; Lai, de Bruyn, Lask, Bryant-Waugh, & Hankins, 1994; Treasure, King, Gordon, Wheeler, & Russell, 1985).

Amenorrhoea, together with the derangement of other hormones, contributes to a loss of bone mass and the risk of osteoporosis. This process starts early in the illness—a period of amenorrhoea lasting 6 months or more can already lead to a significant reduction in bone density (Grinspoon et al., 2000). In a Hong Kong study involving 42 adults with a history of AN, the duration of illness and the lowest BMI also predicted a low bone mineral density (Wong et al., 2004). In the longer term, the risk of bone fractures is increased. The most effective way of ameliorating the situation is prompt weight restoration and return of menses. However, the loss may not be entirely reversible.

There are relatively fewer studies on the effect of self-starvation on body height. What data there are show that the onset, duration, and severity of illness all contribute to the final height that the adolescent attains (Lantzouni, Frank, Golden, & Shenker, 2002; Swenne & Thurfjell, 2003). Children whose illness has a prepubertal onset and was preceded by a long period of poor weight gain fare the worst and may never catch up with their expected height. Adolescents with onset after menarche appear to be the least affected, perhaps because these patients had already achieved their expected height by the time the illness started.

Radiological imaging of the brain has shown alterations in brain structures, most likely also as a result of starvation. There is widening of cortical sulci and enlargement of lateral ventricles. Though largely reversible with weight gain, persistence has been observed in some patients. Other studies have found a significant reduction in both gray and white matters even among those with a relatively short duration of illness. The significance of this is hitherto unclear (Zipfel, Lowe, & Herzog, 2003).

Psychiatric Morbidities

Patients with AN are at an increased risk of suffering from a range of additional psychiatric disorders, the most common of which are depression, anxiety, and obsessive-compulsive disorders (Lewinsohn, Striegel-Moore, & Seeley, 2000; Steinhausen, 1997). In Steinhausen's (1997) review of 31 follow-up studies involving 941 children and adolescents, an average of 21% suffered from affective disorder, 26% from anxiety disorders, and 12% from obsessive-compulsive disorder sometime during the follow-up period. These rates are at least double those in the general population and may precede, occur simultaneously as, or follow the onset of the eating disorder. However, the presence of these disorders is more likely only before the patients have recovered from AN (Herpertz-Dahlmann et al., 2001; Wentz, Gillberg, Gillberg, & Rastam, 2001).

Feeling depressed, irritable, and anxious is very common in the acute phase of the illness (Rastam, 1992; Smith, Feldman, Nasserbakht, & Steiner, 1993). This is in part due to the effects of starvation and caloric deprivation, which produce physiological and psychological symptoms that resemble a depressive episode. Typically the mood becomes increasingly depressed with weight loss and improves with weight gain. In a proportion of cases, however, depression and AN become intertwined. These young people present with a full range of depressive symptoms, including sleep disturbance, fatigue, social withdrawal, loss of interest and drive, loss of enjoyment in activities, pessimistic thoughts, and, when severe, suicidal tendencies. In a community study of Canadian adolescents with a range of eating disorders, approximately 50% suffered from a concurrent diagnosis of depressive disorder (Geist, Davis, & Heinman, 1998). Careful assessment and monitoring of the patient's mental state are therefore very important.

Family and twin studies have consistently confirmed a genetic link between depressive illness and AN (Mangweth et al., 2003; Wade, Bulik, Neale, & Kendler, 2000). Not only are depressive disorders more common among patients with AN, but also family members of the anorexic patient have an increased risk of developing a depressive disorder themselves.

The rate of anxiety disorders is similarly increased by the illness. Lifetime prevalence of anxiety disorders among patients with anorexic nervosa range from 33% to 72%, a figure that is 2 to 4 times that found in the community (Godart, Flament, Perdereau, & Jeammet, 2002; Kaye et al., 2004). Of the different types of anxiety disorders, obsessive-compulsive disorder is the most consistently increased. For many, it predates the onset of AN and involves themes unrelated to their eating pathology (Kaye et al., 2004; O'Brien & Vincent, 2003). Other anxiety disorders such as social phobia and generalized anxiety disorder are also overrepresented when compared to community populations. The presence of anxiety disorders has again been suggested to be genetically related and exacerbated by the development of eating pathologies (Kaye et al., 2004; Keel, Klump, Miller, McGue, & Iacono, 2005). Others suggest that caloric deprivation may also aggravate a preexisting tendency toward anxiety (O'Brien & Vincent, 2003; Pollice, Kaye, Greeno, & Weltzin, 1997). There is indeed a suggestion that anxiety and obsessiveness are persistent personality traits of patients with AN.

Etiology

AN is a complex, multifactorial illness where genetic, psychological, familial, and sociocultural influences predispose, precipitate, and maintain the illness. Because adolescence is the typical age of onset, a developmental perspective is essential. It is necessary to understand how these multiplicities of biological and psychosocial factors lead to the development of the illness at this particular stage of the adolescent's life. Once the physiological effects of starvation take hold, a range of physical and psychological responses are triggered that perpetuate the cycle of self-starvation.

Genetic factors. Genetic factors have a definite but complicated role. The illness clusters in families. Both family and twin studies confirm an eleven-fold increase in risk among female relatives of an anorexic patient. All of these observations support the hypothesis of a genetic component of the illness (Mangweth et al., 2003; Strober, Freeman, Lampert, Diamond, & Kaye, 2000; Wade et al., 2000).

Familial clustering is not limited to the illness itself, but some personality traits associated with AN also appear more often among female relatives than by chance, such as avoidant, dependent, perfectionistic, and obsessive-compulsive traits (Kaye et al., 2004; Lilenfield et al., 1998), again suggesting a genetic contribution.

The search for candidate genes is in its infancy, but existing data suggest a role for the serotonin-related genes, which regulate the level of the neurotransmitter serotonin in the central nervous system (Steiger, 2004). Other biological systems and genes are being examined, but the results have thus far been inconclusive (Klump & Gobrogge, 2005).

Psychological factors. Patients with AN are typically described as perfectionistic and obsessive and dominated by a sense of ineffectiveness and low self-esteem (Jacobi, Paul, de Zwaan, Nutzinger, & Dahme, 2004). Many psychological theories have been proposed to explain these observations, and these tend to converge on one common theme—the patients perceive a lack of control in their life, the need for which is displaced onto their eating behaviors (Surgenor, Horn, Plumridge, & Hudson, 2002). Bruch, from a psychodynamic perspective developed from Bowlby's attachment theory (Bowlby, 1969), described the anorectic to have failed to develop a sense of self, which has stemmed from the parents' failure to respond appropriately to the child's needs (Bruch, 1978). During adolescence, when the developmental task is to strive for autonomy and search for identity, the anorectic experiences "a paralysing sense of ineffectiveness" (Bruch, 1973, p. 254). Her subsequent "control" over her body and "success" with weight loss bring a feeling of achievement, which perpetuates the self-starvation cycle. In a similar vein, Crisp (1995) argued that the anorectic has failed to master the developmental tasks of adolescence and the illness allows the patient to "regress to a simpler existence, without the conflicts of growth, sexuality and personal independence" (p. 91). While these theories remain hypothetical, issues concerning control and personal effectiveness are indeed repeated themes in clinical encounters.

Family factors. Family dynamics have, for a long time, been considered to play a crucial role in the etiology. Famous family therapists such as Minuchin (1978) and Palazzoli (1978) have described characteristic patterns of interaction in families with an anorectic daughter. Minuchin described enmeshment, overprotection, rigidity, and lack of conflict resolution, while Palazzoli highlighted supreme loyalty and rigidity in family beliefs. It is clear that these are neither specific to the disorder nor invariably present in these families. Moreover, even in the presence of apparent family dysfunction, it cannot be assumed that the family is the cause of the problem. Having a family member with AN takes a heavy toll on the family. Clinical experience attests to the fact that families can be functional before the onset of the illness, but conflicts emerge while attempting to handle the illness. Nevertheless, the family context is important, and family dynamics may be very relevant predisposing and/or perpetuating forces. The painful effect the illness has on family relationships is very real and needs to be addressed in the course of treatment.

Sociocultural factors. A commonly cited predisposing factor for the development of the disorder is a society's endorsement of a thin body ideal. This has been used to explain the rising incidence among Westernizing cultures (Lee & Lee, 2000). In support of this notion is the recognition for a long time that those whose occupation or interests necessitate an emphasis on weight and shape, such as ballet dancers, gymnasts, and jockeys, are high-risk groups. The increasing concern among non-Western girls for their weight and shape and their desire to be thin are thought to be the result of the spread of Western culture and all that is encompassed by having a slim body.

Precipitating event. Against this array of background factors, precipitating events that trigger the onset of the eating problem are similarly varied. The illness could have started following a chance remark about the girl's weight or shape, or there could have been severe trauma such as sexual abuse (Schmidt, 2003). Such stresses are best conceptualized as general risk factors for psychiatric morbidity and not as specific to AN (Fairburn, Cooper, Doll, & Welch, 1999; Romans, Gendall, Martin, & Mullen, 2001). They further jeopardize a precarious psychological balance, accentuating the perceived lack of control, which is then displaced onto eating behaviors, weight, and shape (Surgenor et al., 2002).

Prognosis

AN typically runs a protracted course. Symptoms recover at different rates. Weight and physical recovery (which includes a return of menses) may not be accompanied by improvements in eating attitudes, mental status, or psychosocial functioning. In Steinhausen's (1997) review, an average of 50% of the child and adolescent patients followed up over varying periods of time achieved full recovery (which includes normal physical and psychosocial functioning), while improvement without full recovery was documented in less than a third and a fifth remained chronically ill. In general, improvements in eating disorder symptoms fared slightly better, with two thirds achieving a normal weight and a return of menses, while a smaller number (50%) resumed normal eating behaviors. Medium- to long-term studies document that recovery continues many years after the onset of the disorder and that recovery rates in the range of 70% to 80% are possible (Halvorsen Andersen, & Heyerdahl, 2004; Herpertz-Dahlmann et al., 2001; Rastam, Gillberg, & Wentz, 2003; Steinhausen, Boyadjieva, Griogoroiu-Serbanescu, & Neumärker, 2003; Strober, Freeman, & Morrell, 1997). Unfortunately, there is also continued mortality during the follow-up period. Vigorous ongoing treatment and follow-up are warranted.

The course of recovery is often complicated by the occurrence of other psychiatric disorders during the follow-up period, such as mood disorders, obsessive-compulsive disorder, and anxiety disorders. Figures commonly lie in the range of 40% to 50% (Halvorsen et al., 2004; Herpertz-Dahlmann et al., 2001; Wentz et al., 2001). Steinhausen's (1997) review found a quarter to have suffered from anxiety disorders, a fifth had some form of mood disorders, and 12% had obsessive-compulsive disorders. Progression to binge eating behaviors or frank bulimia nervosa occurred in 20% to 30% of cases, which most often occurred during the first few years of the recovery phase (Herpertz-Dahlmann et al., 2001; Strober et al., 1997) but could be a transition phase to recovery. A follow-up study of Chinese adult patients evidenced similar patterns (Lee, Chan, & Hsu, 2003). Ultimately, when complete recovery from the eating disorder is achieved, patients have a good chance of overcoming other psychiatric disorders as well (Herpertz-Dahlmann et al., 2001; Wentz et al., 2001).

The mortality rate among patients with AN is relatively high. Among adult patients, the standardized mortality ratios, which compare the number of actual deaths to the number of expected deaths for a healthy population of the same age and gender, are as high as 10. Causes of death include physical complications of the eating disorder, suicide, and substance abuse. A longer duration of illness, bingeing and purging, and depressive disorder are all related to the increased mortality (Birmingham, Su, Hlynsky, Goldner, & Gao, 2005; Franko et al., 2004; Herzog et al., 2000; Keel et al., 2003; Ruuska, Kaltiala-Heino, Rantanen, & Koivisto, 2005). These figures appear somewhat better for the younger age group, in that follow-up studies have found relatively few deaths: The mean crude mortality rate (the actual number of deaths among patients with the eating disorder) ranged from 0% to 11%, averaging approximately 2% (Steinhausen, 1997). A careful assessment of the patient's mental state throughout treatment for comorbid psychopathologies and suicide risk is essential.

There is so far no clear consensus about the relationship between illness characteristics and outcome. Intermediate to long-term follow-up studies seem to indicate that adolescent patients have a higher recovery rate and a lower mortality rate than do adults (Halvorsen et al., 2004; Herpertz-Dahlmann et al., 2001; Rastam et al., 2003; Steinhausen et al., 2003; Strober et al., 1997). Some studies have found symptoms such as vomiting, purging, bingeing, chronicity, and obsessive-compulsive personality traits point to a less favorable outcome. There is also a suggestion that ongoing family relationship problems are associated with a more chronic and relapsing course (Hsu, 1991; Strober et al., 1997).

Management

As patients value their thinness, they are often very reluctant to receive help. Motivating the patients and their families, helping them understand that they need help, and helping the families persevere in the face of strong resistance from the patients are very important first steps. Careful and repeated explanations about the risks of the illness and the benefits of recovery and understanding the reasons for resistance may help to overcome some of the reluctance. Giving information about what the treatment involves and the targets to be achieved will also be helpful.

In the initial phase of treatment, weight restoration is usually the primary goal. This can be achieved in outpatient, day-patient, and inpatient settings. Suggested indications for hospitalization include (a) low or rapidly dropping body weight, such as when the weight is below 80% of the ideal body weight; (b) evidence of physical complications, such as electrolyte imbalance and cardiovascular decompensation; (c) persistent self-induced vomiting or laxative abuse; (d) family inability to supervise the patient's diet or severe conflicts over meals; (e) presence of psychiatric comorbidities and/or suicide risk; and (f) failed outpatient treatment. The use of compulsory admission, though legal, has to be carefully weighed (Manley, Smye, & Srikameswaran, 2001; Watson, Bowers, & Andersen, 2000)—it is necessary to be clear on the objectives and alert to the possible consequences of such a crucial decision. When treatment is "enforced" on the patient, whether it is actually coercion (physical or legal) or merely a subjective feeling thereof, an empathic attitude from the treatment team is usually appreciated by the patient and the family and will help in establishing a treatment alliance.

To restore weight, a diet should be phased in to achieve a weight gain of around 0.5 kg per week. Weight should not be allowed to increase too rapidly because the body may not be able to cope with rapid changes and complications may ensue (refeeding syndrome). Careful monitoring of the patient's physical state, including cardiovascular, pulmonary, and neurological functioning as well as hemodynamic and electrolytic balance, is essential. Dietary advice is often necessary at this stage, but the patient should not be allowed to dictate the range of foods, as this will inadvertently put the focus on her eating symptoms once more. Oral feeding is a much better option than nasogastric feeding, as the latter is a very coercive procedure and the patient may feel psychologically traumatized and resentful that all the control has been taken away from her. Nasogastric feeding should be a last resort, when life is at risk. Close supervision during and after mealtime is necessary to ensure that food is actually consumed and the chance of vomiting minimized. Restriction of daily activities may be necessary to facilitate weight gain. Because of delayed gastric emptying, patients often complain of gastric bloating in the initial stages of refeeding, and reassurance and explanation are needed.

A "target weight" needs to be borne in mind. Guided by studies that have tracked the development of the ovaries during weight gain, this target weight should be approximately 95% of the ideal body weight (Key et al., 2002; Lai et al., 1994; Treasure et al., 1988). However, this should serve as an indication of the approximate weight at which menses is likely to return and should not be rigidly set. It is especially not helpful to have repeated discussions with the patient about the actual weight that needs to be achieved because this may once again put the treatment focus onto her weight and create unnecessary struggles with the treatment team. A behavioral approach, such as being allowed more privileges as weight improves, can be useful in motivating the patient at this stage.

During this stage of treatment, some patients may be very resentful and uncooperative while others may be surprisingly compliant. While clinical decisions are ultimately the responsibilities of clinicians, patients must not be left feeling that clinicians have taken over their life and that they no longer have any control. Since the issue of control is central to the psychopathology of AN, a delicate balance has to be struck: on one level to ensure weight gain and on the other hand to empower the patient to take on responsibility for herself. This needs to be handled sensitively.

Helping the patient gain weight is treating only a symptom and not the illness itself. AN is a psychiatric disorder, with the implicit understanding that it has important underlying psychological issues that must be dealt with before recovery is possible. As treatment progresses, the focus must shift from the physical to the psychological. As the patient's physical state is gradually stabilized, psychological treatment to understand the illness to foster the development of autonomy and responsibility for herself takes center stage. This shift in emphasis may be quite confusing for the patient and her family and at times for the treatment team. There may be changes in the patient's behavior and in the alliance with the family at these times. There must be close collaboration among members of the treatment team, and the treatment objectives have to be openly communicated among all concerned.

As part of the psychological treatment, individual exploration with the patient about her experiences, family relationships, feelings, and difficulties can help her make a link with her eating problem and shed light on the meaning behind her self-starvation. For children and adolescents, the addition of family therapy should be routine practice, as studies have confirmed that family therapy is more effective than individual psychotherapy among patients whose illness begins before the age of 19 and lasts for less than 3 years (Le Grange, 1999; Ma, Chow, Lee, & Lai, 2002; Russell, Szmukler, & Dare, 1987). The premise of family therapy is that family relationships have been altered by the illness and may be perpetuating it; no causal relationship is implied. The reason for involving the whole family in treatment is to mobilize family resources to help the patient and is not fault finding. Our experience with Hong Kong Chinese adolescents has revealed four underlying themes in the family context regarding the meaning of self-starvation: (a) self-starvation to gain love and control; (b) coalition of the anorexic daughter with her powerless and helpless mother to fight for a better position in the family, by triangulating herself in the parents' marital conflicts; (c) family loyalty, including sacrificing herself for the good of the family; and (d) the anorexic daughter acting as emotional support for her helpless and powerless mother (Ma et al., 2002). Such dynamics have to be explored and addressed in the course of treatment. For older patients, there is still a paucity of conclusive treatment research data, and family therapy has not been found to be more effective than other forms of psychotherapy.

There is little convincing evidence that drug treatment is effective in the management of AN per se. However, in the presence of psychiatric comorbidities such as depressive or anxiety disorders, the use of antidepressants such as selective serotonin reuptake inhibitors may be indicated. Atypical antipsychotic drugs such as olanzapine have been reported to be a useful adjunct if the psychopathology takes on a delusional quality (Hay, 2004; Zhu & Walsh, 2002).

Successful treatment requires a truly multidisciplinary approach with team members who are able to work closely and collaboratively together. The team should include at least psychiatrists, psychologists, family therapists, and social workers. Expertise from pediatricians or physicians and dieticians will also be required, especially during the initial stage of treatment when the physical health of the patient is at risk. Because patients and their families are often ambivalent about treatment, which may be reflected in their attitudes and behaviors, the treatment team must be skilled in understanding these complex feelings and be able to deal with them sensitively. Good communication within the treatment team is crucial to ensure difficulties and issues encountered are discussed and directions are agreed on and understood. It is also essential for the treatment team and the family to maintain a strong treatment alliance so that concerted effort can be made to help the patient overcome her very severe illness.

CONCLUSION

AN is no longer confined to the Western world. It now exists in many different cultures and across different social classes. Not only does it affect adolescent girls and young women, but prepubertal children may be affected too. The approach to management must be multidisciplinary. There must be a careful assessment within a developmental framework of the interaction among the multitude of contributing factors. Underlying psychological factors and psychiatric conditions have to be delineated. Comprehensive treatment does not stop at weight recovery. The management of underlying psychological and psychiatric issues, which may well be prolonged, is essential in enabling patients to return to a fully functional physical, psychological, and social self.

Practice Guidelines

1. Anorexia nervosa is a complex, multifactorial illness where genetic, psychological, familial, and sociocultural influences predispose, precipitate, and maintain the illness. Physical complications and coexisting psychiatric disorders contribute to the increased rates of morbidities and mortality.
2. Helping the patient gain weight is treating only a symptom and not the illness itself. As treatment progresses, the focus must shift from the physical to the psychological.
3. Many patients with anorexia nervosa feel a lack of control in their life and therefore tend to resist treatment. An empathic attitude from therapists will help in establishing a treatment alliance.
4. Family therapy should be a routine part of the treatment process for children and adolescents with anorexia nervosa.
5. Recovery is protracted, so continued vigorous treatment and follow-up are warranted.

Part II

The Family Treatment Model and Clinical Issues in Managing Anorexia Nervosa

Chapter 3
Underlying Theoretical Perspectives

INTRODUCTION

Since anorexia nervosa (AN) was first identified as a mental disorder, social discourses on this disorder have multiplied. Like other mental disorders, AN has become an object of study by different people at different times and from different disciplinary perspectives such as medicine, psychology, psychiatry, sociology, social work, anthropology, and law.

In this chapter, four theoretical perspectives, namely the psychoanalytical perspective, family perspectives, the feminist perspective, and the sociocultural perspective, are presented, with these perspectives representing the underlying theoretical strands of the family treatment model, Micucci's model (1998), that this therapist has used in working with young people with AN and their families. The treatment model is described in detail in chapter 4.

PSYCHOANALYTICAL PERSPECTIVE

The psychoanalytical perspective views AN as being brought about by the unresolved intrapsychic conflicts or traumatic childhood experiences (Ogden, 2003). This perspective looks at the unconscious and the conscious meanings of self-starvation in terms of the patient's history and experiences in the family of origin. Intake of food symbolizes basic desires and needs. Food refusal is perceived as a deliberate attempt to repress lust, greed, and desires unacceptable and psychologically repulsive to the adolescent and young woman. Weight loss induces a sense of false control to avoid fear of pregnancy, to arrest youthful growth and maturity, and even to reject female sexuality. While the fantasized symbolic meaning of AN is difficult to prove, the results of Western studies (Maine, 1999; Neumark-Sztainer, Story, Hannan, Beuhring,

& Resnick, 2000) have partially supported the theoretical argument of the psychoanalytical model on the unresolved intrapsychic conflicts arising from sexual abuse. For instance, Neumark-Sztainer and her research team (2000) have shown that the history of physical and sexual abuse increased the risk of disordered eating among adolescents. About 40% to 50% of women with eating disorders have a history of sexual trauma (Maine, 1999, p. 3). An Australian study (Brown, Russell, Thornton, & Dunn, 1999) indicated that 75 out of a total of 117 eating disordered patients have experienced one or more types of abuse (child sexual abuse, physical abuse, or adult sexual abuse). The result of this study has supported the association of symptomatic dissociation and history of sexual abuse (both child and adult) with eating disorders.

Bruch (1973) argued forcefully for the influential role played by early childhood experience in developing AN; the mothers of these patients have tended to nurse their child since infancy with excessive care and concern, often out of their own needs rather than the child's needs. Parents reportedly described the patient as obedient, conforming, loyal, and meticulous before puberty. In short, the child has learned to live by meeting her parents' expectations. Under this form of upbringing, the afflicted child would not have developed an ability to identify her hunger need and differentiate it from other biological needs. The growing child would develop a strong sense of ineffectiveness and, by chance, could learn to use self-starvation as a protest against the overwhelmingly unbearable parental control, as a personal crusade for personal autonomy and individuality and as a means to master the uncontrollable life.

The psychoanalytical perspective has reminded the therapist to look for the metaphoric meaning of self-starvation and to work on the core problem of these self-starving young people, namely their strong sense of incompetence, personal ineffectiveness, poor self-esteem, and self-image; as a consequence, treatment needs to incorporate fostering their sense of competence and repairing the damaging self-esteem. Both goals can be achieved by the professional attitude of the therapist as well as by the therapeutic experiences created in treatment through developing trustful therapeutic rapport. In terms of attitude, the therapist should respect the patient as an individual who is capable of feeling, judging, and acting, even though it may be contrary to other people's expectations, including the therapist's. During the therapeutic encounter, therefore, the therapist would permit the patient to assert her own views to fulfill her personal needs and to encourage the young person to try new ways of relating to the parents and the therapist—even, for instance, to try being rebellious against her parents and the therapist.

However, Bruch's (1973) exclusive focus on the mother–child relationship and the past family context has limited her conceptualization (Minuchin, Rosman, & Baker, 1978). She has overlooked the father's role in maintaining the status quo of the family. Nor has she paid any attention to the here and now family context. Even though she did recognize the significant role played by the mother in the child's problem, her involvement with the mother in treatment has been peripheral and minimal. The pathological analysis of the mother–child relationship could easily be misinterpreted as a mother-blaming attitude. The clinical model developed is predominantly child centered and individual oriented. Experienced psychoanalytical psychotherapists such as Selvini Palazzoli (1985, p. 165) confessed, "Now it was precisely this enormous personal effort (aside from the vast expenditure of time demanded by the psychotherapeutic treatment of many of these patients) when viewed against the paucity of the results, at least in numerical terms, that impelled me to search for new conceptions and new ways of more effective therapeutic intervention." Selvini Palazzoli finally landed on the destination—family psychotherapy as a new orientation.

FAMILY PERSPECTIVES

Family perspectives are based on systems theory (Dare & Eisler, 1995; Minuchin et al., 1978) in conceptualizing the disorder. The symptoms of AN are believed to be context dependent, and self-starvation can be better understood in light of the immediate sociocultural context. There are two stages of development for family perspectives. In the early stage of development in family perspectives, a pathology model is developed, with the afflicted families viewed as a site of pathology. The pathology model is later replaced by a strengths model, which emphasizes family strengths and resources.

Earlier family therapist masters such as Minuchin et al. (1978) and Selvini Palazzoli (1985) have made significant contributions in developing the pathology model. They have identified common characteristics of families suffering from AN, for example, enmeshment, overprotection, conflict avoidance, and cross-generational coalition (Minuchin et al., 1978); family values and beliefs that are rooted in agrarian societies (Selvini Palazzoli, 1985); and rigid family beliefs and role prescriptions transmitted across generations (White, 1983). Labeled as psychosomatic, these families change slowly and adapt inflexibly to the changing demands of an industrial and modernized society.

The pathology model views AN as the tip of an iceberg, a symptom that reveals the structural defects of the family, its communication problems, and the inflexibility of the family structure in trying to adapt to changes brought about by internal factors such as maturation of the child or by external forces such as economic depression and unemployment. The model has demystified self-starvation by contextualizing AN in the family context; in doing so, it has thrown new light on the linkage of emaciation to family malfunctioning (Beresin, Gordon, & Herzog, 1989; Steiger, Stotland, Trottier, & Ghadirian, 1996; Tozzi, Sullivan, Fear, McKenzie, & Bulik, 2003).

With the paradigm shift from the psychoanalytical perspective to the systems perspective, family therapy has become an adjunct to conventional psychiatric treatment. Family treatment aims to identify the dysfunctional family structure and family relationships and to effect changes accordingly. The involvement of family members in the care of the sick child is a step forward from psychoanalytical psychotherapy. Family therapists have succeeded in involving the previously invisible father in assessment and treatment. As acknowledged by Luepnitz (1988, p. 68), "Minuchin himself has helped make thousands of families less father-absent by bringing peripheral fathers into treatment." Most importantly, the recovery rate of the emaciated children and adolescents is high; 86% of them have recovered after family treatment (Minuchin et al., 1978).

In the 1980s, Western family therapists (Eisler, 1995; Lock, Le Grange, Agras, & Dare, 2001) developed the strengths model and assessed treatment efficacy. Represented by the Maudsley approach in the United Kingdom (Eisler, 1995, 2005; Lock et al., 2001), the strengths model assumes that a family is basically an adaptive social system capable of balancing between stability on the one hand and the changing needs of individual family members on the other. Emphasis is on identifying differences among family members and discovering the strengths and weaknesses of different family transactional styles and how family members cope with adversity. The treatment goals are twofold: (a) to motivate the emaciated young person to take charge of her treatment plan and to be responsible for recovery and (b) to collaborate with the parents in helping the young person to regain weight rather than to control her.

Clinical studies (Dare, Eisler, Russell, & Szmukler, 1990; Russell, Dare, Eisler, & Le Grange, 1992) have shown that family therapy was superior to individual therapy in helping adolescent patients younger than 18 and with an illness history of shorter than 3 years. The positive outcome has been maintained at 5-year follow-up, indicating that age and the history of the illness significantly influence the treatment outcome. The treatment efficacy of a family approach has also been demonstrated in clinical studies conducted in Toronto (Martin, 1985) and Buenos Aires (Herscovici & Bay, 1996).

Despite the efficacy of a family approach in treating AN, Eisler (1995, 2005) has critically challenged the psychosomatic family model as an explanatory model for AN as theoretically flawed and empirically weak. From a systemic perspective, the family features observed can be the cause as well as the consequence of the disorder. The family patterns of interaction discerned in treatment can be interpreted as the family's attempt to accommodate the caring demands of the emaciated patient. The disorder not only has devastating impacts on the emaciated young person's life but also has spillover effects on the well-being of each of the individual family members and on family life as a whole. With the onset of the disorder, families sooner or later reorganize themselves around the disorder with the following characteristics: (a) allowing the symptoms to take a central role in family life, (b) narrowing the time focus on the here and now, (c) amplifying aspects of family function, and (d) diminishing the ability to meet family life-cycle needs (Eisler, 2005). In the face of a life-threatening disease such as AN, parents may reprioritize their concerns, say by putting aside their marital conflicts, if any, in order to channel their time and efforts into coping with the child's health condition.

Besides family treatment, the treatment team at Maudsley Hospital has initiated an intensive day program using multiple family therapy (MFT) to help adolescent patients with AN (Dare & Eisler, 2000). MFT refers to treating a number of families together (Asen, 2002). Families having similar problems are grouped together to tackle their difficulties based on the principle of mutual help and support. MFT has been practiced with demonstrated effectiveness in Germany (Scholz, Rix, Scholz, Gantchev, & Thomke, 2005) and the United States (Asen, 2002).

Despite the inadequacy of the family model as the explanatory paradigm, the conceptual map offered by the family model has helped to identify different family contexts that may have maintained the symptoms of the disorder and hindered recovery. The results of recent studies in the United Kingdom (Treasure et al., 2001; Whitney et al., 2005) and Germany (Graap et al., 2008) have provided evidence to support viewing the family context as one of the crucial factors maintaining the disorder. These studies are of importance even in other cultures and societies, and in general it will be of great clinical utility for Hong Kong family therapists to identify the varied family contexts that have unfavorably affected the recovery and to adapt a family treatment approach to effect changes effectively.

FEMINIST PERSPECTIVE

Dissatisfied with the failure of the past literature in explaining why the majority of patients suffering from AN are female and in addressing the gender- and culture-specific issues related to this life-threatening illness, feminist scholars (e.g., Chernin, 1986; MacSween, 1993) have attempted to identify a solution to this complex problem at the structural and cultural levels. AN is regarded as a protest or as a means of personal control to master an uncontrollable life in which options are limited and potentialities are circumscribed by the social structure and patriarchal culture in which the person is embedded. It is necessary to analyze the social position of women in a patriarchal society (Orbach, 1986), the socialization of women to please and comply with others at the expense of denying their own individual needs (Lawrence, 1984), and the irreconcilability of individuality and femininity in a bourgeois patriarchal culture (MacSween, 1993). Luepnitz (1988) found the mother-blaming attitude of family therapists totally offensive, oppressive, and unacceptable, while Andersson (1995) has recognized the potential healing power of the intimate mother–daughter relationship in treatment. Both of them have been upset with the loss of women's voices in the existing literature. Andersson has shifted the therapeutic emphasis from a dysfunctional family structure to language systems, meaning systems, and problem-dissolving systems. She has perceived the mother–daughter connection as a potential healing force in treating eating disorders. Hearing the voices of these self-starving adolescents and young adults and learning of their family experiences are important means to uncovering the mystery of AN.

SOCIOCULTURAL PERSPECTIVE

While hysteria was postulated to be associated with the sexually repressive society in the Victorian era, AN is believed to be related to Westernization and the acculturation of the Western standard of beauty, that is, slenderness and slimness, for the general public and for special professional groups such as ballet dancers, athletes, and fashion models who place high value on physical appearance and a thin body shape (Piran, 1999). Both Asian (e.g., Lee & Lee, 1999) and Western studies (e.g., Abrams, Allen, & Gray, 1998; Becker, 2004) have shown that eating disorders are related to the degree of Western acculturation, either in society or in a given segment of the population that accepts the Western standard of feminine beauty. An anthropological study (Becker, 2004) surveying the change of the body shape and standard of beauty in the Fiji islands has shown that, with the introduction of Western television programs on the Pacific islands, young people shifted from their traditional standard of robust body shape and disinterest in reshaping the body to an awareness of thinness as a beauty standard and an expressed wish to fix their own body shape. As revealed by the narratives of young adult women in the Fiji islands who dieted vigorously, their dieting behavior is closely linked to the acquisition of the Western standard of beauty through daily exposure to the media.

Nasser and Katzman (1999) thought that as a concept Westernization is too general to be useful. It is better to dissect the broad concept into underlying and individual social forces, including urbanization, global markets, the threat to national identity, the experience of discontinuity, and the disappearance of traditional cultural idioms for articulating personal distress. Under the influence of globalization, the dietary habits of the non-Western countries such as China, Japan, and India have undergone significant changes, especially with the introduction of Western fast food chains. The change in dietary habits has given rise to obesity and subsequent anxiety and overconcern over body shape (Nasser & Katzman, 2003).

For example, Hong Kong over the past several decades presents a prime example of Westernization. A review on beauty pageants (Leung, Lam, & Sze, 2001) from 1975 to 2000 has indicated that fragility and thinness are the ideal beauty standard in contemporary Hong Kong society. Body dissatisfaction is also prevalent among college and secondary school students (Caritas-Hong Kong, 2004; Lee, 1993, 1997). Dissatisfaction with body shape has become a normative discontent; slenderness as a key feature of feminine identity is now pervasive not only in the West (Robin, Silberstein, & Striegel Moore, 1985) but also in many rapidly Westernizing parts of Asia.

Apart from changes in dietary habits, the shifting of mealtimes is another factor that may contribute to obesity. In highly urbanized cities in Asia, it is not uncommon for people working long or irregular hours to skip a meal, usually lunch, and to have a heavy meal in the evening. The results of a survey (Wong, Ma, & Lau, 2003) have shown that about half of the respondents worked over eight hours per day, leaving little time or energy for physical exercise after work. The lack of exercise, the change in dietary habits, and the tendency to combine two meals into one heavy meal may account for the rise in obesity and the subsequent dread of fatness in society. This dread is further perpetuated by the promotion of slimness as an ideal standard of beauty in the mass media and by the commodification of beauty products in society.

Leung, Lam, and Chan (2001) disagreed with the claim that obsessive preoccupation with body weight is the result of Westernization. They argued that fragility and thinness were the ideal beauty standard in ancient China, except in the Tang Dynasty (618–907 CE). For example, King Ling of Cu in the Qin Dynasty (221–206 BC) favored willowy waists, and his wives and concubines starved themselves almost to death to keep the tiny waist (Chin, 1978; Pak, 1978). The weeping willow tree (*liu*) became a metaphor to describe the beauty of women in the noble and gentry class much adored throughout history. Lady Hsu of the Sung Dynasty (960–1279 CE) described vividly the tiny waists in her poem:

> The Palace ladies in front of the hall,
> Have all slender waists;
> For the first time learning to ride on horseback,
> They are greatly afraid. (Gulik, 1961, p. 212)

In ancient China, fetishistic emperors, noblemen, and powerful members of the gentry set the ideal beauty standard in terms of tiny waists and bound feet. Wang's (2000, p. 48) observation is insightful: "Foot binding thus became an efficient way to keep women in their place—the inner Chamber—physically, mentally, and symbolically." Such cultural practice aroused ancient Chinese men's erotic feelings toward women and protected the chastity of their exclusive possession, that is, their women. In view of the disparate power between men and women under the patriarchal culture, ancient Chinese women had no choice but to maintain tiny waists and to bind their feet obediently amid pain and suffering. When the daughter reached the age of 8 or 9, a sweet and loving mother would suddenly become cruel, turn a blind eye to the torment and suffering of her struggling daughter, and show no mercy in response to her tears and screams. The mother would be coerced to bind her little daughter's feet because she knew too well that the prospect of her daughter's future marriage was tied intimately to the size of the tiny feet (Jackson, 2000; Ko, 2001).

Modern Chinese women are luckier: They can move around, dance, and exercise with their healthy feet, but shackles remain. The adoption of natural feet in the late Manchu Dynasty and the beginning of new Republic of China (from 1911 CE) signified a shift in meaning of the physical body: from serving the monarch, the noblemen, and the gentry to serving the country (Hwang, 2001), which could hardly be regarded as a personal triumph for gender equality and individuality. For modern Chinese women, the options and choices in the selection of ideal body shapes and body images are still subject to constraints—often imposed subtly through advertisements for beauty products and messages that plumpness equates to poor self-control and unpopularity. The ideal standard of beauty, that is, slenderness and thinness, which has exerted considerable influence on young people in modern Asian societies, typifies the subordinate and submissive relationship of women in society and the power inequality between the genders.

In the premodern societies such as the Fiji islands, the robust body shape was perceived as a sign of a woman's good child-rearing ability, while in modern societies a sexy woman must be slender and thin. Apparently the postulations of women as the childbearing machine in traditional societies and as a sexy object in modern societies are critically challenged by feminist scholars as denying women's autonomy in many areas of their lives (Mac-Sween, 1993).

The sociocultural perspective has equipped family therapists with a wider lens in assessment. A family therapist would be more empathetic with the patient's ambivalence to change and perceptive to identify the linkage of the patient's ideal body image to gender inequality and the beauty standard in society and her dietary habit and its relationship to the pressures of urban life.

SIMILARITIES AND DIFFERENCES

The different theoretical perspectives undoubtedly enrich understanding of AN. They differ from one another in different areas of concern and focuses of assessment; for instance, the psychoanalytical perspective looks into early childhood development and the subsequent onset of AN, the family perspectives emphasize the here-and-now interactions and their linkage to the disorder, and the sociocultural perspectives examine the interrelationship between sociocultural forces such as urbanization and Westernization, and eating disorders.

All these theoretical perspectives, except the psychoanalytical perspective, acknowledge the difficulty of identifying the real cause of the disorder and have focus more on the consequences of the disorder and on factors that have maintained the symptoms. For instance, the strength-oriented family perspective identifies the constricting family process that may have maintained the symptoms of AN while the sociocultural perspectives bring out the reinforcing effects of the beauty standard in society on the emaciated young person's pathological pursuit of slimness, despite a decline in health.

Although the meaning of context varies according to different theoretical models, they all appreciate the importance of context in shaping the disorder. To the psychoanalytical perspective, social context refers to the rearing environment in infancy; the sociocultural perspectives refer to the sociocultural forces (e.g., urbanization, modernization, society in developmental transition) that govern society at large; while the family perspectives emphasize the ingrained family conflicts, the rigid and repetitive family interactions, and other constricting processes such as cross-generational alliances and the role played by the emaciated child in the family.

A core theme emerges. The disorder should not be simplistically viewed as a problem of eating and body weight. It is a personal attempt to gain control over and cope with problems of disconnection, transition, and oppression, which are context based (Katzman & Lee, 1997).

CONCLUSION

Different models of psychotherapy are based on different theoretical perspectives in explaining the development and maintenance of the disorder (Eisler, 2005). Advances in science have provided compelling evidence that the complexity of human behavior has to be understood on multiple levels (Ridley, 2003). This multiple-level understanding of the disorder has pointed to the fact that effective treatment does not dichotomize the body and the mind of a patient but treats her as a whole person shaped by a family and social context (Churven, 2008).

Chapter 4
The Family Treatment Model

INTRODUCTION

The conceptual perspective adopted to understand anorexia nervosa (AN) influences the choice of strategy in helping, and because of systemic understanding of AN, family therapy has been found to be of particular utility in treating young people suffering from AN. In the ecological systemic perspective (Bronfenbrenner, 1989), a social context consists of the microsystem, mesosystem, exosystem, and macrosystem. The microsystem refers to the immediate social systems such as family and school, which have direct influence on the individual. The mesosystem refers to the interrelationship among social systems such as family, school, and peers that have direct effects on the individuals. The exosystem refers to social systems (e.g., social service provision, community facilities) that have tremendous influence on the entire family but may have no direct effects on individuals. The outer layer of the ecological system is the macrosystem (e.g., the cultural values and beliefs and economic condition of the country), which has significantly shaped individual coping and family functioning. AN can be understood as embedded in complex systems that are in reciprocal interactions with one another to attain an equilibrium. By working with the patient and her family together, family therapy starts to effect change on the microsystem and the mesosystem levels.

Family therapy is an approach for treating human problems by bringing together the members of a family to help them work out conflicts at the source. According to Eisler (1995, p. 155), family therapy is a treatment *with* families rather than *of* families. It aims to help families find ways to resolve their problems. The underlying assumption of family therapy is that people are products of their context and behavior will change as a result of the changes in the social context.

While family is the most relevant context in understanding human behavior, family therapy also emphasizes the importance of larger social systems such as the school and social service systems in shaping families and human behavior (Fishman, 1996). Family therapy effects changes not only in the entire family but also in the relevant social systems that have effects on the family and on individuals.

Since the late 1970s, different family therapy approaches with different treatment emphasis have been developed for helping patients suffering from AN. For instance, Minuchin, Rosman, and Baker (1978) have stressed the change of the family structure characterized by enmeshment, overprotectiveness, rigidity, and conflict avoidance. Therapists such as White (1983) and Stierlin and Weber (1989) have targeted the intergenerational beliefs in family cohesion, self-sacrifice, and denial that seriously interfere with individuation. The Maudsley approach (Dare & Eisler, 1995; Lock, Le Grange, Agras, & Dare, 2001) first aims at the restoration of body weight by externalizing the illness and by soliciting the parents' cooperation and collaboration in refeeding the child. Only after the symptoms have completely disappeared the Maudsley approach help the families deal with normal developmental issues such as autonomy and control.

Among all the family treatment models developed for AN, the Maudsley approach has been manualized (Lock et al., 2001) for the widest application and is evidence based (Le Grange & Eisler, 2008; Rhodes, 2003). Although the Maudsley model (Dare & Eisler, 1995) is evidence based, the Maudsley approach may fail to address the conflicts between the emaciated young person and her parents, which seems so central to the disorder (Churven, 2008). The manualized approach has weakened its flexibility in meeting the needs of diverse families encountered in practice. Families often come from different walks of life; the poorest families have to rely on government welfare subsidy, while in modestly high-income families, both parents work as professionals or in business. Their family structures, family shapes, family history, and family resources are varied. Take the example of multiproblem families with AN; the Maudsley approach does not state the principles for helping these poor families. Also, it does not pay sufficient attention to the issues of control and power that the patient has to struggle with (Churven, 2008).

There is growing recognition that to have a better chance of success intervention strategies should (a) focus on both individual and family maintaining factors (Schmidt & Treasure, 2006), (b) address the patient as a whole person in a family/social context, (c) help resolve the power struggle between the emaciated young person and the parents (Churven, 2008), and (d) elicit the active participation of the parents in supervising the young person's eating (Le Grange & Eisler, 2008).

This chapter describes selected Western treatment approaches in helping the Chinese emaciated young people and their families, the rationales for adopting the model, and the characteristics of the modified treatment model. In chapter 5, each of the treatment steps is elaborated. Intertwined throughout the different treatment steps are case vignettes, which illustrate the treatment principles and techniques.

MICUCCI'S TREATMENT MODEL

The treatment approach adopted is modified from that of Micucci (1998), which in turn is based predominantly on structural family therapy developed by Minuchin (Minuchin et al., 1978), but it conceptually integrates feminist psychodynamic perspectives and is technically eclectic. For instance, the model incorporates the techniques of the narrative school such as externalization of the problem (White, 1983).

The treatment model of Micucci (1998, p. 100) differs from the Maudsley approach (Lock et al., 2001) in its emphasis on helping the adolescent and the family to disrupt the symptomatic cycle that has maintained the symptoms, to challenge the conflict-avoidance coping, and to relieve the profound isolation and disconnection underlying the apparent closeness and harmony in the family, without losing sight of the importance of helping the parents to refeed the emaciated young person. The ultimate treatment goals are to help the family to transcend the constricting family process and to open up options and possibilities for the young person to recover.

Rationales for Choosing the Model

The model (Micucci, 1998) has the advantage of dealing directly with the family politics arising from anorexia. The therapy addresses the intense power struggle and control between the emaciated young person and the parents. Family assessment explores the battleground over eating and how the current family relationships have been damaged but without assigning blame.

The second strength of Micucci's model is the care and concern toward the emaciated young person's pains and sufferings, her sense of profound isolation, and her strong sense of uncontrollability in life while effecting changes on the entire family. Winning the trust of the emaciated young person through establishing good therapeutic relationships is as important as mapping out the family conflicts.

The third strength is that Micucci's view of reality is complex. Micucci reminds the therapist to look for both the family strengths and the family pathology in assessment. A strengths-based approach undoubtedly helps the therapist to identify the individual and family resources to combat the disorder, but severe parental psychopathology, in terms of an undiagnosed mental disorder of one or both parents, may become a great obstacle to treatment.

In the framework of the structural family therapy school (Minuchin & Nichols, 1993; Minuchin, Nichols, & Lee, 2007), the basic assumptions are compatible with those of Micucci's model—families are richer in resources and more complex than how they perceive themselves. Family therapy training equips the therapist with the knowledge and skills.

Theoretical Perspectives of the Model

Micucci's (1998) model comprises three major theoretical perspectives: family systems perspectives, feminist psychodynamic perspectives, and sociocultural perspectives. Since these perspectives were thoroughly discussed in chapter 3, only the major constructs are briefly summarized here.

Family systems perspectives. Originated from general systems theory (Bronfenbrenner, 1989), the family systems perspectives believe that human behavior can be better understood at multiple system levels: individual, family, and society (e.g., social service systems, education system, and medical social service systems); these systems interact with each other reciprocally rather than linearly. Changes at one level of the system result in reciprocal changes at other levels.

Family is a semiopen system subject to the operation of two mechanisms: metamorphosis and homeostasis. Minuchin et al. (1978) found that families with AN shared the four characteristics of psychosomatic families: enmeshment, overprotection, rigidity, and involvement of the symptomatic adolescent in parental conflict. These families are stuck and fail to change to cope with the challenges and difficulties arising from the disorder. Subsequently, the developmental needs of both the afflicted young people and the families are arrested and become unfulfilled. Despite its inadequacy as the explanatory model of the disorder, the psychosomatic model has helped scholars to understand how the symptoms would have been maintained by the stifling family context.

Feminist psychodynamic perspectives. The feminist psychodynamic perspectives have challenged the inadequacy of the classical psychodynamic theory in conceptualizing the problem of the young person with AN merely as an issue of autonomy and in perceiving the mother as a toxic agent hindering the recovery of the emaciated young person. The perspectives reiterate the importance of hearing the lost voice of the emaciated young person and of being empathetic toward the highly distressed mother whose diminishing caring capacity is often attributable to marital distress and lack of spousal support.

Sociocultural perspectives. The sociocultural perspectives stress the linkage of the disorder to the powerful influence of the culture of thinness, the symbolic meaning of weight as power and control, and the tensions and stresses placed on women because of traditional sex role expectations, the achievement anxieties of women in modern society, and women's personal ineffectiveness and vulnerability (Micucci, 1998).

Key Family Processes

Three major family processes are fundamental for change: isolation and conditional acceptance, control versus genuine connection, and symptomatic cycle. The three processes are interwoven in the course of the disorder.

Isolation and conditional acceptance. Although family members suffering from AN appear to be closely related to one another, with diffused boundaries and cohesiveness, beneath their interaction is the profound isolation and rejection subjectively experienced by the emaciated young person. Parental love is conditional on the basis of the young person's achievement and performance.

Control versus genuine connection. When a child has grown to adolescence, the parents may fail to perceive the changing needs and fear the loss of parenting power. They may exert tighter control over the adolescent's behavior, which in turn deepens the sense of isolation and disconnection. From the perspective of the young person, parental love and care may be perceived as parental control.

The symptomatic cycle. An afflicted young person may be under great distress and start excessive dieting for reasons such as peer rejection and peer pressure, family conflicts, and pursuit of an "ideal" body shape. With the onset of AN, the afflicted young person's changing behavior has effects on members of the family. Conscious of increasing weight loss, the parents may first try indirect means to persuade the young person to eat, but usually to no avail. When their attempts fail, the anxious, frightened, and helpless parents exert tighter control, which in turn increases the young person's resistance; both the parents and the daughter become locked in this self-defeating symptomatic cycle of interaction. Family life sooner or later becomes organized around the symptoms, leaving little energy and attention to take care of the needs of the healthy family members or other aspects of family life. The parents gradually believe that the emaciated young person has become "crazy" and only mental health professionals can "fix" her "craziness." Blamed as the troublemaker, the young person feels more isolated and disconnected in the family.

Under the constrained family narrative, parents may overlook the multifaceted self of the emaciated daughter: obstinate, oppositional, and sullen but at the same time perceptive, caring, and self-disciplined. They can also lose sight of the fact that she may be an achiever in school. The same is applicable to other family members. The overloaded mother may despair that her husband would reprioritize his work and be more available physically and emotionally at home. In the eyes of the emaciated young person, the family members' attempts to help overcome her problem would easily be misinterpreted as another means of control or coercion.

Treatment Principles

Family treatment involves transforming the presenting problem as an individual difficulty to a constricting family process that has impeded parental efforts in helping and reinforced the young person's ambivalence for change and recovery. Family assessment is shifted from resolving the symptoms to identifying the symptomatic cycle of interactions between the young person and the family (Micucci, 1998). A shared purpose in treatment is developed with the family to activate their collective efforts to disrupt the symptomatic cycle of interactions and learn new ways of relating with each other. The goal of treatment is to cultivate a therapeutic context characterized by mutual and genuine emotional connection on the basis of which each family member can assist the emaciated young person to drive away the disorder.

There are three treatment principles in this model: (a) to collaborate with the young person and the family to disrupt the symptomatic cycle of interaction, (b) to heighten the awareness of the family on the multifaceted self of each family member and the malleability for change, and (c) to expand the constrained family reality and provide more options and possibilities to drive away the disorder (Micucci, 1998).

Treatment Process

The model comprises the following treatment steps:

(a) Negotiating a treatment contract by shifting the family's focus from the symptoms to the symptomatic cycle or the constricting family process that has maintained and escalated the symptoms of AN

(b) Encouraging parental collaboration by supporting them to help the starving daughter gain weight rather than to control her

(c) Addressing unresolved conflicts and improving the family relationship

(d) Handling relapses by preventing the reemergence of the symptomatic cycle and further enhancing family relationship

(e) Supporting individual development

(f) Supporting the transformation

These treatment steps are cyclic rather than linear; each treatment step overlaps with the next throughout the treatment process. However, *it is essential to postpone working on the developmental issue until the symptomatic cycle that has maintained the symptoms has been resolved.*

MODIFICATIONS TO MICUCCI'S MODEL

It has been found to be necessary to modify Micucci's model for application to the Chinese families in Hong Kong. Minuchin, the master of structural family therapy, once said, "I am not a structural family therapist. I am working with the family."[1] The needs of the family rather than any theoretical approach should determine how the therapist works with the family.

The modified treatment model is distinguished from Micucci's model in three aspects: (a) enrichment of the cultural perspective in assessment and treatment, (b) motivational and engagement work with the emaciated young person, and (c) work with family problems (e.g., financial difficulty, parents' mental health problems, and suspected incest).

Enrichment of the Cultural Perspective

In the examples and vignettes presented, the afflicted young person, the family, and the therapist share the same traditional Chinese cultural heritage.

---

[1] Minuchin said this during his clinical supervision with a group of Chinese family therapy trainees including the author ten years ago.

Enrichment by adopting a cultural lens helps the therapist in assessment and treatment.

In assessment, the therapist's conceptualization of the family should be compatible with the definition of the family in Chinese societies. In Chinese societies, for example, it has been pointed out (Wen, Chang, Chang, & Chu, 1989) that the Western concept of a nuclear family is foreign, and the translation of the word *family*, *jia ting* (家庭), connotes a concept with no exact equivalent in traditional society. In traditional society, family is conceptualized as kinship, *jia* (家) or *jia zu* (家族), which is subjective in nature and can be fluidly defined by different kinship groupings under different social circumstances. For instance, *jia* would be more narrowly defined in the context of a family funeral or more broadly defined in a family business. Understanding the subjective definition of such terms and the fluidity of such definition would broaden the assessment from the immediate household unit to the extended family including the paternal and maternal families of origin.

In treatment, the therapist utilizes emotional intensity to activate the family changing mechanism, to shift the family's attention from the symptom to the constricting family process, and to assist the family in resolving their conflicts in ways that are receptive to the family and that synchronize with the culture in which the family is embedded. For instance, in eliciting the hidden family conflict, the therapist has to be perceptive enough to pick up nuances and the hidden connotations of verbal statements and nonverbal cues used to indicate negative meanings. Being protective of and loyal to their parents, some emaciated young people do not wish their parents to lose face, *mianzi* (面子), in front of the therapist, who is a stranger to them especially in the first few sessions. They use evasive and restrictive language to express disagreement or discontent toward the parents, "I don't know; I don't want to think about this," rather than directly opposing the parents' decision regarding schooling or career choice. Even though the young person is able to express her discontent or anger toward the parents, she often seeks the approval of the parents through eye contact and facial expressions.

It is imperative for the therapist to attend to the relational issues rather than substantial issues in conflict resolution. Some (or all) of the parties involved may wish to have a gracious exit from the presenting conflict—and may even want this to be unspoken and not openly acknowledged. Such wishes need to be respected, and each party must be allowed not to confront or handle the conflict or not to respond to the therapist's suggestions (Chen, 2002). For example, a mother came into conflict with her emaciated daughter over eating. The therapist invited the father to help mediate; the father said no. The therapist respected the father's decision—but used it as an entry point, such that further exploration revealed that the father did not feel competent to deal with the conflict and was generally unprepared to deal with this and other family conflicts. He had grown up in a highly conflicted family characterized by frequent marital friction between his parents and also conflicts between his mother and his paternal grandparents—while conflicts with mothers-in-law are not uncommon and indeed the subject of many jokes in the West, in Chinese societies the relationship is regarded as intra-family, and indeed with all parties often under the same roof. He would lock himself up in his room to avoid facing the conflicts by reading and listening to music. Pressing this reluctant father to intervene in the mother–daughter conflicts would also make him lose face, *mianzi*, and feel intimidated. A more respectful way is to allow psychological space and time, so that he could work through his resistance and begin to question and perhaps even dislike his habitual coping, before getting him to change.

Motivating and Engaging the Ambivalent Young Person

Young people with AN are typically ambivalent toward change and often have low motivation in seeking help and participating in treatment (Bruch, 1973; Selvini Palazzoli, 1981). This ambivalence is a cause of dropout in treatment, which in one study was 10% (Hoste, Zaitsoff, Hewell, & Le Grange, 2007) for adolescent patients and 38% to 63% for adult patients. Engaging the young person in treatment and motivating her to assume an active role in recovery are critical especially in the initial stage of treatment.

Such a treatment goal can be achieved by accepting resistance as part of the treatment challenge, with the therapist responding empathetically to the pains and sufferings of the emaciated young person at multiple levels, inside the body, with her friends, parents, and siblings, and with mental health professionals, heightening the young person's awareness of the devastating impact of the disorder on different aspects of her life and contextualizing her pain and suffering in order to understand the metaphoric meanings of the disorder.

In a nutshell, in the modified model engaging and motivating the emaciated young person to assume an active role in recovery are as important as disrupting the symptomatic cycle of interactions in the family. Ways of engaging the young person and motivating her to assume personal responsibility are discussed in detail in chapters 6 and 7, respectively.

Help to Overcome Other Family Problems

Before the onset of the disorder, the family functioning of some afflicted patients has been adversely affected by negative life events such as the death of the father, parental divorce or separation, especially when caused by extramarital affairs, unemployment, undiagnosed mental illness of the parent(s), and in particular serious traumatic events such as incest. Although it remains unknown how these predisposing factors interact with AN to affect family functioning, one can hardly doubt that such negative life events can generate series conflicts and tensions, both overt and hidden, in the family. In helping these multiproblem families, the therapist has to collaborate with other helping professionals such as psychiatrists and social workers to help the family overcome these difficulties. In doing so, the therapist can concentrate her or his effort and time in assisting the family to resolve problems and difficulties that have arisen directly from the disorder.

INTERDISCIPLINARY COLLABORATION

The modified treatment model cannot be operated in isolation. There should be medical backup from a multidisciplinary mental health team with knowledge and skills in managing AN. Medical backup is extremely important in the family treatment of the adolescent and young woman with AN; many physical complications arising from malnutrition require medical care and attention. Family therapists with no medical training must team up with a psychiatrist, a family physician, or a pediatrician who has clinical experience in caring for emaciated patients. In our situation, the author has teamed up with the adolescent and child psychiatric team of our university in managing the emaciated young person.

Even with medical backup, the family therapist still has to monitor the patient's body weight throughout the course of the treatment. Before the start of every treatment session, the adolescent or young adult woman is weighed. Any change in body weight is an indicator of the patient's health and her response to treatment. A sudden and severe drop of body weight requires the therapist to deal with the crisis immediately, if necessary with hospitalization.

For families with multiple problems, social service support from the community is part and parcel of the overall management for the emaciated young person and the family. Working closely with a family-oriented community social worker in the active role of a case manager of the family is highly beneficial.

Chapter 5
Treatment Process

THE THERAPEUTIC PROCESS

Stage 1: Shifting the Family's Focus From the Symptom to the Constricting Family Process

In response to the patient's unpredictable and bizarre behaviors, parents are in a state of bewilderment and emotional intensity, characterized by guilt, shame, anxiety, and uncertainty (Harden, 2005; Karp & Tanarugsachock, 2000). They do not know how to react behaviorally and emotionally, and the parents' psychological and social well-being is subsequently affected. Many parents blame themselves for inappropriate parenting and perceive it as the major contributing factor for their daughter developing anorexia nervosa (AN). The parents' culpability is typically expressed by the mother as "my being too indulging as a parent; my being ignorant of this disorder" and by the father as "my being too demanding and punitive; my being too stoic and old-fashioned." The couple also tends to blame each other for causing the problem.

Nevertheless, the family therapist needs to assess the positive aspects of the parents being in this state. The emotional intensity can be an impetus for parents to seek information, to explore new ways of parenting, and to experiment with new ways of relating to one another as well as to reexamine family values and beliefs. It is critical for the family therapist to make use of this opportunity to restore the parents' competence and confidence and to mobilize their resilience to collaborate as a team in rescuing the emaciated daughter. The first step toward this goal is through shifting the family's conceptualization of the problem.

In the first session, the attention of both the young person and the parents is on the symptoms. Parents might not have a clear idea of what caused the disorder, nor do they know what family therapy is. Somehow one day they suddenly find that their daughter is on a diet and is rapidly losing weight. Parents tend to perceive that something has gone wrong with their daughter that has caused her become "crazy" to start dieting. They blame the young person for food refusal and use ways to control her rather than to care for her. The young person naturally resists by fighting back and gripping tightly onto the problem. Feeling desperate, devastated, and angry, parents become hopeless, helpless, and powerless. The only alternative and option left is to seek professional advice; some parents even invite professionals to take over their roles.

The young person adopts a similar mind-set to understand her own problem. In the first interview, the young person typically responds to the therapist evasively but concretely that she likes being slim and thin. Losing weight has given her a false sense of control and a personal ideal in life. No wonder most of these young people come to receive treatment only halfheartedly. The motivation for change varies from one person to another. Some are ambivalent toward change, some perceive it as parental demand, while a minority, alarmed and tormented by the feeling of losing control, wish to take the opportunity to fix the problem of food refusal.

As both the afflicted young person and her parents perceive AN to be an individual problem, it is logical for them to expect the therapist to help fix the young person's abnormal thinking and change her dieting behavior accordingly. Their perceived solution would be simple and straightforward—that the emaciated young person has to change, and there is no part for members of the family to play in her recovery. Therein lies the paradox: The attempted solution constitutes the problem (Watzlawick, Weakland, & Fisch, 1974). Their conception of the problem results in excessive preoccupation with body weight, food, and dieting; hence they overlook other options and possibilities that are readily available.

While acknowledging the need for the young person to be responsible for her own health and to take charge of her recovery, the family therapist's principal task in the initial stage of treatment is to expand the problem conceptualization by introducing a new frame and by shifting their attention from the symptom to the constricting family process that has limited their options and possibilities in coping. The paramount concern is not to find out the cause of the disorder but to identify the stifling family context that has maintained and escalated the symptoms of AN.

Governing the shift of the treatment focus is the current knowledge on the disorder and the belief toward the family. As shown from patient narratives, the etiology of AN is multifactorial. From a systemic framework, it is an arduous task for the therapist to single out any factor that has caused the disorder. The task of identifying the cause would be especially complicated for those young people with a long history of the illness. It is widely recognized that the maintenance of food refusal is context dependent. Examining AN within its immediate family context may unveil the mystery of the disorder and may illuminate ways of finding the "key" to free the deadlock of the family in facing AN.

The family story presented is problem saturated; it reflects only part of the family life but usually does not provide the full picture. The family is believed to be more complex and richer, in terms of its experience and resources, than what the family might appreciate or articulate (Minuchin & Nichols, 1993; Minuchin, Nichols, & Lee, 2007). It is essential for the therapist to listen to their problem-saturated stories as well as to assess strengths and resources that the family may be unaware of.

To effect the shift is to translate the problem of food refusal from an individual frame to a relational frame, to link the symptoms of self-starvation to the constricting family context, and most importantly to help the young person and the family to perceive the linkage between the symptoms and the constricting family context. A case vignette illustrates the process of problem translation.

Case vignette. An 11-year-old AN daughter, Mary, had suffered from AN for two years.[2] She started dieting after attending a class on nutrition and health. She had been hospitalized three times, had restored her body weight quickly during hospitalization, but had each time relapsed soon after being discharged. The psychiatrist sent an ultimatum to the parents upon the second relapse and strongly suggested they attend family treatment. At the first family interview, the daughter weighed 29 kg at a height of 146 cm (BMI = 13.6). She looked skinny and pale. She was unfriendly to the family therapist. The parents were exhausted, helpless, and hopeless, believing that they had already been defeated. Like most of the parents, they hoped that the therapist could educate the emaciated daughter and let her realize how foolish she was in self-starvation. About 30 minutes into the treatment, the

---

[2] All the names used in this book are pseudonyms to protect the privacy of the patients.

mother mentioned that the paternal grandmother was living with them. She was the major caregiver for the daughter since her infancy, as the mother needed to work during daytime. The grandma would do whatever she could in order to please the granddaughter. The therapist then turned to ask the 5-year-old little brother if he enjoyed similar privileges from the grandmother.

The son replied, "No, grandma would do everything for her [Mary], but not for me."

The therapist responded with curiosity, "I see. Who is the most powerful person in this family?"

The son uttered, "My sister."

The therapist said, "Oh, really! Then who is the second powerful person in the family?"

The son replied sweetly, "Dad."

The therapist expressed appreciation for his sharpness in observation and asked, "How about your mom and you?"

The little son said, "My mom is the third most powerful person in the family. I am the least powerful person."

The therapist continued along this track and asked, "When did your sister become so powerful?"

The son said, "After she was ill. Before that, she is not like that."

The 5-minute exploration revealed that Mary had become the most powerful person at home after the onset of AN and that her position of power was higher than that of her parents. Apparently Mary's self-starvation was maintained by a reversal of the hierarchical organization between the parents and the daughter; this explained the parents' inability to refeed Mary at home. Further exploration showed that the parents had handed over their power to the daughter upon professional advice. The inexperienced mental health professionals whom they had consulted previously had suggested that they reduce Mary's psychological stress. When she was not stressed, she would have an appetite for food and her body weight could be restored accordingly. The parents interpreted the well-intentioned professional advice as having to please their daughter unconditionally. The family therapist talked to Mary and the little brother respectively, in front of the parents, to learn if they liked their parents to be so weak and incompetent. Both felt bad about this. Mary was upset that the parents expected her to make every decision, even those that were apparently beyond her ability. The voices of the two children moved the parents. Looking puzzled and confused, they began to question their old way of conceptualizing the problem and handling it.

In this case, the therapist utilized the information given by the mother on the relationship between Mary and her paternal grandmother to explore if there was any change in the parent–child relationship and to identify if such a change was related to the symptoms of AN. The process of exploration was also a process of problem translation. The son's description of the reversal of the parent–daughter hierarchical organization and the daughter's protest against having an age-inappropriate task of decision making thrust upon her were powerful messages to the parents—that their present coping was ineffective and self-defeating; they could respond to the disorder differently.

However, the therapist had to be extremely careful at this point, by holding a nonblaming attitude toward the parents, being supportive, and being empathetic. This could be achieved by complimenting the parents' efforts in sacrificing their own needs and abdicating their parental power in order to rescue the emaciated daughter, by acknowledging their pain and suffering, but also by reiterating the ineffectiveness of their sacrifice in helping. The nonblaming attitude of the therapist would be warmly welcomed and received with great relief by most guilt-ridden parents.

There is one caveat. In translating the problem the therapist must not play down the physical danger of the disorder. On the contrary, using a grave and earnest voice, the therapist should stress in different ways the gravity of the problem and the mortality rate resulting from severe emaciation. The intensification of the crisis is useful for those protective parents who have denied or minimized the problem of food refusal. The emaciated daughter needs to hear such a powerful message too.

Change of the problem definition and identification of the problem-maintaining system, if successful, would energize the family to participate actively in treatment. It can be regarded as *a prerequisite* to the next stage of treatment, namely to encourage the emaciated young person to perceive the urgent need of seeking help from the parents and to foster parental collaboration in refeeding the self-starving child.

Stage 2: Collaboration With Parents Through Empowerment and Instilment of Hope

In the second stage, the therapist aims to (a) foster parental collaboration to fight the disorder and (b) encourage the emaciated young person to perceive the urgent need of seeking help from the parents.

Collaborating with Chinese parents in refeeding the self-starving young person is by no means easy. The difficulties lie in the parents' expectation of family therapy: "You the expert should help fix the problem." Unsurprisingly they feel confused, puzzled, and bewildered in learning from the therapist that they have to assume the bulk of responsibility to refeed the emaciated daughter. How to engage them and win their trust becomes the primary concern in the initial stage of treatment, which can be achieved through joining and emotional connection.

Emotional connection. It is crucial to establish emotional connection with each parent, to tolerate unpleasant emotions, in particular, tension, frustration, and anger, and to let them feel understood and accepted (Diamond & Liddle, 1999). Female therapists can especially connect with the emaciated young person and the mother.

Successful engagement and joining with the father is culturally strategic and practically necessary. Despite modernization, the father is still the head of household and the decision maker in the majority of Chinese families. Most of the fathers are as distressed and desperate as the mothers. Overlooking their needs for care and concern would be a disservice. Female therapists might make use their gender constraint to join the father by saying, "As I am a woman, I may be unable to understand your experience as a father in going through the illness of your daughter. Can you share with us your experience here?" Following such an invitation, most Chinese fathers are happy to share their experience of the illness. By taking care of the emotional need of the father and understanding his coping and strengths, the therapist is able to win his trust and convince him of the importance of his active participation in treatment. In treatment, some of the parents' intense negative emotional and behavioral responses, including parental rejection toward the patient's emaciation, may be unintelligible to the therapist, suggesting the need to explore parents' history of upbringing.

Understanding parents' history of upbringing. In working with Chinese parents, it is crucial to understand their family of origin, the history of their upbringing, and their position and responsibility in the family of origin. The exploration allows the therapist to assess each parent's personal and social expectations in parenting, elicit the hidden meanings of the parent–child conflicts, and deepen the children's empathetic understanding toward the burden of care shouldered by either or both parents.

Political upheavals, urbanization, and migration from village to town are common themes in development in Asia. For example, the elder generation of many families in Hong Kong migrated from villages in rural China and perhaps went through the turmoil of the Cultural Revolution. Behind an angry father could be a story of a young man who had suffered from poverty and/or political upheaval and had to be the major breadwinner in his family of origin, often in the ancestral rural village. In light of the upbringing of this father, the daughter's self-starvation was unbelievable and totally unacceptable. His rage and anger toward his emaciated daughter seemed to be natural and appropriate.

Encouraging the emaciated young person to seek help from the parents through externalization and the use of metaphor. Mutual blaming by the parents and between the emaciated young person and the parent(s) is common and impedes their cooperation and collaboration to fight the disorder. How are we going to face this difficult situation?

This paradox can be tactfully resolved by employing White's (1983) technique of externalization, which refers to the process of changing the patient and the parents' understanding of AN to see it as an enemy from the outside and not a psychological problem or pathology of the patient. The process of externalization involves the therapist's attempt to elicit the adverse effects of AN on different members of the family, using the art of questioning to help them identify AN as their common enemy, and in doing so to energize them collectively to face the imminent threat. This is another way of changing the family's definition of the problem. This technique can effectively engage the parents in collaborative action without blaming them.

The use of metaphor is also clinically useful and acceptable to the parents. The therapist invites the parents to imagine that their daughter is suffering from cancer or a life-threatening disease that demands their quick action to save her. Do not underestimate the power of this metaphor. It is graphic enough to heighten the parents' awareness of the severity of the disorder, to increase their anxiety, and to prepare them for change on the one hand and to remind them of their past competence in parenting on the other. Most importantly, the parents would blame neither themselves nor the child for illnesses such as cancer.

The techniques of externalization and the use of metaphor are quite effective in working with families with emaciated children and teenage girls. The therapeutic effect is remarkable for Chinese families with good family functioning prior to the onset of AN. It works with those couples who have covertly and overtly mitigated, undermined, and even defeated each other in parenting due to their disparate problem conceptualization and handling. These techniques also stop the father from blaming the mother and alleviate the mother's sense of culpability.

Externalization of the problem can enhance the patient's motivation in treatment and alleviate her self-blame. The therapist delivers an intense message to the patient: "I am saddened by the fact your enemy has almost controlled your mind and overtaken your body. There is no time to lose. You have to fight back in order to restore your health." Externalization of the problem offers a legitimate reason for the therapist to encourage the young person to invite her parents to help her fight the enemy. The therapist says to the emaciated young person, "In order to drive away your enemy, you need allies. Would you invite your parents to be your allies?" This step is extremely important: It makes the young person assume responsibility for her recovery, so that she feels respected and in control. As a result, her sense of personal ineffectiveness is reduced.

On the other hand, externalization, if used indiscriminately, runs the risk of being interpreted by adult patients as the therapist's rejection of the important aspect of her personal identity, denying her personal experience of the illness, and depriving her of her choice between striving for recovery or remaining sick (Vitousek, 2005). One has to be cautious of some of the potential risks and problems involved in employing this technique for adult patients: the problem of underutilizing the positive aspect of the anorexic self, the problem of imposed reality, the problem of excluded reality, the question of responsibility, the question of agency, and the question of truth. To minimize these risks, the patient and the parents need to understand that the therapist is adopting a metaphor to help them to work toward an acceptance of a complex self (Vitousek, 2005).

For a young adult woman with AN, it is more promising to acknowledge her obstinate self that has been so powerful to restrain her from the bodily desire for food and drinks, and to positively reframe it as her unique personal quality which can also propel her to recover.

The therapist could say, "Most successful people in society are as determined and self-disciplined as you are. Once they have identified their life goal, they channel all their time and energies to it. You probably do not know that you have this personal quality too. Your stubbornness is a gift. I believe that once you made up your mind to fight the disorder, you would be able to do so." The therapist sometimes tells a story of a great man with such personal attributes to make it more persuasive to the young person.

Externalization has limited therapeutic effects for those families with multiple problems and difficulties such as severe marital discord, an undiagnosed or diagnosed mental disorder in the family, and unemployment before the onset of AN. In multiple-problem families, it is not surprising to find that the emaciated young person is healthier than her parents. In these cases, the onset of the AN can be used as a gateway for the family to work on their long-standing problem(s), which can hardly be handled simplistically by externalization and the use of metaphor.

Working on the core family problems. Burdened by their own problem(s), parents of multiproblem families are too exhausted to help their afflicted daughter. To encourage parental collaboration, the therapist must assist the family to work on the core problem(s), which could be multiple, for example marital crisis, unemployment, poverty, and physical or mental illnesses of the parent(s). Referral of a hitherto undiagnosed mentally ill parent to psychiatric treatment or referral of poverty cases for the welfare subsidy should be made as soon as possible. Once the family recognizes the therapist's helping role in generating hope and alternatives for tackling their difficulties, they are more willing to shift their attention from their own problem(s) to help the emaciated young person.

Eliciting parental competence. The therapist can make use of the here and now therapeutic context to elicit the parents' competence in parenting and to empower them. Therapy differs from education in its emphasis on experiential learning and its focus on the irrationality of human life. The therapeutic impact of creating a context for the parents to revitalize and reconfirm their competence in parenting is more influential than simply telling them that they have been competent parents.

Take the example of Mary's family: In the second session, the parents were as weak, helpless, and powerless as before; they lacked confidence and the competence to refeed their daughter. They looked for a miracle from the therapist. While the parents were complaining to the therapist, Mary struck her little brother when he asked her to play with him. The brother cried. The parents did not stop Mary or show their disapproval. By capturing what had happened, the therapist invited the parents to manage Mary's misbehavior. The mother responded immediately to the invitation and went to stop Mary and comfort her son. The father ordered Mary back to her own seat and to apologize to her brother. The aggressive and unreasonable "monster" responded to her parents' demand obediently. She apologized to her brother and sat down in silence on the sofa. The therapist congratulated the parents for their competence in managing Mary's misbehavior and asked them if they could exercise their parental power in a similar manner at mealtime. The parents beamed with hope for the first time since the therapy started and promised to try. The therapist ended the session by reiterating that the parents needed to support each other and be psychologically prepared to fight a hard battle with AN at home during mealtime in the coming week, including facing the yelling and screaming of Mary when they changed to asserting their parental authority to refeed her.

Stage 3: Addressing Unresolved Conflicts Using Culturally Appropriate Strategies

Food generates conflicts for the self-starving young person; it is also a means to express her conflicts, discontentment, and anger toward the parents (Ogden, 2003). The parent–child interaction is often restricted by their excessive attention on eating and noneating. Their continual struggle results in anger, frustration, hopelessness, and helplessness. Sometimes, the negative consequences of AN are so severe that it leaves the family with little energy to take care of other aspects of their lives or unfulfilled needs (Eisler, 1995).

The therapist has to be psychologically prepared to work with intense emotions, to tolerate the messiness arising from the conflict, and to accept her or his own feeling of impotence and lack of control amid the family chaos.

Prior to helping to disrupt the negative symptomatic cycle, an assessment should be made to understand the different aspects of conflict: the nature of the conflict, the content of the conflict, the process of the conflict, the number of actors involved (who and whom), and the availability of conflict resolution method, if any. The next two case vignettes illustrate the importance of family conflicts for assessment and treatment.

Case vignette. Fan had been suffering from AN for 7 years. She was the first child of a large family and was 22 years old at the time of referral. She had two younger sisters and two younger brothers. Her two sisters were college students while her two brothers, aged 17 and 14, were in secondary school. The father was a foreman and the mother a housewife. The family lived in a public housing estate. She was still under hospital treatment at the time of the first family interview. Fan burst into tears when she told the family therapist that she was suffering immensely as she was caught in a great dilemma. She wished to go home from the hospital for weekends but was very unhappy during these home visits, as her parents did not allow her to prepare her own meals and forced her to eat those foods that were prepared and assigned by the parents.

Fan cried hysterically, "Why can't you trust me? I've grown up and I have the right to choose my own food. It is my body and my own health. Why do you [parents] force me to do things against my will?" The parents looked pale and enraged. Her mother explained, "We can't leave it to you. I have tried in the past. The result is that you relapsed again and again. You will starve yourself to death and we have to take charge of your body."

Fan fought back and said, "You can control other aspects of my life, but you can never control my body."

The family therapist asked, "Are you suggesting that you choose to starve yourself as a means to protest against your parents?"

Fan nodded her head and said, "Yes. That's the only way I can win."

The family therapist replied empathetically, "I see."

Fan's siblings allied with their parents and lectured her for her stupidity in doing so. Apparently Fan was a loner, and no one was willing to listen to her voice in the family. Self-starvation seemed to be her crusade against all odds.

Case vignette. Lily, aged 13, was the second child of a family of four. She had a 15-year-old elder sister. Her parents had been separated for a year, and her mother had moved out to live on her own. She had been suffering from AN for 6 months. Lily came from a lower class family. Her father, an illiterate and unskilled worker, was the victim of an occupational injury. He was paralyzed for a year after falling down from a high wall. Fortunately he regained 90% of his mobility a year later, though he still suffered from constant bodily pains and numbness. Lily's mother was an Indonesian Chinese who had married Lily's father to escape from poverty in her homeland. She was beautiful and attractive. Before the economic depression, she had worked as a waitress in a restaurant. At the time of the referral, the whole family was on welfare assistance. In the first interview, Lily told the family therapist that her AN was attributable in part to her wish to save money for the family and in part to her unhappiness at home. Her mother returned home every day to look after the children but had stopped talking to her husband for at least 6 months. Apparently this family was unfavorably affected by multiple problems including poverty, unemployment, parental marital discord, and the father's injury. A family secret was disclosed in the second interview.

The father told the family therapist, "My wife rejected me because I am useless after the injury. I can't work and I can't support the family financially."

Instead of talking to her husband, the mother turned to the therapist and said furiously, "No. That's not true. When I married you, you were not rich. You know what you've done. You deserve the punishment."

Lily and her eldest sister were in great distress. The air in the room froze. The father lowered his head and remained silent.

"What has happened to the family that you need to punish him?" asked the family therapist with care and concern.

Following a long silence, the mother finally uttered with tears falling on her cheeks, "He sexually abused my 15-year-old niece, who was living with us two years ago. She is my sister's eldest daughter. She came from my village to help look after our children. That morning he wished to make love with me. I was still sleeping and I turned him down. He went out and did that. He pressed his body on top of my niece and molested her. At that time my niece was sleeping in the sitting room. My sister and my mom kept blaming me for not reporting the case to the police. I wish to protect him. I do regret that I didn't call the police at that time."

The father whispered with great pain, "Heaven has already punished me by giving me the injury. I've already said sorry to you several times and you still won't forgive me."

Lily and her eldest sister crawled on the sofa and their bodies were shivering. The mother continued sobbing and said, "How can I forgive you? How? Please tell me how."

Apparently this family was still haunted by the father's disgraceful sexual molestation of his niece, and the pain and suffering of each family member were great.

Diagnostic value of family conflicts. The above two case vignettes illustrate the diagnostic and therapeutic values of bringing conflicts out into the open. In both cases, the family therapist successfully elicited the family conflicts through enactment (Minuchin & Fishman, 1981; Nichols & Fellenberg, 2000), a technique commonly adopted by the structural family therapy school to direct family members to talk or interact together in order to observe and change problematic transactions.

The family conflicts discerned in treatment enable the therapist to assess the linkage of AN to the family context and to identify if the family context has maintained or escalated the problem of food refusal. In the case of Fan, the area of conflict was meal preparation. Fan and her parents were first involved in the argument, and her siblings later joined in. Sadly, none of Fan's siblings supported her in her fight with her parents. The family process observed suggested that Fan was weak and powerless in the family; and all the family members treated her as insane. Fan's self-starvation had become her only effective weapon to gain power and retain her sense of dignity in her family. If the presenting transactional pattern among Fan, her parents, and her siblings would not change, the possibility of Fan giving up self-starvation would be slim.

Although the family drama discerned was messy and unpleasant, it was diagnostically useful, as it pointed the way to formulating the treatment strategy. The strategies of helping for this family were primarily threefold: (a) to help the family to be aware of their process of conflict and to understand its linkage to the child's self-starvation, (b) to collaborate with them to break the self-defeating pattern of transaction that has maintained the self-star-vation, and (c) to help Fan to fight her parents, which is developmentally normal for adolescents and young adults, not only in areas of concern other than self-starvation. The family therapist employed a key treatment strategy to achieve the goal of helping, namely identifying a potential healer in the family, in this case the younger sister, toward the end of the session. Sympa-thetic to Fan's difficult position, she was able to recognize this dysfunctional transactional pattern of interaction and to find ways to interrupt it by inviting Fan and her parents to try new ways of interacting with one another.

The family conflict in Lily's family was as overt as that in Fan's family, but its nature was utterly different. Sexual abuse is a taboo in many societ-ies, including Chinese societies (Ng & Ma, 2004). Its occurrence within the family would indeed be a great shame to the family. The wife was courageous in disclosing it to the therapist. The disclosure uncovered the unresolved family trauma that had haunted the family for a long time. Lily's self-starva-tion can be interpreted as a cry for help as well as a response to the intolerable and tense family environment. The hurt between the couple was a big hurdle for them to join hands and cooperate as a team in helping Lily to recover.

Disrupting the family's negative interaction using means that synchronize with the culture. To disrupt the negative interactions of such families, treat-ment strategies such as normalizing the parent–child conflicts, helping to shift the conflicts from eating to other aspects of life (e.g., personal privacy, relationship with peers), and helping them to identify an essential dynamic of the parent–adolescent conflicts and to repair the quality of their relation-ship (Diamond & Liddle, 1999; Eisler, 1996; Ogden, 2003) are clinically useful. For example, in the case of Fan's family, the therapist acknowledged the developmental need of Fan to rebel against her parents but reiterated the importance of not using her own body as the battlefield to fight with her parents. The therapist solicited the parents' collaboration to allow Fan to be rebellious in areas other than eating. These treatment strategies were applied to help Fan's family with success.

Cultural heritage can also be a resource for treatment. It is an art for the therapist to effect changes under different therapeutic contexts by tapping into the specific cultural resources, for instance, the cardinal rule of filial piety in Chinese societies. The afflicted young person has an encouraging response toward the therapist's positive interpretation of the doctrine by downplaying the element of parental control and emphasizing self-responsibility to take care of her own health and citing a millennium-old Confucian saying, "Your body with your hair and your skin is a gift from your parents. You must treasure this gift to be filial" (*Xiao Jing*, 1960, p. 1).

Stage 4: Handling Relapse by Preventing the Reemergence of the Symptomatic Cycle and Enhancing Family Relationships

In the course of family treatment, any relapse would stunt the progress of the treatment. A trap that the patient, the family, and the therapist may fall into is to focus on the body weight and dieting again. An easy way for the therapist to get out from this trap is to review any episode that had affected the young person or the family and that may have caused the relapse. Holding a sympathetic, concerned, and patient attitude, the therapist can easily find out what has happened in the young person's life or in her family that has resulted in behavioral change. Once a full picture has been gained of what has actually happened, the therapist should next look into whether the patient and the parents had done anything to prevent this relapse before the treatment.

Take the example of Mary: After a steady gain in weight from the second session onward, there was a drop of 1 kg when she was weighed at the sixth session. An assessment revealed that the family was shocked by the sudden death of the paternal grandmother a week ago. The grandmother had fallen down on the floor of the kitchen one day, became unconscious, and was dead on arrival at the hospital. As the only son and having been brought up single-handedly by his widowed mother, the father was deeply grieved. The death of the paternal grandmother was a blow to Mary too, as she had been looked after by the grandmother since birth. The therapist was keen to know whether the grandmother's death had affected the parents' previous achievement of refeeding Mary and whether Mary's appetite was adversely affected. Fortunately, although the parents' mood was very low, they still functioned as a team at mealtime. Mary was sad, but her appetite was only slightly affected. The therapist created a supportive and permissive context for the family to share their loss and express their grief. It took two more sessions for the family to go through the grief. To the relief of the therapist, Mary's body weight continued to rise and was back to normal 2 months later.

The young person's relapse can be read as a signal of help or as a stress threshold, indicating that she is facing a stressful event that she is unable to cope with. Ann was a 17-year-old whose body weight had dropped from 46 kg to 41.5 kg when she was studying hard for a public examination. Brought up in a postdivorce family, Ann was living with her 40-year-old mother and her three siblings. The family was on welfare, as her father had refused support after his remarriage. As one of the bright children in the family with good grades at school, Ann knew very well that it was only through education that she could climb the social ladder and lift her family out of poverty. To Ann, good grades on the public examination not only could represent the fulfillment of her personal dream in becoming a professional but also would be a tribute to the family by a filial daughter. She told the therapist that she had no time for meals and that she needed to concentrate all her efforts on studying in order to gain admission to the more prestigious local universities. Ann liked studying in a community library, took her two meals outside, and returned home late. One of Ann's classmates called her mother one night and informed her that Ann often missed her meals during study. Alarmed and shocked, the mother responded immediately. She prepared lunch for Ann and demanded that she came home for dinner. She followed her mother's advice obediently. Ann had insight on her own problem. She knew the detrimental effects of skipping meals but lacked the strong will to break her own habit. The timely intervention helped Ann to prevent the relapse and recover subsequently.

Review through ongoing assessment. Ann's story illustrates that an assessment of different aspects of the patient's life such as her studies and peer and family relationships has to be an ongoing process. To Ann, the source of stress was studying. Since studying had such an important meaning in Ann's life, it became a psychological burden. Like most young people with food refusal problems, Ann was at risk of relapsing to cope with stress. She was lucky because there were two healers in her immediate social network: her mother and her good friend. They were perceptive enough to prevent the relapse by stopping Ann's self-defeating cycle of coping.

For those young people with unsympathetic parents or unsupportive peers at school, a review in the session would help tremendously. The review will elicit the parents' compassion and increase their understanding of the young person's struggle. In hearing the young person's struggle and learning about her difficulties, the anger of the family members toward the young person's relapse may be alleviated. They may become more supportive instead.

Conduct the review flexibly. The review must be flexibly conducted subject to the young person's response and the nature of the precipitating event. The therapist has to provide sufficient psychological space for the parents to explore the matter jointly with the adolescent. When the parents run into difficulties, the therapist can initiate a dialogue with the adolescent; once the ice is broken, the parents are invited to join in the conversation and to take over the therapist's role. The therapist aims to serve as a bridge to help the parents review jointly and collaboratively with the adolescent.

The therapist should not rule out the possibility of meeting the young person alone if the subject matter is sensitive and private in nature in the eyes of the young person. Sometimes the therapist may solicit the help of a sibling to take up the task of reviewing. On other occasions, the therapist may need to ask the siblings to stay away from the subject matter as illustrated by the following case vignette.

Case vignette. Ying presented as a 15-year-old girl with a 6-month history of AN. Treatment had progressed well; her body weight had returned to normal at the month session, and her menstruation had returned, and the therapist was ready to declare success and terminate treatment. Then suddenly she lost 1 kg. The therapist tried to explore what was bothering her, but Ying was reluctant to talk. The therapist solicited the help of her mother, but in vain. Ying's reticence suddenly offered a hint to the therapist. Perhaps it was embarrassing for Ying to discuss the subject matter in front of her siblings. The therapist asked Ying if she would be more ready to share her concern with her mother, with her siblings out of the room. Ying nodded. While the siblings waited outside the treatment room, Ying told her mother that she had been worried about constipation for over a week. She feared that it might be related to the amount of food that the mother had prepared for her. The therapist cleared up her doubt by providing advice regarding the appropriate types of foods that she could take for regular bowel movements rather than reducing the amount of food at meals. Ying was relieved.

This story illustrates how sometimes a relatively trivial and unrelated matter can intrude into treatment and if not discovered and dealt with can prove to be the stumbling block. The art is obviously a sensitive ear for words unsaid; once the problem is identified, the remedy is easy.

Sometimes a relative can help to break through an impasse encountered in treatment.

Case vignette. Josephine, a 16-year-old girl, was in a family of four: father, mother, and an older brother age 19. The brother was already working, but Josephine was still in school but was very unhappy there. She wanted to quit and go out to work, but her mother insisted otherwise, even as she acknowledged Josephine's unhappiness. Probably as a result of the mother–daughter conflict, Josephine had suffered from AN for 12 months, and no progress was made in three sessions. The situation was aggravated when in the course of treatment her mother decided to divorce her husband—in fact, the precipitating factor surfaced in one session when she learned that her son was totally disappointed with his father, who was described as irresponsible, lazy, and egocentric. The father moved out, leaving Josephine and her mother to struggle with each other over the close but suffocating mother–daughter relationship. They fought with each other over trivial matters every day. At this point, and recognizing that the intense relationship may benefit from an outside catalyst, the therapist invited the mother and the daughter to identify a close relative whom they trusted and involved her in treatment. The aunt joined the subsequent session, and she did a marvelous job to elucidate why the patient refused to progress further. Josephine wished to quit her studies and go out to work. Her mother insisted that she continue schooling even though she was fully aware that the patient had a lot of unhappy experiences there. The therapist was impressed by the aunt's skilful way of opening up the mother–daughter conflict and facilitating their negotiation. The mother finally gave in without losing face, and Josephine won her battle. She succeeded in finding a job as a saleslady shortly after the session. The mother was pleased to see Josephine's steady gain in weight and the return of the patient's menstruation, in addition to the improvement of her well-being.

In short, the rule of thumb in conducting the review is to listen for the voice of the young person and respect her views. As long as the family members can take up the task of review, the task should be entrusted to them. The therapist is no more than a facilitator in the process.

Stage 5: Supporting Individual Development

In the latter stage of treatment, emphasis should be placed on supporting the young person's individual growth and development, which have previously been arrested by the disorder. Having broken the symptomatic cycle, there will be rippling effects on the family. The family will gradually function better, and the patient will be free from the control of the disorder. All these will perpetuate the patient's differentiation from the family, with her outlook and concern redirected back to the outside world. Some families embrace the patient's change and development with a warm welcome, while some are full of anxiety. It is critical to help parents to learn to let go in this stage.

Help parents to learn to let go. In some Asian societies including Chinese societies, the traditional culture makes it even more difficult to let go. Bound by the traditional Chinese culture value of filial piety, the individuation of Chinese adolescents is discouraged by strong loyalty to the family and the parents. Such cultural expectations prescribe a similar norm in parenting. For example, there is an old Chinese saying, "Once a parent; always a parent." Reading between the lines, there is the strong message that a dutiful Chinese parent is expected to take care of his or her child for life, which in part explains the excessive involvement of the parents in the young person's daily life even though the child is at the stage of gaining independence from the family. This cultural expectation in parenting is further reinforced by current social norms in some societies, which place the welfare of the child as the priority in society (Ma, Lai, & Pun, 2002).

Letting go of an AN child would be even more difficult. The dilemma is that at the initial stage of treatment, the therapist stresses parental collaboration and assertion of parental control in combating the disorder. Suggesting that parents let go at a later stage would result in confusion and unease, especially for parents carrying vivid memories of visceral anguish and worried about relapse. Conflicts between the parents and the young person are inevitably increased when the young person fights for more autonomy.

This demonstrates the need to support the growth and development of the parent(s) in order to support the growth and development of the patient. Take Josephine as an example; her mother had anxiety about letting Josephine go out to work, partly because she thought that Josephine was still too young and partly because the mother's meaning and life had been revolving around Josephine since her illness. Having divorced her irresponsible husband, the mother's life was empty. Caring for Josephine had become her only purpose in life. Making use of hypothetical questions (Stierlin & Weber, 1989), the therapist redirected the mother to search for new meaning in her life: Suppose your daughter fully recovers, how are you going to spend your time and plan your activity? Suppose Josephine starts dating, what will you do to make your life more interesting? These questions are future oriented. They attempt to open up alternatives and options without pressuring for change. A surprising outcome was that Josephine was enthusiastic in making several good suggestions to her lonely mother on ways of expanding her social circle.

An unfriendly and nonsupportive environment can discourage the young person's growth and development. The therapist must refrain from being overly optimistic and must acknowledge the possibility of setbacks due to unfavorable environmental factors such as an unfriendly work environment or failure to gain admission to a university, for example. Actions speak louder than words. In such circumstances, the therapist should practice what she or he believes—that she or he would never give up on the young person—by retracing the path back to the early steps of treatment.

Stage 6: Supporting the Transformation

In this stage of treatment, the therapist's task is to continue appreciating the recovered young person and the family's self-perpetuating process of change and the progress in their growth and development. Congratulating their achievement without owning the success is crucial. The role of the therapist in this stage is peripheral. The therapist can lengthen the interval between interviews, disengage the family gradually, and prepare for termination. Separation anxiety may need to be dealt with during the termination, and evaluation regarding the helpfulness of the treatment can be made.

AN OVERVIEW OF THE TREATMENT PROCESS

This chapter has described different stages of treating young people suffering from AN with some culture-specific factors relevant to the Chinese cited in particular. Table 5.1 summarizes the essential therapeutic tasks in each stage of treatment. Nevertheless, these stages serve only as signposts for the therapist to track the progress of treatment; they must not be followed and applied rigidly and sequentially. In family therapy, family assessment and treatment are inseparable. The above stages, when put into practice, are cyclic and dynamic rather than linear and stage specific. Therapeutic change should continuously evolve and oscillate among stages and should be consolidated and reinforced throughout the process of treatment. Nevertheless, caution should be exercised that the therapist would not work on the developmental issues of the emaciated young person unless the family has broken the symptomatic cycle that had maintained the symptoms.

The process of change will largely depend on the family's readiness to adopt relational perspectives to understand AN and their capability to identify alternative ways of resolving the intense control and power struggle between the emaciated young person and the parents in treatment, which in turn will pave the way for the parents' success to act as a team in refeeding the emaciated daughter.

Therapy is a process of co-construction between the therapist and the family. Karl Tomm (1998) is right: The family has granted the therapist the privilege of stepping into their private life. The treatment success has to rely heavily on the active participation of the emaciated daughter and the family, their commitment to change, and most importantly the flexibility of the therapist to adjust the roles and functions to changing family contexts and to modify treatment strategies accordingly.

The focus on the constricting family process and the interpersonal

dynamics does not mean that the therapist should play down the importance of intrapsychic needs, decision-making capacity, and responsibility of
individual family members. Getting to know each of the family members,
developing a good therapeutic alliance with the young person, and winning
her trust must never be underestimated, compared to the task of empowering
the parents.

Table 5.1: Therapeutic Process and Therapeutic Tasks in the Five Treatment Stages

Treatment Process
Stage 1: Shifting the family's focus from the symptoms to the constricting family context   • Identify the young person's and the parents' conceptions of the disorder   • Explore whether the symptoms are maintained and escalated by the family context   • Reframe the problem of AN in a relational lens   • Identify the family strengths and family resources
Stage 2: Collaborating with parents through empowerment and instilment of hope   • Make an emotional connection with the parents   • Understand the parents' history of upbringing   • Encourage the emaciated young person to seek help from the parents through externalization of the problem and use of metaphor   • Help to resolve the core family problem(s) (e.g., family poverty, unemployment, parents' mental health problems)   • Elicit parental competence
Stage 3: Addressing unresolved conflicts using culturally appropriate strategies   • Identify the source(s), nature, frequency of family conflicts   • Identify potential family healer(s) in conflict resolution   • Disrupt the family's negative interaction using ways that synchronize with the Chinese culture   • Utilize cultural assets and cultural resources

Table 5.1 (Cont'd)

Stage 4: Handling relapse by preventing the reemergence of the symptomatic cycle and enhancing family relationships

- Review through ongoing assessment
- Conduct the review flexibly
- Disrupt the symptomatic cycle of family interaction that maintained the relapse
- Enhance mutual understanding in the family

Stage 5: Supporting individual development

- Help parents to learn to let go
- Support growth and development of the recovering young person

---

Stage 6: Supporting the transformation

- Appreciate and validate the recovered young person's effort in maintaining her health and expand her social life
- Prepare for the termination

Chapter 6
Developing a Therapeutic Relationship

INTRODUCTION

Developing therapeutic rapport with young people suffering from anorexia nervosa (AN) is never easy. Malnutrition has significant effects on different aspects of their lives. At very low weight and under the physiological effects of starvation, the patients seem to be in a "toxic" state that is beyond the reach of significant others as well as the therapist (Dare & Crowther, 1995). They are highly sensitive, unfriendly, unapproachable, and hostile and exhibit great mood swings. Some patients argue with and scream at their parents over trivial matters, while others simply ignore their parents or express their anger and frustration in cold silence. They also tend to project their unresolved relational difficulties with their parents onto the patient–therapist relation (Hughes, 1997). The patient–therapist relation is an enactment of the disturbed and conflicting relationship of the patient with her parents.

Due to self-starvation, these adolescents often wrestle with their parents over the issue of control. The parents wish to control their self-starving daughter by forcing the adolescent to eat while the daughter asserts her will and fights back by further reducing the amount of food intake. From the perspective of the parents, these adolescents are defiant and obstinate. Thus they are bad girls. The experience of these young people with their parents is unpleasant and uncomfortable. In the eyes of the emaciated young person, parents are often perceived as domineering, demanding, intrusive, and authoritative.

The psychiatric diagnosis of the disorder somehow may temporarily soften their entanglement and struggle for control. Knowing that their bad daughter is suffering from an illness may make the parents more tolerant of the daughter's insane behavior and become more caring and protective toward her. Paradoxically, their care and protection unwittingly reinforces the daughter's infantile behavior and encourages her to behave younger than her age. The psychological consequence arising from the psychiatric diagnosis for the patient is typically described by Stierlin and Weber (1989, p. 85): "Once diagnosed as a 'condition,' the mode of behavior becomes objectified, separated off, and torn out of its context; it is declared to be the problem of one single individual." Options for cure become limited, and only the doctor as an expert has the knowledge to treat the patient. The metaphor of "illnesses" will give the patient a legitimate reason to continue behaving irresponsibly. The problem is not simply how the patient sees herself but how our mental health service has supported the patient's reality that she is incapable of being competent.

There are a few critical issues that the therapist has to handle in the early phase of the treatment. The first is the therapist's tendency to be induced into an emotionally charged deadlock between the emaciated adolescent and her parents. Once caught in their self- defeating system, the therapist finds it impossible to maintain her or his neutrality and distance herself or himself from it in order to have sufficient psychological space for assessment. As part of the system, the therapist is tied down by their strong sense of helplessness and hopelessness. The adolescent may perceive the therapist siding with the parents, while the parents may fail to see any difference between the therapist's way of handling the problem and their own.

The second issue is how to make the adolescent feel that the therapist is different from her parents and other adults who try to help by controlling her. The emotional connection is fundamental for the therapist to motivate the adolescent to participate actively in treatment, to break out from her cocoon, to take up the responsibility of recovery, and to join hands with the parents and the therapist in combating self-starvation.

In this chapter, an attempt is made to identify and examine some difficult scenarios encountered in practice, to state principles for overcoming these difficulties, and to discuss ways of winning the emaciated person's confidence toward the therapist and family treatment.

VIGNETTE 1: THIS IS NONE OF YOUR BUSINESS

Maria, who was still staying in the hospital, entered the treatment room with her parents reluctantly. On the way to the treatment room of the hospital, Maria kept muttering, "I don't have any problem and I don't need any treatment. Please leave me alone in the ward." Her parents managed to settle her down on one of the sofas. Maria made no attempt to greet the therapist and remained detached in the first half of the session. The therapist leaned forward and started talking with her. She asked Maria for how long she had been hospitalized and what her experience at the hospital was like. Maria was agitated, showing no interest in any conversation with the therapist. She remained mute and sullen for a while. When the therapist attempted to engage her in conversation, Maria shouted rudely, "Who are you? This is none of your business. Please leave me alone." She turned to her parents, burst into tears, and cried like a baby, "I wish to go back to the ward. I don't wish to see this Dr. M [the therapist]. I want to leave this room. Let me go." Apologetic and embarrassed, the parents explained to the therapist that their daughter never behaved like that before the onset of self-starvation. She had always been polite and considerate toward others.

Maria's rejecting attitude put the therapist in a dilemma. If the therapist had persisted, she would have been repeating what her parents had done all along; and in doing so, she would have increased Maria's resistance toward her. Had she retreated, however, it might have reinforced Maria's belief that she could defeat the therapist in the same way she had defeated her parents and those who were concerned about her, thereby enabling her to win the upper hand in the struggle. In the face of this dilemma, the therapist did not have many options but to shift the exploration to her parents. The therapist chose to break the dilemma by asking the parents if similar situations had happened at home and how they had responded to Maria's rejection. The therapist went further to understand the impact of Maria's unreasonable behavior on each of the parents and on the family as well. The more articulate the parents, the easier it would be for the therapist to elicit their stories. At the end of the session, the therapist understood the parents' perspective but the patient's story remained obscure and unknown.

The core of the dilemma is often this: the patient is simultaneously saying "don't bother me" (explicitly) and "please reach out to me" (subtly). What should the therapist do to get out of this bind? How can the therapist connect with the patient without actively pursuing her?

VIGNETTE 2: I AM A FIGHTER AND I AM NOT AFRAID OF FIGHTING

Helen was the second child of a family of five: herself together with her father, her mother, her elder sister Susan, and her younger brother Eric. The three children were studying at university. Susan started losing weight during her first year of study when she felt rejected by her new friends in the university. The whole family attended the first family interview punctually. Helen's mother was very anxious, and her anxiety and worries drove her to dominate the conversation soon after the session began. After listening to her mother for a while, Helen cut in and argued with her mother on the incorrect information that she had given to the therapist. She was provoking, offensive, and rude to her mother. Displeased and offended by Helen's way of talking, her brother, Eric, reminded her to be polite toward her mother; the father and Susan followed suit. The drama emerging was striking. Helen, the fragile adolescent, was fighting a lonely battle against the united front of her parents and her siblings.

The therapist attempted to join Helen by re-presenting what she had observed in the room and by acknowledging her difficult position at home. To the therapist's disappointment, Helen became furious and hostile to the therapist. She said angrily, "I am sick of you professionals, who are so keen to analyze people's situation; that's all that you can offer." Judging from her tone, she was prepared to do everything to provoke the therapist to fight with her. The therapist learned from the mother that Helen had been referred for individual psychotherapy 6 months earlier. Every time Helen ended up arguing and quarreling with her psychotherapist and quit after three sessions. To Helen, various events in the past had confirmed that the outside world was dangerous. Her friends and classmates had rejected her, her siblings were not on good terms with her, her previous therapist had attempted to control her. Hostility and aggression seemed to work well as protection from hurt.

It is crucial for the therapist not to repeat the mistakes made by Helen's first therapist. But how can the therapist achieve this?

VIGNETTE 3: I AM FRIGHTENED AND
I HAVE TO FLEE

Ginny, a 16-year-old adolescent, was the second child of the family. She had an 18-year-old brother, and he was the mother's favorite child. As part of a traditional Chinese family, Ginny's mother valued a son more than a daughter. Ginny was displeased that her mother cared only about her brother and neglected her. It was the second time that Ginny missed the appointment. Her mother told the therapist that Ginny had refused to get out of bed. Ginny kept saying that she was very tired and wished to sleep. After several attempts, Ginny's mother went to see the therapist on her own. Ginny's mother was always punctual. She did not think that Ginny was sleepy or tired; she just wanted to avoid seeing the therapist. Ginny's treatment progress was not as smooth as expected. After the first session, the father missed several sessions too, in part because the treatment time clashed with his working hours and in part because the mother disliked attending the session with him. Ginny's mother was a new immigrant with a low level of education. She felt looked down upon by her husband and her in-laws. Constant quarrels and fights characterized the marital relationship. Ginny's mother had once moved out and went back to her village. She returned home a week later as she missed her two children very much. Before the onset of AN, Ginny enjoyed a very good relationship with her father. They had a lot of activities together, and her father often sided with her against her mother and her brother. However, it was strange that Ginny started to detach herself from her father after the onset of AN. She refused to be alone with him or to talk to him even during hospitalization.

Relating to Ginny required a lot of patience and acceptance. She was not unfriendly to the therapist as Maria and Helen were. She greeted the therapist and smiled back when the therapist joked with her. She was willing to share with the therapist parts of her life such as her studies and her views of different teachers. However, she would become vigilant when the therapist explored the family dynamics, especially the marital relationship between her parents and her relationship with her father. Her answer to the therapist's questions was always, "I don't know" or "I don't wish to say more." Moreover, from time to time she sought reassurance from her elder brother, leaving the therapist with the impression that she needed to hold back something. During the fifth session, the mother told the therapist that she had learned from Ginny that a night before Ginny's onset of the illness, her mother went out to play mahjong with her friends and her father went into her room. She stopped telling the mother what had happened and wept ceaselessly. The therapist invited the mother to make use of the session to learn more from Ginny about the father's behavior. The mother talked to Ginny patiently and reassured that she would protect her if any bad thing had happened. Ginny shook her head and refused to utter a word on the subject. There was something hanging in the air, but neither the mother nor the therapist knew what it was about. Perhaps Ginny was too frightened or too loyal to her father to disclose the secret. The therapist suggested seeing Ginny individually in the next appointment, but Ginny turned it down immediately. Thereafter, Ginny failed to turn up for treatment in the two subsequent sessions.

Ginny was fleeing. If you were the therapist, what would you do to engage her back in treatment?

VIGNETTE 4: IT IS TOO MUCH FOR ME AND
I AM DISSOCIATING

Fan, a 22-year-old young person mentioned in the past chapter, had been suffering from AN for 7 years. She had relapsed many times and was finally referred for family treatment. Fan started self-starvation in junior secondary school. Both Fan and her parents failed to recall what had caused her to dieting excessively. The cause had been lost in the history of the illness. Fan weighed only 32 kg. With a height of 160 cm, she was physically fragile and psychologically unstable. Fan had been receiving individual psychotherapy for a year with little progress. Her emaciation was as serious as before, and there was practically no gain in body weight. Family treatment was regarded as the last resort in the eyes of the parents and the patient. Fan came from a working-class family. Her father was hardworking though not well educated. His supervisor and his coworkers recognized his performance at work. Her mother was a full-time housewife and had to look after five children. Fan was the eldest daughter and had two sisters and two brothers. Her two sisters were college students and her two brothers were in secondary school.

Fan impressed the therapist as suffering from extremely low self-esteem and self-image. The therapist was deeply struck by the description of her own problem that was full of psychological jargon. She said, "My emaciation was caused by the fact that I had no self-confidence and I did not have any sense of competence. I am the cause of my own problem." Unsurprisingly, when she interacted with her family members, she was fearful of asserting her own view when repeatedly put down by her siblings and her parents. Her parents and siblings were caring of and concerned about Fan, but they blamed Fan for being "mad" and were the principal source of tensions and stresses at home. Fan internalized their views, became self-critical and felt culpable, but continued justifying her self-starvation by her poor self-image and self-esteem. In the first session, the therapist suggested a new frame for Fan and her family to understand her problem: that her unstable mood had a biological basis. She was suffering from chronic malnutrition that had impinged on her perception of the world, her psychological well-being, and her sense of mastery in life. Food was her immediate prescription. Fan should seek the help of her parents and her siblings in resuming normal meals.

The therapist was able to gain Fan's trust and the family's cooperation in achieving the goal of refeeding. Though the process was by no means smooth, Fan's body weight increased steadily. In the process of treatment, the therapist helped Fan fight her parents by shifting her battle with her parents from eating to other issues and by soliciting the support of her second sister in the process of resuming normal meals. The treatment lasted one and a half years. During the tenth session, Fan got into a heated argument with her parents regarding her freedom in preparing her own food. The parents turned down her request right away, and it was at this point that Fan became hysterical. She screamed and cried like a 2-year-old toddler. Suddenly she was dissociating. She asked her parents, "Who are you?" She turned to the therapist and kept shaking her head.

If you were the therapist in the room, how would you respond to Fan's dissociation?

PRINCIPLES FOR DEVELOPING
THERAPEUTIC RAPPORT

AN has been viewed as a disorder of the self (Bruch, 1973; Miller, 1991). The relentless pursuit of thinness can be regarded as a symbolic expression of the patient's self as "imperfect." Those young people with a vulnerable self-organization tend to resort to using the body to bolster themselves (Miller, 1991). Emaciation can be understood as the patient's concrete self-experience and as an attempt to gain control to remedy her imperfection of self and to feel more secure in an insecure world.

It has been postulated that the patient's sense of insecurity and inability in interpersonal relationship is linked to the quality of her relationship with her attachment figures during infancy (Dallos, 2004; Treasure, Schmidt, & Troop, 2000). There is an evolutionary need for the infant to seek physical comfort and develop emotional attachment to the parents for the purpose of survival. This early childhood experience is significant because the child appears to learn a set of expectations regarding the mother's responses, and such learned responses tend to be generalized to the child's relationship with others when he or she grows up (Bowlby, 1969). Infants under the care of a sensitive and responsive mother are more likely to adopt a secure attachment strategy in relating to others compared to infants who are repeatedly disappointed by their unresponsive mothers; the latter tend to become insecure, anxious, dependent, and avoidant in pursuing their own needs in relation to others.

In reviewing the history of the upbringing of these young people, Bruch (1973) found that their mothers had brought them up as the compliant child who lived according to the parents' wants and wishes rather than according to their own needs. Under the excessive nurturance and protection of the parents, these adolescents had difficulties in individuating from their parents and becoming independent and autonomous. It is believed that self-starvation crystallized their wish for autonomy.

The evidence of Shoebridge and Gowers's (2000) study indirectly supports the attachment theory. The study compared 40 young people with AN to matched controls using obstetric records and maternal interviews. Index mothers reported higher rates of near-exclusive childcare, infant sleep difficulties, severe distress at the first regular separation, high maternal trait anxiety levels, and later age for first sleeping away from home. More index families experienced a severe obstetric loss prior to the birth of the patient. The results of this study indicated that high-concern mothering in infancy is associated with the subsequent development of AN; they also suggested early insecure attachment patterns.

Both the attachment theory and Bruch's postulation have been criticized as unnecessarily narrowing the investigation on the mother–child dyadic interaction. A cross-cultural study (LeVine, 1990), which compared the maternal behavior of middle-class full-time American mothers to that of mothers of an African tribe in Gusii, Kenya, showed that American mothers spent twice as much time during the observation in talking to their infants at 3–4 months and 9–10 months compared to the Gusii mothers and three times as much looking at their infants. On the other hand, the Gusii mothers were more concerned about the physical survival of their infants, as the infant mortality rate was high in Kenya. The American mothers put more emphasis on stimulating the intellectual growth of the infant than on physical survival, owing to the low infant mortality rate in their country. Unlike the American mothers, the Gusii mothers had to busily engage in their labor-intensive agrarian work while taking care of their baby. The Gusii infants could have multiple attachment figures, as kinsmen in the village helped in child rearing. The Gusii children, when grown, were less articulate and expressive; yet they were also less demanding and less dependent on their mother's love and attention. This in turn brings less psychological damage to the child should the quality of the mother–infant relationship be poor. The author concludes that an infant's early development and his or her subsequent relationship with other adults are shaped more by the ecology of the rearing environment than by the quality of the mother–infant relationship alone.

The systemic perspective has expanded Bruch's psychoanalytical view by emphasizing the sensitivity of the family members to assess accurately and respond appropriately to one another for mutual fulfillment of personal needs (Hill, Fonagy, Safier, & Sargent, 2003). The obsession with food, calories, exercise, and weight only diverts the patient's and the family's attention from recognizing her real needs to the bodily symptoms. An early interpretation of the symbolic meanings of the symptoms is received with strong resistance. To these psychologically fragile young people, the therapist's interpretation is another adult's attempt at telling them how and what they should feel and think. This explains why Helen reacted so strongly when the therapist re-presented to her the family pattern observed. Besides, interpretation demands the patient to understand her experience at an abstract level, which does not synchronize with her concrete self-experience that "things are no more than what they appear to be at face value" (Josephs, 1989, p. 495).

Attitude of the Therapist

Helen's strong reaction reminds the therapist to put aside her expert role and change her orientation of practice from certainty to uncertainty. While acknowledging the power of scientific discovery in understanding diseases and illnesses, clinical practice based on certainty is limited by the premature closure and denial of genuine uncertainties in clinical work (Gerrity, Earp, DeVellis, & Light, 1992). Uncertainty refers to the constructive use of the therapist's ignorance (Bruch, 1973) and the creation of a state of curiosity in the mind of the therapist (Cecchin, 1987). Both attitudes lead to the exploration of the adolescent's different aspects of life in the immediate social context. The adolescent is invited to be a collaborator to enrich the therapist's understanding of her concrete self-experience, the stresses she was facing as well as her experience in relating to her family, her significant others, and the outside world. Adopting a not-knowing position is strategic for it conveys the therapist's due respect for the patient's decision as to which areas she would like to share with the therapist, her degree of self-disclosure, and her way of relating to the therapist, which in turn induce the difference that makes the difference (Stierlin & Weber, 1989).

For young adult women with a chronic history of the illness, it would be more important for the therapist to adopt a nonconfrontational position that emphasizes the client's agency to decide whether to remain unchanged or to actively consider struggling for recovery, to participate in the selection of different treatment and care plans, and to be responsible for her own progress (Geller, Williams, & Srikameswaran, 2001).

Therapeutic Strategies

Family therapy has often been criticized for neglecting individual stories and overlooking the needs of individual family members. However, family therapists who are experienced in treating AN patients, such as Micucci (1998), Eisler (1996), and Fishman (1996), have already stressed the importance of working with emaciated patients at the individual level while effecting changes in the family.

The following six treatment strategies are often useful in both motivating and engaging the patients in treatment. These treatment strategies comprise (a) eliciting the patient's story through creation of psychological space, (b) involving the unfriendly adolescent without actively pursuing her, (c) heightening the patient's awareness of her feelings and recognition of her needs, (d) addressing the patient's concern, (e) permitting the patient to shield behind the symptom, and (f) using crises timely.

Eliciting the patient's story through creation of psychological space. Eliciting the patient's story as early as possible is the foremost task for the therapist in the first session. The desperate and anxious parents usually dominate the conversation at the beginning of the session. The therapist should follow the parents' stories for a while and shift to learn about the patient's story by creating sufficient psychological space for the patient to tell her story. The adolescent will find it easier to respond to the therapist's fact-finding questions. For instance, to a college freshman, the therapist would ask how she had adjusted to university life, how many fellow students she had befriended, and what kinds of extracurricular activities she had participated in; to a secondary school student, the therapist would be interested to know about her school life, the academic subjects that the patient liked and disliked, her teachers, her classmates, and even her hobbies. Sometimes the parents interrupt. Sometimes the parents take over the patient's role in narrating her life experiences. The therapist must stop the parents politely and respectfully by explaining to them the importance of letting the patient tell her experience.

Involving the unfriendly adolescent without actively pursuing her. Creating psychological space for the emaciated adolescent to tell her story does not work for those patients who have low motivation for treatment and a hostile attitude toward the therapist. Maria is a typical example. Her rejection of the therapist's involvement in her life was very similar to her rejection of her mother. Her maternal grandmother had taken care of Maria since birth. Her parents performed their parental roles only during weekends. Maria went back to live with her parents at the age of 6, when they started employing a maid after the birth of her youngest sister. She missed her maternal grandmother very much and failed to develop strong emotional ties with her mother, but her mother's relationship with her younger sister was very good.

The therapist had to address Maria's anger and hostility by permitting her not to be involved in treatment. With the benefit of hindsight, the therapist would ask Maria to settle comfortably on an armchair at the corner of the room. Then she would make use of her conversation with the parents to learn about Maria's different aspects of life and watch out for any opportunity to arouse Maria's interests to get involved in the conversation. Sometimes the adolescent may start joining the conversation by correcting some misinformation given by the parents; sometimes the adolescent may provide additional information. In one instance, an adolescent supported her brother's criticism of the paternal uncle, who was suspected of being mentally ill and who had brought many troubles to the family. These strategies usually succeed in involving the adolescent without actively pursuing her.

Heightening the patient's awareness of her feelings and recognition of her needs. The therapist must help the patient to see that she has the capacity to feel, to judge, and to act as an individual, especially in expressing her anger and frustrations (Bruch, 1973; Selvini Palazzoli, 1985). Take the case of Helen. The therapist congratulated her for her ability to express her anger toward the therapist and acknowledged her unpleasant experience in relating to the therapist and her position in the family in the following way: "I am glad that you are able to verbalize your anger and hostility. I do hope that you can continue to do so. I believe that the more you are able to express your anger and hostility, the less you need to rely on your body to protest for you." Such therapeutic intervention is helpful for AN patients since they have been suffering from an overwhelming sense of inadequacy and have not developed a positive sense of existence. They are doubtful of their own feelings and experience. To quote Selvini Palazzoli (1985, p. 152), "Nothing they themselves experience can be legitimate." Having been negatively affected by the consequences of the disorder such as large mood swings, parents and the significant others may be too frightened to validate their feelings and their experiences. Validation of the patient's subjective experience would help the patient to affirm the positive side of herself.

Patients are either ambivalent about change or resistant to change because they have psychological gains from the disorder such as a false sense of control over their uncontrollable life (Treasure et al., 2000). The process of storytelling and the responses of family members toward the adolescent's story are golden opportunities for the therapist to increase the patient's awareness of her feelings, legitimize her experiences, and recognize her needs, on the basis of which the therapist can motivate and engage her in treatment. Being real to the patient is essential in engagement (Beumont, Russell, & Touyz, 1995).

The following case example illustrates how the therapist made use of the process of storytelling to help the patient become aware of her ambivalent feelings toward her mother and motivate her for treatment.

Rebecca was a 22-year-old young adult woman who had been suffering from AN for 4 years. The psychiatrist referred Rebecca for family treatment upon her second admission to the hospital. Rebecca's father had just died 2 weeks before meeting the therapist. Rebecca's experience of hospitalization was quite negative. She had to follow the doctor's instruction to stay in bed throughout the day. She identified the therapist as part of the medical team, and hence her attitude toward the therapist was suspicious and unfriendly. She told the therapist that only her mother wished to have family treatment; she had no such need. She wished only to be discharged as early as possible. When the therapist asked her about the mother–daughter relationship, she shook her head and uttered that their relationship was unremarkable except that her mother would frequently scold her without any reason. Significantly, Rebecca never stopped crying while she told her story. She stared at her mother with hostility and anger while denying any relationship problem verbally. Using the patient's crying as an entry point, the therapist asked Rebecca if she was aware of her painful feelings in the process of telling her story and worked to explore further what had caused her to be so pained— the death of her father a month ago or her relationship with her mother. After a long pause, Rebecca explained that the death of her father did not inflict much pain on her as her relationship with him was detached. Her pain was attributable to her mother's disrespect of her privacy and the abuse of her parental authority. Two weeks ago her mother shouted at her in front of her relatives during her father's funeral. Her mother also hit her after she threw a tantrum that week. Rebecca called the police for help to stop her mother's violent behavior. The recollection of these unhappy events helped Rebecca to get in touch with the ingrained hurt she had been suffering and her need for privacy and respect. Rebecca no longer denied the problem, and she perceived the need to receive treatment to resolve their relationship difficulties.

Addressing the patient's concern. The way the patient tells her story will help the therapist formulate an appropriate course of action to respond to the patient's concern. Take Ginny as an example. Her readiness to talk about her studies with the therapist and her great reluctance to mention even a word on her relationship with her father suggested that Ginny simply wished to hide a family secret. Her deliberate attempt to miss the appointment twice was an additional signal: "Don't press me anymore. I am not going to tell you anything about the family secret." I told Ginny's mother that I read her message and I would respect her decision to keep the secret. After being reassured, Ginny came back for treatment for the subsequent appointment. In the session, Ginny denied any connection between the family secret and her self-starvation. She preferred to sequester the family secret inside the walls of her home forever rather than to disclose it to anyone, including the therapist. She promised to take charge of her own recovery so long as the therapist kept her promise. Besides, her mother also reassured Ginny that she would not stay overnight outside and would protect her from being alone with her father. In short, the therapist helped Ginny and her mother to deal with the family secret by not disclosing the details.

Permitting the patient to shield behind the symptom. Self-starvation can be regarded as a shield for the patient to escape from coping with the world and as a denial of existing problems. By avoiding the pains of having feelings in their mind, the patients expressed their pains and suffering by degrading their body (Dare & Crowther, 1995). The therapist should be perceptive enough to understand the subtle meaning of this communication and be empathetic of the patient's need for regression without reinforcing it. Take the example of Fan. During her dissociation, the therapist suggested the family allow the patient to remain unchanged, be empathetic of her need to be in a state of dissociation, and provide sufficient psychological space for her to regain her sense of reality. In this particular circumstance, the therapist responded to the patient's impulses, desires, and actions in the manner of a permissive parent who was nonpunitive, accepting, and affirming (Faber, 2002). This permissive attitude is of paramount importance when a patient is very much underweight. Any therapeutic effort to push for change will place additional psychological burden on the malnourished patient and may trigger more primitive defense mechanisms (Brown, Russell, Thornton, & Dunn, 1999).

While respecting the defensive functions of dissociation for AN patients in coping with the stress, the therapist must try to discover if there could be some relationships among dissociation, history of sexual abuse, and eating disorders (Brown et al., 1999); hence, exploration for a history of trauma should be undertaken in assessment, if necessary.

Timely use of crises. Some of the difficult and less motivated patients can be engaged during a crisis. Self-mutilation, such as burning, cutting, or hitting oneself without suicidal intent, is common among patients suffering from AN. Stealing is even more prevalent for the bulimic subgroup (Krahn, Nairn, Gosnell, & Drewnowski, 1991). Most of those patients who shoplift or steal do so for biological and psychological reasons. Emaciated patients try every means to suppress their eating desire. The more they suppress their eating desire, the more the images of food appear before them. This strong internal impulse dictates patients' behavior and makes them vulnerable to loss of self-control, especially in an environment full of food such as a supermarket. Some of these patients realize that they have stolen food only when they are caught. Others deliberately choose self-destructive behavior such as shoplifting, self-mutilation, and fighting as a means to lower their pain and sufferings, as a form of revenge, or as a way of seeking love and attention from their parents.

With the exception of a few "lucky" patients, most of these patients are caught, arrested, and tried, with the risk of being committed to custodial psychiatric care. Due to public ignorance of the disorder, these young people would be treated like criminals rather than disturbed psychiatric patients. Arrest and trial pose an immediate crisis to the afflicted patient and her family. The crisis can be a danger as well as an opportunity. Without timely professional assistance, this crisis undoubtedly will be a danger, for punishment does not resolve the psychological issues and would aggravate the sense of depression, dejection, and futility.

However, such a crisis is also an opportunity for the therapist to engage the ambivalent and less motivated patient in treatment. Some dropout patients come back for treatment immediately after arrest because they finally realize that if they continue to do nothing to combat the disorder, the disorder will sooner or later destroy their future.

CONCLUSION

Stone Fish's view (2000, p. 508) reminds us of the crux of relating to an adolescent: "When therapists do not view conflict as growth potential for the relationship, the therapist may be sending the message that struggle can be avoided which may lead to withdrawal from the relationship." Developing a therapeutic alliance with emaciated patients such as Maria, Helen, Ginny, Fan, and Rebecca requires the therapist to be honest, warm, genuine, and real with the patient; to be tolerant of a mixture of complex and intolerable emotions such as anger, hostility, fears, and rejection; to allow for the continued struggle between the young person and the therapist; and to formulate treatment goals that are mutually acceptable to the young person and the therapist. Last but not least, the therapist should have the courage to contradict and challenge the tunnel vision of these young people and to motivate them to take charge of their own change and recovery.

Chapter 7

Risk Assessment and Clinical Management

INTRODUCTION

Family therapists are often taken aback by the emaciated young person's ambivalence toward and lack of motivation for change (MacDonald, 2002). It is usually the parents, the teachers, and the doctors who seek help on behalf of the reluctant patient, who seems quite contented with her fragile health. These young people refuse to gain weight despite their severe emaciation. The relentless pursuit of thinness has become the priority in life. The results of Tan, Hope, and Stewart's (2003a, 2003b) qualitative study conducted in England have shown that anorexia nervosa (AN) is an important part of the patient's personal identity; recovery is painful because it requires patients to relinquish part of their personal identities. An AN patient expresses her ambivalence of change in treatment: "My disorder is just like an old torn doll; it's no good but it's still the only thing that I can hold on to. I won't give it up until I have a better one."[3] The patient's inability to perceive the risks and adverse consequences of her behavior arouse great anxiety for the parents and the therapist.

Clinical management of AN is a huge challenge for therapists. There is a tendency for the therapist to confront the emaciated young person on her denial of the gravity of the problem. Such a therapeutic response only increases resistance to treatment (Treasure & Ward, 1997). Developing a good therapeutic relationship with the young person may decrease resistance to change and recovery. The use of motivational interviewing, which is borrowed from the field of addiction, has been found to be promising in enhancing the emaciated young person's motivation, confidence, and

---

[3] A patient aged 30 under the care of the author.

readiness in treatment (Feld, Woodside, Kaplan, Olmsted, & Carter, 2001; Gowers & Smyth, 2004; Vitousek, Watson, & Wilson, 1998).

In the process of treatment, the therapist may have to face a drastic drop in the patient's body weight and an increase in risks to health. The principle of nonmaleficence (Gladding, Remley, & Huber, 2001) obliges the therapist to exercise professional authority tactfully through persuasion, coaxing, and manipulation to press for immediate hospitalization. Hospitalization is a joint decision between the parents and the therapist. It must be based on a comprehensive risk assessment on the individual and interpersonal factors that have maintained and escalated the symptoms.

Despite the patient's protest against hospitalization and the undesirable short-term effects on the therapeutic relationship, ambivalent patients often view compulsory treatment as a push for recovery (Tan, Hope, Stewart, & Fitzpatrick, 2003). After recovery, they are able to understand the importance of intervention.

This chapter proposes a risk assessment framework for a joint decision between the parents and the therapist on hospitalization, using a case illustration.

CASE VIGNETTE

Ada was referred for family treatment at the age of 13; she was at a height of 160 cm, with body weight of 36 kg. She started dieting and excessively exercising at the age 12. Her body weight had dropped from 44 kg to 33 kg in one year. Extremely alarmed, anxious, and worried, her parents sought psychiatric treatment from a child and adolescent psychiatric service in the public hospital system and then family therapy as well. Ada came from a working-class family. Both parents were working full-time, and she had a younger brother aged 7. The family life was reportedly uneventful except that Ada's mother was a breast cancer survivor; four years ago she received the cancer diagnosis with shock, but she had recovered after mastectomy and chemotherapy. With the onset of AN on the part of the daughter, the previously close and harmonious mother–daughter relation deteriorated and became characterized by frequent quarrels and intense day-to-day conflicts especially during mealtimes. The same was true for Ada's relationship with her father and her younger brother. Ada was friendly to the therapist. She was quite honest in explaining why she engaged in excessive dieting: She liked to be slim and beautiful. She was not particularly keen to take care of her own health, as she failed to perceive any risk involved, though her concentration span had been affected. As revealed in the lunch session in treatment, both parents were helpless, ineffective, and exhausted in trying to convince Ada to eat her lunch. Ada was as stubborn and resistant as a rock in refusing her parents' advice. Knowing Ada's need for control, the therapist tried to make use of every opportunity to let Ada make her own decision, including the target weight set for the end of each week. To the therapist's disappointment, Ada broke her promise repeatedly. Her body weight dropped from 36 kg at the first session to 31 kg at the second session but recovered to 33 kg for the third and fourth sessions. The task of refeeding Ada had become increasingly difficult to her parents. However, they were ambivalent about hospitalization and looked to the therapist for professional advice.

The proposed framework for risk assessment, as follows, helped the parents and therapist to decide whether hospitalization was required for Ada.

RISK ASSESSMENT

Risk assessment is complex in the case of AN. Besides body weight and body mass index (BMI), a family therapist must take into account the patient's health condition, her motivation for change, the parents' degree of understanding toward the gravity of the problems, family dynamics, entwined family difficulties, family resources, and the interpersonal context of the therapist–patient relation.

Health Condition

Body weight and BMI are two key indicators of health. Family therapists have to be highly vigilant when the patient is seriously underweight, (15–20% below the expected body weight) and continues to lose weight despite treatment (McKenzie & Joyce, 1992). These indicators point to immediate hospitalization. Consultation with a psychiatrist or medical practitioner should be sought as soon as possible because there may be complications such as low blood pressure, low heart rate, and low white blood cell counts due to malnutrition, which would imply an increased risk to health and life.

Motivation for Change

Motivation for change varies from individual to individual, and the therapist must assess the patient's confidence and readiness to change. Using the transtheoretical model of stages of change originally developed in the field of addiction (Prochaska & DiClemente, 1983) and later adapted for AN

(Treasure & Ward, 1997), there are four stages. Patients at the precontemplation stage deny having a serious problem; hence they lack self-initiative to
seek professional help. At the next contemplation stage, patients somehow
recognize that the disorder has already grown out of control, to an extent that
they can hardly disregard the problem, but are still ambivalent about change,
most probably attributable to the secondary psychological gains derived from
the sick role (Treasure & Ward, 1997). In the preparation stage, as the name
suggests, patients are getting ready for the final action stage.

The literature in the West (e.g., Feld et al., 2001; Treasure & Ward, 1997)
has shown that the majority of AN patients are at either the precontemplation or the contemplation stage, with a few at only the preparation or action
stage of change. Unlike patients in the preparation and action stages, these
patients are unprepared to take any action unless the therapist addresses their
ambivalence to change.

Treatment resistance emerges as a result of the social interaction
between the patient and her significant others. Treatment resistance may
symbolize the intense struggle of the emaciated daughter against her parents
for autonomy and control; the patient may see recovery as losing the battle in
the fight with her parents.

To a few highly resistant patients, treatment refusal can be the reflection
of a peer subculture in a ballet school, a dancing class, or a school of performing arts, which glorifies thinness as the beauty standard. Such a peer norm
and belief not only fosters the patient's self-denial of the disorder but also
reinforces her treatment nonadherence. School bullying can also contribute to the onset of AN. Sometimes treatment resistance becomes intelligible
when contextualized in light of being bullied in school on account of fatness
and clumsiness.[4]

The risk of further deterioration is high, if many unfavorable factors are
present: (a) the patient's motivation for change is at the precontemplation
stage or contemplation stage, (b) the patient has employed excessive dieting
as a means to fight with her parent(s) for control and autonomy, and (c) there is
a fairly strong peer norm to support the patient's relentless pursuit of thinness.

However, motivation is fluid, and there could be change and malleability as a result of interpersonal interactions. It is here that the therapist has a
significant role to play in assessing the stage of change that the patient is in
but also in effecting change and in bringing the patient from the precontemplation stage to the contemplation stage. Motivational interviewing as a

---

[4]   Two such cases were seen by the author.

therapeutic strategy (Treasure & Ward, 1997; Vitousek et al., 1998) can help to identify the patient's motivational level for change and heighten the patient's awareness of the gravity of her problem.

Although the skill and technique of motivational interviewing have always been associated with the cognitive-behavioral school, actually the Socratic style and an attitude of curiosity—the fundamental attitude and skills in motivational interviewing—are widely employed across different schools of psychotherapy (Vitousek et al., 1998).

In the Socratic method, the patient through responding to the questions raised by the therapist can go through a process of thinking and be reflective of her own condition in a systematical manner. The impact will be greater if the patient can use her own words to assess her own condition rather than being told by the therapist. Nevertheless, the Socratic method is not an interrogation. It must be carried out in accordance to the best interest of the patient rather than from the parents' perspective. Such a therapeutic stance is extremely important to elicit collaboration, cooperation, and trust from the patient.

The advantage of adopting the Socratic method in family assessment is that both the patient and the parents are the audience of the patient's story. The patient's responses achieve the dual purposes of heightening her own awareness of the seriousness of the problem and deepening the parents' understanding of the patient's health condition. In one case, a previously uninvolved father began to realize how seriously ill his daughter was—a realization that was a relief to the mother because her husband had blamed her for her overreaction.[5]

There are two underlying assumptions in the use of the Socratic method. First, the patient's experience of the disorder is unique and subjective. The process of inquiry unfolds the patient's subjective experience without being confrontational and argumentative. Second, reality can be discovered through uncertainty. The therapist is open enough to give up his or her own hypothesis when contradicted by emerging information. But uncertainty does not mean abandonment of professional knowledge or judgment or an appearance of ignorance.

To act uncertain, the therapist uses language of possibility that the patient can disagree with (Vitousek et al., 1998), for example, "I have learned from some young people under my care that they have experienced difficulties in some aspects of their lives after the onset of the disorder. Probably it

---

[5] A case from the author's practice.

may not be applicable to you; hence I wish to hear your story." The journey of inquiry can be navigated with the aid of the following questions: Have you felt cold more easily after excessive dieting? Have you had a lot of hair loss in the past few weeks? Has your skin become drier? Do you find it harder to concentrate on your studies? How about your mood and temper? Have you felt increasingly tired in coping with daily chores? Have you become easily agitated and upset? How often do you find yourself out of control and throw temper tantrums out of the blue? How does the illness affect your relationship with your friends and classmates? How does the illness affect your relationship with you dad, your mom, and your brothers or sisters?

The therapist must validate the young person's unique experience of the disorder in the process of inquiry, conveying a genuine interest toward the patient's self-appraisal of her condition.

Parents' Participation and Collaboration

The parents' cooperation and collaboration can be assessed with the following questions in mind: To what extent do the parents understand the gravity of the disorder? Are they psychologically prepared to take up the urgent task of refeeding their emaciated daughter? Are they too helpless and exhausted to rescue the endangered life of their emaciated daughter? Is there any severe marital discord, which may weaken their team effort to refeed their daughter? For low-income families with dual careers, do the parents actually have the time to supervise eating during mealtimes? If not, can another person in the family to take over the supervision? If not, home-based management may not be tenable.

Family Problems and Resources

The family can be either a source of distress or a source of support and healing. Short-term and long-term difficulties faced by the family are associated with the continuation of emaciation. A comprehensive assessment of family difficulties will help to estimate the risk and predict the treatment response. A multiple-problem family will not have enough energy and resources to take up the task of refeeding compared to those families that are healthy before the onset of AN. Chinese families usually tap into wider family resources including the extended family and relatives.

The contributions of the grandparents and relatives must never be underestimated. Religious and cultural beliefs of the family and formal (e.g., professional help and service support) and informal social support (e.g., friends, neighbors, and church) are also important. Home management is more risky for a multiple-problem family with limited resources.

Interpersonal Context of the Therapeutic Relationship

The patient's struggle for control can easily be projected onto her relationship with the therapist, entrapping the therapist. Imposed treatment, in whatever form, will increase the risk of symmetric escalation (Rathner, 1998); that is, the struggle for control between the patient and the therapist will be further intensified and may result in early dropout from treatment. However, symmetric escalation can be avoided if the therapist establishes good therapeutic communications with the patient, shows reasonable sensitivity to understanding the power dynamics entwined in the therapeutic relationship, and believes that a healthy part of the patient's self that wishes to change can be nurtured and developed to combat the anorexic self.

DECISION MAKING FOR
RECOMMENDED HOSPITALIZATION

Let us return to the case of Ada (see the case vignette above) and the clinical decision of the therapist. While appreciating the therapeutic value of respecting the patient's autonomy, the therapist decided to finally support the parents' wish to hospitalize Ada immediately. The decision was based on the following assessment.

Health Condition

Ada had been ill for 2 years, with a continuous drop in body weight accelerating at an alarming rate. The therapist also learned that Ada was suffering from low blood pressure, irregular heart beats, and declining white blood cell counts.

Motivation for Change

In spite of emaciation, Ada failed to see the devastating effects on her health. She denied a lack of concentration in her studies. She liked her present state of mind. She did not think that her life was out of control. She chose to eat less because it made her stand out in school. Ada's responses to the inquiry suggested that her motivational level was at the pre contemplation stage, that is, she was in denial and refused to take any action for change (Prochaska, DiClemente, & Norcross, 1992).

The mother–daughter conflicts and the incompetence of the father to mediate their conflicts were indeed worrying. During the individual interview in the fourth session, Ada said, "My mom said that if I have a normal meal, I can recover. That's unbelievable. I don't think it is as simple as that. She is deceiving me and deceiving you [the therapist]." The therapist asked, "What is your own wish?" Ada laughed, "Keep the present weight. Of course I can gain weight but I won't do that." "Why?" asked the therapist. Ada said, "I will be the loser if I do. I hate my mom for being so weak and overworried; in being so, she has the upper hand. She has won the sympathy of my maternal grandma, my aunts, and all my relatives." The therapist responded carefully, "Do you mean that you keep losing weight because you wish to defeat your mom?" "Yes," Ada said firmly. The therapist then asked, "It's quite acceptable for young people like you to fight with your parents, but can't you shift your battlefield from food and eating to another area?" Ada said firmly, "I'm afraid I can't do that."

Parents' Participation and Collaboration

Ada's parents understood the gravity of Ada's situation. They both wished to help. Nevertheless, both of them needed to work full-time and were unable to supervise Ada's lunches. They tried to join hands to persuade Ada to eat during dinner, but Ada remained obstinate. The harder they pressed Ada to eat normally, the less food Ada took. The mother said in the fourth session, "In the past week, I couldn't sleep well. I had one nightmare after the other. In one nightmare, Ada was lying on the floor weak and almost unconscious. I went to pick her up and I heard her whisper: 'Mom, I wish to live but it's too late. It's too late.'" At this point the mother cried uncontrollably. The therapist turned to the father and asked with great concern and care, "Do you share my feeling that your wife can't cope with your daughter's illness anymore?" Ada's father burst into tears and said, "Me too. My wife has behaved quite strangely this week. She asked me to hug her many times every day, telling me that she is going to leave us soon; every moment together means so much to her. I was frightened, so was my little son. She never behaved so abnormally before, not even when she was seriously sick during chemotherapy." The therapist responded empathetically, "It must be difficult for you to face this." What was most shocking to the therapist was that Ada laughed mockingly at her mother while she cried. Ada uttered, "You [the mother] deserve it."

Family Problems and Resources

Parental supervision of Ada's meals was practically impossible as both parents worked full-time. The emotional support given by the maternal grandmother was strong, but she was not living with the family and could not offer any practical assistance in supervising the patient's meals.

Interpersonal Context of the Therapeutic Relationship

Superficially, Ada was friendly toward the therapist. The therapist could communicate honestly and openly. Ada's unkind attitude toward her mother made the therapist angry and uncomfortable. The therapist told Ada honestly at the end of treatment, "I wish that I could side with you to fight against your parents. Frankly, I can't do that because I am quite upset and uncomfortable with your way of punishing your mother, who has done nothing wrong except for trying to save you from impending death." Ada shrugged and said she did not care.

DISCUSSION

Ada's case illustrates that the threat to the patient's life poses a great challenge to the family therapist in clinical management. The young person's lack of motivation for change and the rapid deterioration in health require the therapist to respond quickly and decisively.

Such a decision has to be backed up by the therapist's competent risk assessment. The use of the patient's capacity and competence as assessment criteria is problematic for patients suffering from AN (Tan, Hope, Stewart, & Fitzpatrick, 2003). Risk assessment for AN patients should be multidimensional and include the patient's motivation for change, the family dynamics revolving around emaciation, the parents' collaboration, the presence of multiple family problems and the availability of family resources, peer norms, and the interpersonal dynamics of the therapeutic relationship.

In the face of strong resistance or treatment refusal, the therapist must offer options and choices to the patient; a position of non-negotiability will be adopted only when the patient voluntarily refuses the options offered and her health condition worsens. However, the clinical management principles that precede compulsory treatment must be followed when the patient's health is not seriously under threat (Rathner, 1998).

Treatment is a co-constructed process, which can be realized with the active participation and contribution of the patient and the therapist (Anderson

& Goolishian, 1992). From this perspective, the treatment decision is a shared process, in which the therapist shares with the emaciated young person the assessment and concerns and with her parents or significant others the factors to be considered in risk assessment and the pros and cons of hospitalization.

A family therapist may feel uneasy and indecisive if immediate hospitalization is forced as a recommendation. If there are doubts and confusion, it is strongly advisable to obtain a second opinion from either an experienced family therapist or a psychiatrist with substantial clinical experience in this area (Rathner, 1998).

Recommended hospitalization and compulsory treatment help the patient's recovery provided there is a team of caring hospital staff experienced in dealing with eating disorders who provide quality care with empathy and a psychological orientation (Colton & Pistrang, 2004). Ada's story provides additional anecdotal evidence to support this observation.

The outcome of Ada's recommended hospitalization was positive. After being hospitalized, Ada wrote to the therapist twice, indicating that she still trusted the therapist. In her first letter she pleaded with the therapist to rescue her from the harsh ward management and, if possible, to fight for her discharge. The therapist wrote back immediately to encourage her to fight for her discharge through weight gain. In her second letter to the therapist, Ada proudly reported her positive progress and expected discharge. She finally recovered from AN and was free from AN symptoms 2 years after the completion of treatment.

Family therapists have significant contributions to make in managing treatment resistance and treatment refusal. They can play multiple roles in the process of helping—for example, as an assessor balancing the risks and benefits of home-based treatment versus inpatient treatment in meeting the needs of the patient, as an educator and as a coach to provide health education and instructional guidance, and last but not least as a facilitator to help identify factors that have hindered the patient and the parents from making a rational and appropriate treatment decision and, if possible, to enable them to arrive at a joint decision in treatment.

An interview 6 months after the completion of treatment showed that Ada perceived the experience of hospitalization as unpleasant and uncomfortable, but she did benefit from it. The strict hospital management had unexpectedly become an impetus for her to recover as soon as possible. Soon after admission, she gradually realized that the only way to be discharged and regain her freedom was to resume normal eating.

Ada's feelings toward the family therapist were mixed. She disliked the therapist's support of the parents' decision to hospitalize her, but she appreciated the therapist's courage to challenge her unkindness toward her mother. To Ada's parents, family therapy had provided them with a context to work on the unresolved problems arising from AN and had given them hope and support and provided professional advice without which they could hardly have coped with the challenges and threats of the illness.

Part III

The Journey of Healing:
Case Illustrations

Prelude

The next three chapters document the healing journeys of three families suffering from anorexia nervosa (AN).[6] Since AN is a problem often deeply embedded in the family, both as a collection of related persons and as a social construct, the issue of cultural specificity is an intriguing one that gives rise to much of the impetus for the present work, especially in exploring the features of Chinese culture that differentiate some of the cases from those reported in the West. Jing's family illustrates a response to the inner voice of the therapist. Jing's mother had become a hostage of her own mother, which in turn had drained much of her energy and time, caused chronic tensions and stresses on her marriage, and intensified her conflicts with the emaciated daughter, Jing. It was not easy for her to break free from the emotional chain because filial piety, a virtue of Confucianism, was still highly cherished in the Chinese society in which this family lived.[7] The symptomatic cycle discerned in treatment had made it difficult, if not impossible, for the couple to collaborate and cooperate as a team to help their daughter Jing recover. The therapist assisted the family in disrupting the symptomatic cycle by unfolding the invisible pain of the husband and by eliciting the help of Jing and her father to assist her mother in setting up reasonable boundaries with her family of origin.

In the second family, the hostility and anger of the emaciated daughter, Ling, toward her parents was projected onto the two family therapists. Both therapists found it hard to develop a therapeutic relationship with Ling. However, since the focus of family therapy was to remove the symptomatic cycle that hinders recovery, the therapists were able to collaborate with the multidisciplinary team at the hospital to empower the parents and help them to break the vicious patterns of interaction with Ling.

The third family illustrates how the onset of AN typically compounds the distress of a multiproblem family suffering from migration, family violence, divorce of the parents, and financial difficulty. Besides providing family therapy, the therapist perceived the need to collaborate with a community-based social worker who took up the role of case manager and

---

[6] These cases were chosen from the patients under the author's care for different reasons.

[7] This case is another one from the author's practice in Hong Kong.

responded to the service needs of the family by providing social services and mobilizing community resources. This case vignette also demonstrates how a lonely, helpless, and highly anxious mother regained her confidence in parenting through enactment, a technique that encouraged the mother to talk to her children directly and to resolve her conflicts with her emaciated daughter.

Chapter 8

Coping With Anorexia Nervosa in an Extended Chinese Family, *Jia*

INTRODUCTION

All these cases are situated in Hong Kong. According to a recent census report (Hong Kong SAR Government, 2001), about 66.2% of Hong Kong families are nuclear families, many of which are nevertheless embedded in an extended family, that is, the *jia* (家) or *jia zu* (家族).

The concept of family in traditional Chinese culture is fluid, dynamic, and changeable according to the circumstantial requirements. The current translation of family as jia ting is alien (Wen, Chang, Chang, & Chu, 1989). There is only *jia* or *jia zu* in Chinese culture. According to *jia gu wen* (甲骨文), the first pictorially written Chinese on oracle bones, *jia* is a picture showing a pig under a roof (Zu, 1999); the pig is literally interpreted as family property. *Jia* or *jia zu* refers to the immediate household or the nuclear family, the husband's family of origin, and close relatives within the same clan.

Influenced by structural functionalism borrowed from sociology (Wong, 1975), an easy mistake is to conceptualize the family as a household unit, which loses sight of the cultural characteristics of Chinese families and unnecessarily narrows the assessment. *Jia*, in a traditional sense, is patriarchal, patrilineal, and patrilocal. However, modernization and Westernization have transformed the concept of family in Hong Kong. The results of a recent local study (Lau, Ma, & Chan, 2002) show that Hong Kong women's concept of family is bilineal. According to their subjective definition, they perceived both their maternal family and their husband's family of origin as their family.

The family can be a powerful force to tie down the individual family member and prevent him or her from becoming independent and autonomous while at the same time being a source of support in healing wounds and pains. The Confucian virtue of *xiao* (孝), filial piety, prescribes the transgenerational relationship between the parents and the child. A filial child has to be obedient, should take care of the parents in old age and sickness, and should honor the family and the ancestors.

Chinese parents may have different reasons (e.g., need of companion, need of protection, need of mastery) to exert power over their children, even when they are adults, sometimes even after they are married. Those who are heavily dependent on parental approval for their sense of self become hostage to their parents. On the other hand, a person whose identity is not parent dependent has the ability to say no and set the limit and can create a sense of psychological independence.

Excessive involvement with the family of origin is mutually constructed and reinforced by the married adult children and their aging parents. Blaming the two parties for this would be antitherapeutic, for blame prompts only defense mechanisms and undermines the ability to effect change. Nevertheless, it is critical for the family therapist to explore and assess the upbringing of the parents of the young person with anorexia nervosa (AN) and the influence of their families of origin on the immediate family. A key question to ask is, do the parents' families of origin play a part in hindering the parents' coping with AN?

The following family illustrates the contribution of a cultural perspective of jia, the extended family, in assessment and treatment of Chinese families suffering from AN.[8]

BACKGROUND OF THE FAMILY

Jing, a 16-year-old adolescent girl, was referred to the family clinic by a social worker at a community center. Upon the therapist's advice, the social worker also referred Jing to consult a child psychiatrist. Jing's mother was one of the callers to the hotline set up by the community center to reach out to people suffering from eating problems. She was in a panic over her daughter's body weight, which in 6 months had dropped to 36.5 kg at a height of 156 cm (BMI = 15), from an original weight of 59 kg (BMI = 24.3).

Jing was the only child of a middle-class family. The father was a professional, the mother a part-time administrator. They lived in a pleasant residential district. A year before the onset of AN, Jing went abroad to study.

---

[8] This is a case that the author has worked on.

Her academic performance in school was conspicuously good. Under peer influence, she started dieting over Christmas. The teachers were concerned about her emaciation and her health, studies, and psychological well-being. They suspended Jing's schooling and sent her back to Hong Kong for treatment. Jing's mother was shocked to meet her skinny, fragile daughter at the airport. What maddened her mother most was that Jing refused medical treatment. She argued that in studying abroad, she had already used up much of her parents' savings. Her food refusal continued creating a lot of conflict in the family. When the parents forced Jing to take more food, she fought back by inflicting self-harm on her body or banging her head against the wall.

THE FIRST INTERVIEW

Jing and her parents, Mr. and Mrs. S, greeted the therapist and the cotherapist in the waiting room. The cotherapist, a Ph.D. student, was studying family therapy. Jing was pale and thin, but she was quite friendly and polite to the therapists. The family was ushered into the treatment room, after which Jing was weighed. Her weight had increased from 36 kg to 39 kg 2 weeks after the pretreatment interview. The family took seats on the sofa, with Jing between her parents.

The therapist started the session with her body weight, by tracking the efforts that the family had made to achieve such progress over the past 2 weeks. Jing attributed her progress to improvement of the family relationship, while Mr. S attributed it to their concerted efforts in tackling the problem. The cotherapist asked who had done the most in this family. Jing smiled and pointed to her father.

The mother was depressed and tearful when she presented her views of the problem. In her perspective, Jing's eating problem was caused by scant paternal attention since birth. Mr. S liked a quiet family life and was reluctant to have a child during the early stages of their marriage. He disliked noise and was irritated or upset when Jing cried or made noise while playing. Mr. S would scold her or retreat to the bedroom, leaving Jing alone in the sitting room. In order to minimize father–daughter conflicts, Mrs. S took up most of the child care responsibilities. Problems arising from the care of Jing were tackled alone, without help or support from the father. Mrs. S found it increasingly difficult to deal with Jing's self-starvation. Besides, Mrs. S had to take care of her own mother too. She felt bad about her husband's inadequate participation in helping their daughter and blamed him for his ignorance of the life-threatening nature of the disorder.

She was in desperate need of her husband's assistance, as her daughter would seek her father's approval and validation when she finished every meal at home. To the disappointment of Mrs. S, her husband was too reserved to show his appreciation for the efforts that Jing had made in resuming normal eating. Besides, with the onset of self-starvation, Jing often pressed her mother to eat. If the mother took more food, she would take the same amount. Mrs. S often yielded to her daughter's unreasonable demands. Jing never forced her firm and stern father to eat, nor did she attempt to control his eating. The effects of the self-starvation had affected the mother's well-being, as she felt manipulated and controlled by her daughter. It also aggravated the couple's marital relationship. The mother's story implied that the solution rested on her husband: He should change. She also hinted at the influence of her own family of origin on her coping.

Jing hoped to chat with her father more as she seldom had a chance to do so. After dinner, her father would spend most of his time reading in his bedroom while Mrs. S would be very busy talking to her own mother on the phone. The mother spent 1 to 2 hours every night in dealing with the problems of her family of origin. The maternal grandmother depended heavily on Mrs. S for care and emotional support. Mrs. S's eldest brother was disabled, and her younger brother was irresponsible.

The therapist asked Mrs. S with compassion, "What I've heard suggests that you are your mother's companion, advisor, and social worker. Am I too hasty to make that judgment?"

Jing and Mr. S corrected the therapist and said, "She is more than a social worker. She is the pastor of the maternal grandmother, her brothers, and their families."

The mother burst into tears and agreed. Her own mother had drained so much energy from her that she finally broke down 2 years ago. She suffered from depression and was put on antidepressants. Mrs. S admitted that her inability to say no to her mother's demands had placed her in an extremely difficult position. As perceived by Mrs. S, saying no to an old and sick mother was not filial. The maternal grandmother had become more and more demanding and inconsiderate, to such an extent that Mrs. S had little time and energy left for her husband and her daughter. Some of the family tasks at home were left hanging, and her husband and her daughter were angry with her. This chronic problem had been tormenting the mother and the family for a long time. Mr. S felt as helpless as his wife. He had already given up changing his wife after repeated attempts failed.

He told the therapists, "The first day I dated her, I began to realize how difficult it was for her [his wife] to go out and have fun with me. She dared not go out if her mother disapproved. She would go home early before dinner. Her family was her first priority. The dates came second. I protested many times, but to no avail. She continued to focus most of her attention and efforts on her family. I was defeated. I didn't wish to listen to all these endless phone calls. I felt better reading in my room."

The therapist gradually came to understand the linkage between Mr. S's insufficient involvement in the family and the overinvolvement of his wife with her own mother. He was not an indifferent father or a detached husband as perceived by his wife. On the contrary, his wife had been neglecting him for a long time. With the change of perception toward Mr. S, the therapist felt compassionate toward him. It was amazing that he had been tolerating the continued intrusion of his mother-in-law and the brothers-in-law by stiffening his upper lip. Apparently his pain was invisible to his depressive wife.

The therapist said emphatically to Mr. S, "Have you ever let your wife know about your pain?"

Mr. S shook his head and said, "I don't think she cares about me."

Mrs. S protested, "That's not true. We seldom talk at home. You stay in the room and seem to have no interest in talking with me."

Mr. S remained silent. Only upon the invitation of the therapist did he respond to his wife: "You've forgotten that you spend at least 1 to 2 hours talking on the phone with your mother every evening."

"You two must have gone through a lot of bad experiences because of this," said the therapist, who was searching for suitable words to express understanding toward the couple.

The therapist then turned to Mr. S and asked, "What has made you so tolerant of your wife?" Mr. S said helplessly, "What can I do? I have no choice. I still love her."

Jing joined in the conversation: "I don't like my maternal grandma, my uncles or aunts. They've made my mom exhausted. I must say that I am selfish. It's the only time in my life that my mom has given me so much attention."

The therapist asked for clarification, "Do you mean after your self-starvation?"

Jing said, "Yes."

In replying to whether there was any relationship between her family context and the development of self-starvation, Jing denied it. She started dieting under the influence of her classmates rather than the influence of her parents. However, she was glad that her self- starvation helped her to get back her mother; her dad was now also more concerned about her. Their concern and support were a driving force for her recovery. Jing wished to recover and go back to study as soon as possible. She enjoyed school life abroad and was proud of her achievements in school. In a nutshell, Jing was motivated to take charge of her own health and recovery.

Jing's timely response was extremely helpful. She had expressed her need for more love and concern from her parents and linked her unfulfilled love to the mother's overinvolvement with her family of origin in the past. The therapist punctuated immediately by asking the mother whether she wished to shift her attention back from her own mother to her daughter's health problem should her husband support her. Mrs. S, the filial daughter, welcomed the therapist's suggestion, but she had no confidence in doing so.

While expressing appreciation toward the parents and Jing in achieving the progress in the past 2 weeks, the therapist emphasized that they were still fighting a hard battle to combat the disorder. Their main concern in the following week was to continue collaborating as a team to win the battle.

The wider lens provided by the concept of jia in traditional Chinese culture had broadened the therapist's assessment by gradually moving from Mr. and Mrs. S's own family to Mrs. S's family of origin, especially focusing on its unfavorable effects on Mr. and Mrs. S's collaboration as a team in helping Jing to combat AN. However, what remained unexplored was how the mother's overinvolvement with her family of origin had affected the father–daughter relationship. Besides, the therapists had not learned about the positive aspects of this couple's relationship.

THE SECOND INTERVIEW

Jing's maintained her body weight of 39 kg over 2 weeks. Once seated on the sofa, the mother complained that Jing needed her company during meals and forced the mother to eat even though she was full. The mother dared not resist the daughter's unreasonable request because she wanted her daughter to be happy and to recover quickly.

Jing justified her behavior and said, "I am insecure." She was unsure how much she should take every meal. Jing was facing a dilemma. While recognizing the need for a speedy recovery in order to resume schooling, Jing feared obesity. Mrs. S had made tremendous efforts to help her daughter. Together with Jing, she searched throughout a shopping center in town for Jing's favorite food shop; she had not visited her own mother until the previous night. Mrs. S felt greatly relieved that Jing allowed her to visit her mother and the great-grandmother after Mr. S took over her duties by accompanying her daughter during dinner.

Although Mr. S had started to help his wife, Mrs. S was dissatisfied with his insufficient help to Jing. Jing had told her father repeatedly that she needed his assistance in mathematics, but he disappointed her again. Upon the request of the therapist, Mr. S said that the mathematics homework was difficult and he needed time to think before tackling it. Besides, he needed to deal with the problems at work too. Mr. S's clarification had not reduced his wife's dissatisfaction toward him.

It was amazing to learn that Mrs. S not only had to take care of her own mother but also had to shoulder the burden of caring for her parents-in-law. She was a caregiver to three families: her family of origin, her husband's family of origin, and her immediate family. She was angry that she had to care for her paranoid father-in-law. A week ago, her mother-in-law sought her help to accompany her father-in-law to the hospital. Her mother-in-law had contacted her son, Mr. S, twice, but he had not called back.

Mrs. S's message was clear. She wished her husband would share part of her burden of caregiving. The therapist invited the couple to talk with each other and discuss this matter.

Mrs. S said to her husband, "I don't understand why you don't call your mom. She needed your help to escort your dad to the hospital. You know that your dad was difficult to deal with and your mom can't cope. Are you really so busy in the office?"

The husband said, "It's not as urgent as you stated."

Mrs. S. protested and said, "Do you know how they [the parents-in-law] feel?"

Mr. S. said to his wife, "I don't have time."

Enraged and upset, Mrs. S said, "Your lack of concern makes me suffer."

Jing joined in and said to her mother, "Don't be so nervous. We have many aunts and uncles. They can help too."

Mr. S argued back and said, "There's no need to be nervous."

The therapist said, "You impress me that you know how to set a limit for yourself. If so, you should be the best person to help you wife. Why can't you help her to set limits?"

Mr. S explained, "I don't think so. She never listened to me. She has a psychological problem. In the past 2 weeks, she felt very upset when she didn't visit her mom."

Mr. S continued, "People have their ways of dealing with their problems. She's too nervous."

Jing elaborated, "If my mom does not intervene, things will turn out to be better. When she responds too quickly, people will let her take over their duty."

Mrs. S agreed with her daughter and said, "My problem is that I can't say no. I blame myself for being selfish if I say 'no.'"

Mrs. S thought that she was *yu xiao* (愚孝), that is, foolishly filial. She did wish to learn to differentiate her own needs from the needs of others. She could learn fast if her daughter and husband were more supportive rather than adding to her psychological burden. She disliked being pressed by Jing for company in eating ice cream when she was talking with her sister-in-law on the phone. The sister-in-law called to express her concern and care for Jing, and it would be extremely impolite to end their conversation abruptly. Jing hated all the calls from the relatives as they brought only additional work for her mother. Her self-starvation had become an effective weapon for her to bargain with her mother, defend her self-interest, and fulfill her needs for care and concern. Jing apologized to her mother and promised not to do so in future. In return she hoped that her mother could shorten her telephone conversation from an hour to half an hour.

The therapist asked Mr. S, "Who feels more insecure, your wife or your daughter?"

Mr. S said, "Jing didn't have such a problem before the onset of the disorder. My wife's sense of insecurity is stronger and her problem is chronic."

Jing said, "My mom's sense of psychological insecurity can be lessened when I am on good terms with my dad."

The therapist asked Mrs. S, "Really?"

Both Mr. S and Mrs. S nodded their heads.

The mother explained that when her husband argued with her daughter, she was tense and nervous. She blamed herself for causing their conflicts.

Confused and puzzled, the therapist asked Mrs. S, "What had you done that led to their conflicts?"

Mrs. S replied awkwardly, "It is my fault. I've given birth to my daughter. I should not have done that as my husband never liked children."

Mr. S and Jing disagreed almost at the same time: "That's her problem. She often twisted things around. Something had gone wrong with her. She liked self-blaming so much."

The father–daughter alliance posed an immediate challenge. Their analysis really reflected the mother's problem. Nonetheless, if she accepted their analysis, the therapist would have fostered the mother's sense of culpability.

The therapist attempted to resolve this dilemma through clarification, that is, helping the father and the daughter to explain to Mrs. S why they quarreled.

The therapist asked, "Why did you quarrel with each other?"

Jing said smilingly, "Both of us are strong characters and self-centered. We usually argue over petty things."

"I see. That's nothing related to the unwelcome pregnancy, am I right?" The therapist looked at Mr. S when raising this question. Mr. S agreed with a smile.

Mrs. S's parents were indeed very successful in training her eldest daughter in being so dutiful, caring, and self-sacrificing. Tearful and twisted with pain, Mrs. S recalled how her parents expected her to behave during family adversities.

The therapist said to the family, "Seemingly your family is not as hopeless as before. You two are now on good terms with each other."

Mrs. S expressed once more to her husband and her daughter that she would feel better when their relationship improved.

Mr. S sighed and said to his wife, "It's a vicious cycle. Only if you involve yourself less with your mother will we be better."

The therapist punctuated apologetically, "Pardon me. Please tell me more. It may help your wife."

Mr. S explained that he was indeed very angry at his wife's overinvolvement with her own mother and his parents. The therapist encouraged him to express his anger more, "How did you feel when she was fully occupied with them?"

"Like an orphan," Mr. S moaned with pain. He channeled and displaced his anger and frustration on his daughter rather than expressing them directly toward his wife, as she had already been suffering from depression and was psychologically too fragile to withstand his anger and frustration. It made sense that he refused to join hands with his wife in refeeding their emaciated daughter. He thought that if she loved her daughter, she should spend more time with her and not elsewhere.

Jing stood on her father's side: "I will feel better when she [the mother] put her attention and effort back on our family. All of us will feel better. I enjoy having meals with my mom and dad only. I don't mind having dinner with my maternal grandma, uncles, and aunts once a week, but I hate having dinners with them almost every night."

Surprised, the therapist asked, "Do you have dinners with your grandparents every night even though you live apart?"

Jing replied, "Yes. I hate that."

"How come you can have dinner with your grandparents every night? Are they living close?" asked the therapist.

Jing replied, "Yes, we are living in the same district."

The mother was aware that both her husband's and her daughter's mood would be better when they had their own meals together. She enjoyed having their family meals too.

The therapist wrapped up the session by asking a final question, "Do you like to change?"

Mrs. S replied, "Yes."

"Are you willing to let them [the husband and daughter] help you?"

"Only if they are supportive. . . ."

The mother's answer was reasonable and sensible. The therapist moved her seat closer to Mrs. S in order to support her and repeated her message, "Only if they are supportive," to Mr. S and Jing. They gave board smiles back.

By encouraging this family to talk to one another, the therapist allowed the "neglected" husband to express his anger and frustration but at the same time provided them with a context to perceive the interconnection among the father and daughter's conflict, the marital conflict, and the mother's excessive involvement with the big family, *jia zu*, and how this had constituted a symptomatic cycle that had impacted the parents' collaboration in refeeding the self-starved daughter.

The mother's conflict with her husband and her daughter reflected their disparate subjective definition of family. To the mother, family refers to the extended family; to the husband and the daughter, family refers to the nuclear family. Apart from the disparate subjective definition of family, the overinvolvement of the mother with the extended family had exhausted her psychologically and physically, leaving little energy and time left for her husband and daughter. Mrs. S's depression did not emerge in isolation. When her depression was contextualized in her *jia*, the extended family, the root of her depression emerged: She was the hostage of her mother and her siblings. Jing's self-starvation had provided ample opportunity for the overloaded mother to face the long-standing difficulty, which could hardly be resolved without the active contributions of her husband and daughter.

THE THIRD INTERVIEW

Jing's body weight had increased from 39 kg to 40 kg over the 2 intervening weeks. As usual, Jing sat between her parents on the sofa. They looked more relaxed compared to the last interview. The parents had succeeded in fighting for Jing to attend the school examination in Hong Kong, and her school had already granted permission. Jing went to the nearby library for revision, and her mother accompanied her when she did not have to work. Mr. S took over the role of his wife at least once per week to keep his daughter company too. Jing's eating attitude had changed. She no longer skipped the three meals. Probably due to the study pressure, she had at least one tea break in the late afternoon. Jing felt that her concentration span had increased. Her mind was no longer preoccupied with food, and she could shift her attention back to her studies. Her parents were pleased with the change in her eating attitude as well as her motivation to take charge of her own health. Mr. S thought that his wife had made the greatest effort in helping their daughter to achieve this progress.

The therapist turned to Jing and said, "I am impressed by your progress. How about your mom? Has she made any progress as well?"

Jing smiled and said, "Yes. She has become less upset when she couldn't visit my maternal great-grandmother."

The cotherapist followed and asked, "How was she able to do so? Who has helped her to achieve this in this family?"

The mother replied quickly, "Jing."

Jing explained, "I promise her that I'll be with her when visiting my maternal great-grandma."

Mrs. S joined in, "I only visited my grandmother twice in the past 2 weeks. My mother was angry with my husband and blamed him for being possessive of my time and efforts. She is jealous and often competes with my husband for my time and effort. It's difficult for me. I don't wish my daughter to follow my footsteps and sacrifice her own interest in order to please me."

Jing protested, "That's not true. I went to see great-grandma with you because you've done so much for me."

The therapists turned to ask if Mrs. S had taken care of her husband as well in the past 2 weeks. The couple reported that they had fewer conflicts. Before the onset of Jing's self-starvation, they had related to each other quite well and acted as a team. For instance, Mrs. S was the designer while Mr. S was the workman in decorating their home. Mr. S seldom argued with his wife, and he used to follow her instructions with good craftsmanship. In return, Mrs. S had relieved his burden of caregiving for his parents.

Mrs. S said, "He is a good husband but he is a stern and uncompromising father."

The cotherapist asked curiously, "Was he like this in the past 2 weeks?"

Mrs. S shook her head and replied smilingly, "He has changed in the past 2 weeks. Perhaps I've changed and he became more relaxed."

Mr. S agreed and said to his wife, "You've created less trouble."

Both therapists expressed understanding and said, "So her mood influenced yours very much."

Mr. S replied emphatically, "Definitely."

Jing joined in the conversation: "My dad's mood was influenced by my mom's emotion. When my mom was unhappy, nervous, and uptight, my dad would throw his temper on me. Last week I had a row with my mother. My mother didn't allow me to have a cup of ice cream, for fear that I would eat too much and that it will affect my sleep. I refused to listen. She looked miserable when my dad came home. As expected, my dad scolded me while my mom was cleaning the dishes in the kitchen."

The therapist asked Mr. S, "Are you protecting your wife?"

Mr. S answered with a smile, "Yes. She is weak and vulnerable. She has a lot of negative thinking. I can't argue with her."

Jing supported her father and said, "Her thinking is often distorted. She only thought of the dark side of the story."

Mrs. S muttered, "Yes, it's my problem. I can't help perceiving myself as selfish and irresponsible when I failed to entertain my mother. My two brothers had their own problems, and they were not capable to help much. Am I too selfish if I refuse to help look after them including our nephew, a delinquent?"

The therapist replied, "I am sorry that I can't give you a better answer. Your husband is in the best position to advise you."

The therapist gestured to Mr. S to respond to his wife. Mr. S said, "We should try our best to help if we can, but we can't help in every aspect. Buddha has reminded us that there are underlying causes for any subject matter. If our nephew becomes a delinquent, it's not your fault. There are other factors accounting for that."

Jing challenged her mother and said, "If they die, are you responsible for that?"

The mother spent a few minutes to justify why she needed to offer help to her nephew.

Mr. S reassured his wife and said, "Don't worry too much. It'll be fine sooner or later. We've already helped you to face the difficulties."

The therapist punctuated and asked, "In what way?"

Both Mr. S and Jing laughed. Using their mobile phones they called in one after the other when the maternal grandmother refused to end the call.

Mrs. S had an excuse to cut the line. What a wonderful team they were. The therapists burst into laughter too.

The therapist saw the need for validating the remarkable work they had done as well as helping Mrs. S to understand that her daughter and husband were on her side to help overcome the longstanding difficulty.

The therapist leaned forward and asked Mrs. S in a gentle way, "You need to hear their voices. They are now assisting you to set a reasonable boundary from your own mother and you need that boundary. If successful, you can overcome your depression too."

Tearful, Mrs. S uttered, "Yes, I am the problem."

The therapist reframed Mrs. S's inability of differentiating herself from the family of origin by saying softly, "No, that's not true. You are a good woman and you don't know how to protect yourself."

Mr. S and Jing supported the therapist's positive reframing by nodding their heads.

The therapist repeated the message again, "Please don't blame yourself, and please allow them to help you. You've done a lot for your daughter and your husband. As Jing is gradually overcoming her disorder, it is time for you to take care of your well-being, without which you can't say goodbye to your depression."

Mrs. S's eyes reddened. She thanked the therapists before leaving the treatment room.

The therapists were amazed that the family had activated their resources to help one another. The parents started to join hands and collaborated as a team in helping Jing, while Jing reciprocated their love and concern by helping the mother to set a reasonable boundary from the maternal grandmother. Apparently the marital relationship had improved. There were marked reductions in the mother–daughter and father–daughter conflicts.

THE FOURTH SESSION

Jing had gained 0.5 kg in the 2 intervening weeks. She was busy preparing for her examination. Since she had a conspicuously good academic record in the past, she was worried that she could not keep it up. She was hardworking and spent long hours in the community library. There was a good division of labor between the parents in helping Jing. Mrs. S escorted Jing to the shopping mall as a way of reducing her study stress, while Mr. S accompanied Jing to study in the library during weekends. Mrs. S was very pleased that her husband made such an offer without being asked.

Mrs. S's involvement with her family of origin had been reduced to an acceptable level. The therapist asked how they achieved this.

Mrs. S and Jing burst into laughter: "By lying." Mr. S and the therapists laughed too.

Mrs. S explained, "One of my aunts, who lives in Guangzhou, visited us last week. My mother expected me to show her around town. I didn't wish to do so as I want to have more time with Jing and my husband. If I went out with her, I couldn't cook dinner for them. So I lied to my mother that I promised to have dinner with my mother-in-law. My mother was a bit angry, but she didn't insist on my staying."

The therapist went to shake hands with Mrs. S and complimented her, "That's a beautiful lie." Jing and Mr. S roared into laughter.

The cotherapist asked Mrs. S, "How did you feel after lying?"

Mrs. S said, "Quite uncomfortable and guilty. I seldom lied that way in the past."

Mr. S joined in, "Her aunt was a demanding person and I am glad that she [his wife] started to learn to protect herself."

The aunt had borrowed a large sum of money from Mrs. S's mother and failed to pay back.

The therapist asked Mr. S, "Do you teach her to lie?" Mr. S said, "No, she found her own way."

Jing talked to her mother, "There is no need for you to be guilty. You are just protecting yourself." The cotherapist added, "It is a strategy rather than a lie."

Mr. S and Jing agreed wholeheartedly. Mrs. S thought that her mother was as good as she was and had not learned ways to protect herself even after being cheated by this aunt. She hoped that her mother could also learn how to say no.

The cotherapist observed that Jing appeared to be happier when she talked about her father's company than her mother's company. Using this observation for further exploration, the cotherapist asked Jing, "You seem to be happier when you talked about your father's company than your mother's company. Is there any difference between their ways of relating to you?"

Jing said, "Yes. My mother easily yielded to my demands, but she never told me even though she didn't like doing so. After yielding too much, she would scold me. My father was firm and he would stick to his stance."

Mrs. S turned to Jing and said, "You make too many demands on me."

Jing fought back and said, "You allow me to do so."

Mrs. S said, "My mother and my daughter take advantage of me."

Jing showed no sign of retreating. She protested, "You encouraged me to do so. Prof. M [the therapist] had already said so. Human interaction is two-way and interactive. You allow me to depend on you. It's too comfortable for me to be dependent on you."

Mrs. S challenged her daughter smilingly and said, "If I don't give in, would you relapse?"

Jing stated her objection strongly, "I won't."

Mr. S attempted to mediate their conflict and said to his wife, "There is no need to press her. She is progressing well. Sooner or later she needs to return to school. She needs to learn to overcome her problem of food refusal on her own. I trust her. Please be relaxed. She can take charge of her own health."

Jing became less tense after her father's help. She said, "I am now eating very well. Please don't press me to eat too much. I can't take too much food at one go. You asked me to take the bird's nest soup, followed by Chinese medicine and milk."

Mr. S lent further support to his daughter, "As a matter of fact, there is no urgency. There are still a few months ahead before she returns to school. Actually, too much attention has already been paid to eating."

The therapist sought clarification, "Who has paid too much attention to eating in this family?" Mr. S said, "My wife."

Looking upset, Mrs. S defended her view and said, "I agree with you partially. Undoubtedly she is progressing well, but her menstruation has not come back. She is not yet fully recovered."

Mrs. S expressed with great concern to her daughter, "It's fine for you to keep fit but it's not alright when your menstruation has not been back."

Acknowledging the mother's concern toward Jing, the therapist suggested that Mrs. S ask her daughter if she agreed with her view or not.

Jing replied, "I don't agree with your view. You can't press me too much. I eat more than enough."

Mrs. S protested and said, "Next time don't ask me to share part of your lunch box."

Jing raised her voice and said in an irritated voice, "Dear mom: That was a long time ago." Jing continued, "You love me too much. It's too much. Don't treat me as if I am very young. I'd already shown you the receipt. I've taken a snack an hour before lunch. I know that you won't trust me. So I kept the receipt as proof. However, your expression told me that you didn't trust me. You are too controlling. Your way of expressing your love made me feel like a child. "

The message was clear. Jing wished her mother to let go and trust that she was the master of her own health.

Mrs. S explained apologetically, "I cooked more in order to help balance your body. Your body was too hot due to your overwork. I wish to be helpful. I did not know that you don't welcome that. I'll not do so in the future if you don't like that."

Jing was pleased with her mother's reassurance.

Mrs. S and Jing did find ways to resolve their conflict without any intervention from the therapists.

The therapist appreciated their achievement and asked, "Can you resolve your conflict at home?"

The three of them shook their heads. They tended to be emotional at home when discussing sensitive issues such as eating. They were more rational and calm in the treatment room. Despite Jing's progress, it was still painful for Mrs. S because Jing kept forcing her to eat. For instance, during the weekend, Jing forced the mother to have different types of snacks while shopping. She forced her mother to eat another piece of cheesecake after returning home.

Mrs. S said, "I felt cheated and I had no choice either. If I said no, she kept crying and shouting."

The therapist sought help from Mr. S and asked, "What happened to them?"

Mr. S explained, "She [his wife] yielded too much in the past; she [Jing] has got accustomed to that. They have communication difficulty too."

Mrs. S talked back, "She forced me to eat."

Mr. S replied, "You should stand firm."

Mrs. S turned to her husband to seek further support.

She said, "I can't set a limit."

Mr. S said helplessly, "You've got to learn your way of doing so."

Unexpectedly Jing said to the therapists, "My dad can help to remind her not to do so but she doesn't listen to him. She has no courage to say no to me. I'll feel better if she say no to me when she is upset, rather than suppressing it. I don't like to deal with her suppressed and delayed anger."

Mrs. S became courageous to face her daughter's challenge. She said to her daughter, "If I do so, we shall have more conflicts."

Jing argued back maturely, "This type of conflict is good for us. At least I learn your limit. I don't wish to upset you."

Mrs. S asked sheepishly, "If I were honest, would you throw temper tantrums?"

Jing said sharply, "I've not thrown tantrums for a long time."

Mr. S nodded.

The therapist congratulated Jing and Mrs. S. Both had made good use of this session to express their discontent and to learn about each other's needs; most importantly, they resolved their conflicts constructively.

The therapist adjourned the session by emphasizing that the couple had helped their daughter extensively. As the daughter had begun to take charge of her own health, it was time for them to let go and entrust her with the responsibility of recovery. The couple agreed, while Jing was very pleased with the therapist's suggestion. They wished to schedule their appointment 5 weeks later, after Jing's examination.

THE FIFTH SESSION

Jing's body weight had climbed up to 42 kg. The family went for a 1-week vacation in Japan shortly after Jing's examination. The three of them looked sunny, cheerful, and bright. They spent 10 minutes relating how much they had enjoyed the holiday, including the delicious food, the cool weather, and the beautiful and serene scenery there.

Jing was going to take up a part-time summer job, participate in a 3-day summer camp, and be a volunteer serving people with special needs in a nearby social service center. Jing's school expected her to have some work experiences during the summer. After learning of her daughter's need, Mrs. S approached her boss for help. She was very kind to offer a part-time clerical job to Jing. Jing had expanded her social life; her life was no longer preoccupied with food and eating.

Most impressive was the change in Mrs. S. She narrated, "From the treatment, I learned that I can't always think of meeting others' needs at the expense of my own needs. I started to defend my self-interests. Previously when they [her husband and her daughter] fought with each other, I would mediate actively, but my help is ineffective. Now I let them deal with their conflicts and continue carrying on my activities."

Beaming with a sense of triumph, Mrs. S continued, "I didn't help my nephew to get his school record. Finally his parents went to get it."

Greatly impressed by Mrs. S transformation, the cotherapist wished to understand the effect of her change on Jing and her husband.

The cotherapist asked Jing, "How do you feel about your mother's change?"

Jing replied with a great pride, "Good. Mom learned to invite my paternal aunt to escort my paternal grandma to the hospital. She said assertively to my aunt, 'She [the grandma] likes your company more; can you take a day off?' My aunt took leave from her job without any complaint."

Mrs. S explained, "Yes, I dared to speak up. I knew that if I yielded this time, they'll continue to depend on me. I need to break this pattern and I don't wish to assume this role anymore in future."

Turning to Mr. S, the therapist asked, "Do you feel proud of her?"

Mr. S said subtly, "Yeah."

He said, "She has changed a lot. My mother-in-law seldom phones us now. She has less stress. She becomes less tense. Her psychological state is very good."

The therapist asked, "How about you? Does it affect you?"

Mr. S grinned and said, "Yes. There's no need for me to face her emotional turmoil. My stress level is low. There's time for my hobby."

"Whom has your mother taken more care of, you or your dad?" the therapist asked Jing. Jing replied, "Me."

Mr. S joked, "She wishes to take over my place."

The cotherapist responded humorously, "Like how you sit now."

All of them laughed. Since the beginning of the session, Jing had been sitting next to her mother while Mr. S sat alone on the other side of the sofa.

The cotherapist suggested, "Would you like to change seats with your dad?"

Another burst of laughter filled up the room. Jing changed seats with her dad immediately.

Mrs. S said, "I know that I've got to change. If I continue yielding to her demands, sooner or later Jing will become impossible to relate to. She [Jing] wants me to be strong and assertive. When I was weak and timid in front of my mom and my relatives, she tended to protect me by being impolite to them. I gradually perceived the linkage of my nonassertiveness to her rebellious and rude social behavior. She is repeating what I've done with my mom, but doing everything to protect me."

The therapist sought clarification from Jing, "Do you agree?"

Jing said, "I think so."

In view of the transformation that the family had gone through, the therapist shifted to Jing's study plans after the summer. She planned to return to her overseas school in September. She had confidence that she could keep her health. Mrs. S was slightly worried about her daughter's departure, but her husband reassured her that Jing should be able to make it.

Mrs. S suddenly said to Jing, "Do you want to make use of this session to ask your dad if he loves you or not? It's important for you to ask him directly rather than through me."

"Well." Jing was quite embarrassed. Using her body language, Mrs. S encouraged Jing to talk with her father.

"Do you love me?" Jing whispered.

"Yes, of course. You are my daughter. I was firm and stern to you in the past because your mom was too lenient. I don't wish you to become self-centered when you grow up."

"You never joke with me; nor talk to me much at home," Jing said.

Mrs. S sided with her daughter and said to her husband, "Can you be more responsive to her? Remember once when she was young, she showed you a beautiful flower, hoping that you could share in her joy. You showed no response at all. She was very disappointed." Mrs. S continued lecturing, "You've trained her to please others too much, rather than having her own view. Guess how serious you are toward life. You've already asked her to submit the summer plan for next year. That's too much."

Wearing an embarrassing smile, Mr. S remained silent and uncomfortable.

The cotherapist said jokingly to Jing, "If I were your dad, I would be more demanding toward you as you are so possessive of my wife."

Another round of laughter burst out in the treatment room.

The therapist argued on behalf of Jing and said playfully, "That's unfair to her [Jing]. He hasn't made any attempt to win back his wife." All of us laughed again.

The therapist went to shake hands with them and congratulated them on their transformation.

THE SIXTH SESSION

Although Jing's body weight had increased to 44.5 kg, the family atmosphere was tense at the beginning of the session. Mrs. S was miserable and depressed. Jing looked angry and upset while Mr. S was sullen and self-absorbed. The mother and daughter sat together on the same sofa while Mr. S sat opposite them alone.

Mrs. S wept and narrated, "She [Jing] talked a lot at home about the two popular movie stars and how she adored their slimness and beauty; both of them are patients suffering from AN. She [Jing] was afraid of obesity. When I persuaded her to eat, she accused me of pressing her to become fat. She does not treasure her health and the effort we've put in to help her recover."

Apparently Mrs. S's worry had come back. The therapist suddenly realized that September was approaching and Jing had to leave Hong Kong and go abroad to study. It was uncertain if the mother's old pattern of response was attributable to Jing's departure or to other factors. The therapist turned to Mr. S for the answer.

Mr. S said, "It's normal for her to worry. There's no doubt that she has to rely on herself when she studies abroad. There's not much we can do after this month."

Mrs. S replied angrily, "It depends whether you like to help or not."

Mrs. S was accusing her husband of having insufficient participation in parenting.

The therapist asked with concern and care, "What do you mean?"

Mrs. S said, "They like fighting with each other. Jing woke up late this morning. We had insufficient time for a proper breakfast. When we arrived at the train station, I suggested that we buy a few buns in the nearby bakery. He refused to take any and Jing followed suit. She threatened that if he didn't take it, she would not take any either."

Mr. S protested, "I am not hungry and I don't like eating on my way."

The therapist asked Jing curiously, "Eating is an individual matter. Why did you give up eating when your dad didn't have breakfast?"

Jing said with resentment, "He did it to punish me. He is taking revenge."

The therapist never expected such a strong response. "Oh, is it? Maybe it's true or it maybe it is not. Can you ask him now?"

Jing asked her father, "Is it so?"

Mr. S. replied, "No."

Mrs. S asked her husband, "Why can't you yield to her?"

Angry and frustrated, Mr. S raised his voice and said, "Why do I need to do so? You're worrying too much."

Jing attacked her father and said, "It's because you didn't care enough about me. Last week you scolded mom for doing too much for me, rather than appreciating her effort for doing so. You never recognized her contribution in helping me. You are as selfish as I am. You didn't care about me and the family." Jing was crying.

Jing was siding with her beloved mother to fight against the lonely father. She was too willing to be triangulated into the couple's relationship.

Using an empathetic voice, the therapist asked, "I am surprised to hear about this. I perceive otherwise. What has happened in the past few weeks?"

Jing explained while crying, "I am leaving at the end of this month. Mom is very anxious and dad doesn't care. The family has become very tense and I am in great distress."

"I see. Your departure must be very difficult for your mom to face." The therapist validated and normalized Mrs. S's responses. Since last week, Mrs. S had become very upset. She quarreled with Jing for her obsessive fear of obesity. She was resentful of her husband for his apathy and inertia dealing with Jing's obsessive fear while Mr. S complained of his wife's excessive worry. In a nutshell, their old pattern of interaction had come back.

The therapists had to help the family cope with the anxiety and fear arising from Jing's departure, which in turn activated the old pattern of family interaction. Locked into the old pattern of interaction, the three of them suffered in pain. The therapist decided to address their interlocking pattern of interaction first.

The therapist asked Jing, "When you quarreled with your father, how much did you quarrel for yourself and how much were you fighting on behalf of your mother?"

"Both," Jing said with tears falling down. "I fight for my interest more. He doesn't care about me. Last week I sought his advice on which subject I should take as my major in university study. He said that it was your study, not my study. I should make my own decision."

Mrs. S challenged her husband and said emotionally, "The same applies to how you handled your daughter's guardianship. Her overseas guardian wrote to us for instruction and advice regarding Jing's boarding arrangements. You simply ignored his e-mail. When I reminded you to do so, you said that that was none of your business; it was her [Jing's] business. I felt hurt and upset to hear about this. What have you done for your daughter? Nothing, except keep her company when she was studying for the examination. You're too mean and too selfish. All your effort is concentrated on your study. You only care about your self-improvement professionally and academically. Before she came back to Hong Kong, you took leaves readily. After she came back, you preferred to stay in your office more. It is hopeless. I want to die. Jing said that she would follow suit." Her pitch rose, as did the tempo of her speech. The therapist stopped her politely and respectfully and suggested that she calm down for a while.

Mr. S explained that he was passive because whatever he did could never meet his wife's expectations. He had gradually learned to adopt a strategy of "doing less" in order to avoid being criticized and scolded.

Jing protested and said to her dad, "It's unfair to mom. Mom's English is not as good as yours. She needs your help but you've let her down."

Mr. S replied, "We often use precise English in e-mail writing but your mom disagrees. I am reluctant to offer any help to avoid quarrelling with her."

Jing's intrusion had interrupted the couple's dialogue. The therapist perceived the need to stop her intrusion.

The therapist said to Jing, "I don't agree with you that you are fighting for yourself. What I've observed was that you are fighting for your mom, rather than defending your own interest."

Jing smiled and nodded.

The therapist said to Mrs. S, "Can't you see that your daughter is often on your side. How come you said that you are wasting your time in helping her?"

Jing said, "I need to help her [her mom] because she had done so much for me in the past."

Puzzled and confused, the therapist asked Jing, "I understand your mom's love toward you. But your body weight is increasing steadily. Why does she still feel so anxious?"

Mrs. S said, "She has gradually overcome her self-starvation because of me. If I were not available, she may relapse."

The therapist punctuated immediately, "Pardon me, is it so?"

Jing replied firmly, "No. I eat for my health, for my study, and for my future, not for her. I've repeated this a thousand times at home but she doesn't believe it. What can I do?"

The mother and the daughter continued arguing fiercely.

The therapist invited Mr. S to resolve the conflict. Hesitant and without confidence, Mr. S said, "I am sorry. I can't manage it. She [his wife] was full of negative thoughts."

Jing suddenly raised her hand and said assertively, "Wait. I need to say something more to my mom. Please trust me. I know how to take care of myself. If I didn't have good health, I couldn't cope with the wind chill. I'll take meat and I'll have more noodles and chocolates to ensure I have enough physical strength to face the cold winter there."

The therapist went to shake hands with her and congratulate her: "I am impressed by your strong will to maintain your health. That's indeed the best reassurance to your mom. You've done your part very well. Can you let your parents deal with their discontent directly?"

The therapist wished to set a context for the couple to have direct dialogue with each other by inviting Jing to stay out of her parents' physical space. Jing became cooperative and changed seats with her dad.

The therapist said gently and slowly to the couple, "You need to talk to each other. Learning to let go of a growing child is extremely difficult, especially for a mother."

Mr. S comforted his wife and said, "We can't live with her forever. She is growing up. She has to leave us and learn to be independent. Don't worry too much."

Mrs. S cried, "Once a person has been bitten by a snake, then one will be frightened of snakes. Do you remember how emaciated she was early this year? I am extremely scared. I don't wish to go through the nightmare again. You can deny everything, including a serious problem like her self-starvation. I can't. I feel alone in dealing with her problem. I am alone."

Mrs. S cited another example. Last week Jing threw temper tantrums in the street because of a trivial matter. Mrs. S sought help from her husband. He disappointed her by threatening to return home. The therapist slowed down their dialogue and made use of clarification to help them learn more about each other's viewpoint.

The therapist asked Mr. S, "Are you really selfish as perceived by your wife? Or are you at a loss about how to deal with the conflict?"

"She has overestimated my ability."

Mr. S was weak in handling interpersonal conflicts even though he was good at problem solving. During the conflict he was as confused and upset as his wife. To retreat and take flight, in the perspective of Mr. S, was the best way to avoid fighting with his wife.

The cotherapist asked Mrs. S, "It struck me that you prefer having two decision makers, rather than just one in your family. Is it right?"

Mrs. S said, "Yes. I don't wish to fight a lonely battle."

The cotherapist asked, "In which area would you like to share with him your burden of care?"

Mrs. S said, "Parenting."

The therapist said to Mr. S, "Your participation in treatment indicates that you are a responsible father and husband. Even though your wife kept complaining and blaming, you still listened patiently here, suggesting that you have capacity to deal with your wife's requests. It's quite normal for people to run away from unpleasant and angry feelings. However, is it possible for you to stay rather than flee when your wife wants your help?"

Mr. S was uneasy and remained quiet, suggesting that the therapist might have been pressing too fast. He was in need of support.

The therapist said, "Do you feel angry when your daughter sides with your wife to go against you?"

"Certainly. . . . I feel lonely and rejected."

The therapist intensified Mr. S's message by saying to Mrs. S, "You may be unaware that your alliance with your daughter had unwittingly exacerbated his sense of loneliness, further marginalized him from parenting, and increased his hostility toward you. I believe that you don't do it intentionally and deliberately."

Judging from Mrs. S's facial expression, she was calming down to listen to the message. The therapists conveyed their wish that Jing would enjoy her studies abroad. The family would come back for an interview during Jing's Christmas holidays.

TERMINATION OF FAMILY TREATMENT

It was a delightful surprise for the therapists to meet Jing and her parents 3 months later. What a big difference from 9 months before. Jing's body weighed 50.5 kg. She was cheerful, sunny, and bright. After being promoted to the senior form, she enjoyed her schooling very much. She was a member of the school badminton and basketball teams. She related well to her classmates and participated actively in organizing extracurricular activities for students of the junior forms. She was too busy to think about food. Her parents were very pleased with her progress. Mrs. S felt relieved that her daughter had fully recovered while Mr. S was proud of her independence. Jing called her mother almost every day during the first month after her departure. In the past 2 months she called only once per week. She told her parents that she was too busy to make calls.

The cotherapist wished to learn more about Jing's experience of self-starvation. She asked Jing, "Can you use a metaphor to describe your experience of self-starvation?"

Jing thought for a while and replied smilingly, "Like a cage. I was living in the cage. There was no sunshine, no air, no hope here; it was full of darkness. My greatest concern was food, nothing but food. My mind was full of images of food and my overriding concern revolved around food."

Jing explained, "I have come out of the cage, and food is only a tiny part of my life. I have so much in life: my friends, my extracurricular activities, my study, my badminton, and my basketball; all have given me so much fun and enjoyment. I don't need food to give meaning to my life."

The cotherapist asked the parents, "Does the metaphor apply to your experience too?"

The parents said in unison, "We were living in the cage too. It's the indescribable horror, so painful and awful. Jing was like a wild animal, unpredictable and totally beyond sanity."

"I was like a tamer of the beast in the zoo. My husband was an observer outside the cage. He hadn't changed much; he is still an observer," Mrs. S elaborated.

"It's quite different. He is now an observer with care and concern," Jing corrected her mother. Mr. S smiled sweetly.

The cotherapist asked Jing, "Who has helped you to recover?"

"My parents, especially mom. She's done so much for me."

Mr. S nodded and joined in the conversation, "Jing recovered because of my wife." He repeated twice. Mrs. S smiled but her eyes had reddened.

The therapist said, "I am happy to learn about this. In the past we therapists tended to blame the mother for the daughter's self-starvation. What I heard has refuted such a misconception."

Jing said, "My dad has helped by giving assistance to my mom. I once joked with my roommate that my being too close with my mom is a good reason for my dad to send me abroad to study." Mr. S said naughtily, "Yes. You are right."

The cotherapist asked, "How do you view their relationship now?"

Jing laughed and said, "They are very close to each other since I no longer compete with my dad for my mom's time and space."

Mrs. S learned to set a limit with her mother, who still called her every day. Mrs. S requested her mother to call her in the morning, rather than at night, to minimize its negative effects on her husband and her family. Besides, she could end their conversation with the justifiable reason that she would be fired for being late for work.

As perceived by the couple, the therapists had provided space for them to understand the crux of the problem, on the basis of which they should prioritize their time and energy. They appreciated the therapists' way of working. The therapists offered active guidance but did not prescribe solutions, although they felt quite at a loss after the first session, as their way of treatment was incompatible with the family's expectations.

When asked if we needed to change our way of working, Jing said, "No, we must think about our problem and identify the solution." But the parents suggested that we could actively guide them in the first and second sessions by giving them examples of successful stories in overcoming self-starvation.

The room was filled with joy and laughter. It was time to terminate the treatment. The therapists shook hands with each of them and congratulated them for their joint effort in driving away the disorder.

Table 8.1 summarizes the practice principles for this family.

DISCUSSION

The main concern of family assessment is to identify whether the disorder has been maintained by the stifling family context and to understand those unfavorable factors that have negatively influenced the emaciated daughter and the parents to combat the disorder. Superficially, Jing's family was a typical family with the mother having a very close relationship with the maternal grandmother and the distant and peripheral father. The minimal involvement of the father in parenting had made the mother feel lonely and depressed in shouldering the impossible task of refeeding her daughter single-handedly. The emergence of the family drama suggested that Jing's self-starvation was maintained by the couple's failure to collaborate as a team because of the asymmetric involvement of the mother and the father in parenting.

A cultural perspective has expanded the assessment from the immediate family to the extended family, *jia zu*. In this family, the extended family comprised Mr. S's family of origin and Mrs. S's family of origin in addition to the nuclear family. The family map identified was more complex and larger than originally thought. According to the father's description, the vicious cycle started with the longstanding and extensive involvement of his wife, the filial daughter, with her family of origin, which had brought tremendous stress and frustration to the couple and had negatively affected their marital relationship. Being protective of his psychologically vulnerable wife, Mr. S tended to displace and channel his frustration and anger onto his daughter; this in turn escalated the marital conflict and further sabotaged their effort to act as a team in helping the self-starving daughter.

Such a symptomatic cycle was reinforced by the traditional Chinese cultural belief of filial piety and the submissive and sacrificing role of Chinese women in the family. Mrs. S became hostage of her mother in part because her sense of self was heavily dependent on her mother's approval and in part because a strong sense of filial piety had been inculcated as part of her morality. Mrs. S's failure to perform according to her mother's expectation and demands had evoked immense shame and anxiety, which seemed to have surpassed her love and devotion toward her husband and daughter. In the treatment process, the pains of the husband had become visible to Mrs. S, who blamed the husband for causing most of the misery. The "peripheral and noninvolved" husband was in reality a victim and a silent sufferer too.

Jing's AN was a crisis for the family, a danger as well as an opportunity. The life- threatening nature of the disorder, Jing's declining health, and the day-to-day family conflicts had driven them to deal with their longstanding difficulty with determination. Once the issues were resolved, the mother had more energy and effort to join hands with her husband in helping the emaciated daughter to recover.

The treatment goal for this family was to help the couple collaborate and cooperate as a team in refeeding their emaciated daughter, and this could hardly have been achieved without helping the mother to set an appropriate boundary with the *jia zu*, the extended family, and learn to say no to the requests of the parents-in-law, her mother, her brothers, and her brothers' families. Minuchin (1978) has observed that the family of origin can be intrusive and detrimental to normal family functioning. Mrs. S's change depended considerably on the degree of support she received from her husband and daughter. With the accomplishment of this treatment goal, the therapist assisted the family in resolving the couple's conflict, the mother–daughter conflict, and the father–daughter conflict accordingly.

Bowen (1978) has argued that people with low levels of differentiation are more likely to experience psychological problems and marital distress. The effect of differentiation on health is more significant for women than for men (Miller, Anderson, & Keala, 2004). This case illustration has provided anecdotal evidence to support Bowen's prediction. While recognizing the contribution of Bowen's theory in pointing the way to treatment, the therapists must be culturally sensitive and competent in understanding the differences between the concept of differentiation as originally proposed by Bowen (1978) and the concept as it is manifested in Chinese societies such as Hong Kong. The fundamental value of Western societies is individualism, in contrast to the traditional Chinese values of collectivism and familism. The problem of "poor boundaries," seen in the light of traditional Chinese culture, symbolizes the fulfillment of family responsibility by a filial adult child, the collective orientation of Chinese society, and the cultural expectation of advancing family interests at the expense of the individual self. The critical task of the family therapist is to help the adult child to balance responsibility toward the families of origin (both maternal and paternal) and the caregiving demands arising from AN.

Two concepts are essential for assessment and treatment for Chinese families with AN, namely a power analysis and a loyalty analysis (Luepnitz, 1988). The former enables the family therapist to understand the position and power of women in the extended family, *jia zu*, and their pain and suffering as typified by Mrs. S's story. The latter sheds light on the problem of split loyalty faced by Chinese adults after marriage, in relation to their aging parents and their own family. It is of interest to note one feature of a society in transition between traditional Asian and modernized Western social norms: The nuclear family lives apart from their aged parents (as would be typical in the West) but take up a heavy and expected responsibility in giving care to the aged parents (as would be typical in traditional Asian societies), sharing this with siblings and usually in a context where institutionalized support is relatively week (Lau, Ma, & Chan, 2006).

The process of unfolding the longstanding difficulties of this family in the first and second sessions was a healing process for this family. First, it assisted the family to revisit and examine all of the interlocking issues. Second, the family could no longer deny the problem. Each family member perceived his or her active role in constituting the problem; hence change became the collective effort of the family. This accounted for the transformation of the family from the third session onward.

Although the family resumed the old pattern of interaction in the sixth session when Jing was about to return to school overseas, she was able to achieve a full recovery. The mother–daughter connection was indeed a great healing force in the treatment of eating disorders (Andersson, 1995). Both Jing and Mr. S acknowledged in different sessions the enormous contributions of the mother in the healing process. It is crucial for the therapist not to blame the mother and to appreciate the need of the daughter to rely on her mother temporarily in the process of recovery.

Jing's motivation for recovery was fairly high, and this was undoubtedly an important facilitative factor for recovery. In the last treatment session, Jing used the metaphor of a cage to describe her illness experience. Although her parents had helped to open the cage, she had to come out of the cage herself. Jing succeeded in walking out of the cage because her sense of personal ineffectiveness before the onset of the disorder was not high. She did well in school, and she liked playing badminton and basketball. The disorder did not bring her a lot of psychological gains except parental love. All of these favorable personal factors, when interacting with the supportive family context, accounted for Jing's speedy recovery.

Two follow-up interviews were conducted, one with the couple 2 months after Jing's departure and one with the whole family during the Christmas holidays. The couple related to each other with infrequent conflict while Jing enjoyed her overseas study very much. Her body weight increased to 50.5 kg, and her menstruation had resumed. She enjoyed eating different kinds of food and went out to have meals with her friends for fun. Two years later, she was admitted to a prestigious overseas university. She continued studying very well and started dating too.

The transformation of Jing reflected the triumph of the parents in collaborating together as a team to break the symptomatic cycle maintaining self-starvation and to refeed their emaciated daughter. The positive school life consolidated Jing's transformation and facilitated her development physically, intellectually, psychologically, and socially.

Table 8.1: Practice Principles Employed for the S Family

Treatment Session	Treatment Steps of the Model	Application for This Family
Sessions 1 and 2	• To briefly understand the history of the disorder and the motivation for recovery • To explore and identify the constricting family process that had hindered parental collaboration and refeed the emaciated daughter and hence had maintained the symptoms • To negotiate a treatment contract by shifting the family's focus from the symptoms to the symptomatic cycle or the constricting family process that had maintained and escalated AN • To encourage parental collaboration by helping the parents to help the emaciated daughter rather than to control her	• Jing's history of onset and her motivation for recovery were assessed • The family structure comprising an overinvolved mother, an emaciated daughter, and a peripheral father was identified, accounting for the couple's difficulty in collaborating as a team in refeeding their daughter at home • Further exploration indicated that there were longstanding boundary problems between the family and the couple's families of origin • Through tracking, the therapist made visible the pain and suffering of Mr. S, the angry husband, who was resentful of his wife's long-term neglect; Mrs. S had been suffering from depression in the face of the competing demands for love and attention from her husband, her daughter, and her family of origin, particularly her mother and her parents-in-law • Jing's strong drive for recovery was validated; the couple's strengths were identified • The therapist reiterated the needs of each family member to manage the longstanding boundary problems first with the intrusive maternal grandmother and later with the paternal grandparents and to refeed Jing; the treatment contract was formulated accordingly

Table 8.1 (Cont'd)

Treatment Session	Treatment Steps of the Model	Application for This Family
Session 3	• To continue strengthening parental collaboration in breaking the symptomatic cycle that maintained the symptoms, which in turn would facilitate refeeding • To address unresolved conflicts and improve family relationships using culturally acceptable means	• Appreciation and validation were given to the family, which had already begun to change; Mr. S and Jing started to join hands to help Mrs. S to shorten her daily telephone contact with her mother and to set limits in response to the maternal grandmother's unreasonable demands
Session 4	• To address unresolved conflicts and improve family relationships using culturally acceptable means	• The therapist assisted the mother and the daughter to constructively resolve their conflicts in treatment by ■ Allowing the mother–daughter conflicts to emerge through enactment ■ Suggesting they find alternative ways to deal with their conflicts
Session 5	• To continue addressing unresolved conflicts and improve family relationships using culturally acceptable means	• The therapist appreciated and validated the family's transformation especially on Mrs. S's success in being more assertive to face with her aged mother's unreasonable requests and in having good cooperation with her husband in parenting

Table 8.1 (Cont'd)

Treatment Session	Treatment Steps of the Model	Application for This Family
Session 6	• To handle relapses by preventing the reemergence of the symptomatic cycle and further enhancing the family relationships	• The therapist recognized the intense family emotions and the family conflict, which revealed that the family had resumed the old patterns of interaction: Mrs. S and her daughter allied with each other to fight with Mr. S • Making use of the here-and-now family conflicts, the therapist explored and identified the mother's underlying fear of and worry about Jing's relapse after she went back to study in her overseas school; the therapist facilitated Mr. S and his daughter to help Mrs. S to relieve her anxiety, fear, and worry • The therapist highlighted and firmly discouraged the daughter from playing a role as the "dissolver" of the parents' marital conflict; the therapist encouraged the couple to deal with their marital issues directly in treatment
Session 7 and Two Follow-Up Sessions	• To support individual development • To support the transformation	• Jing's effort to attain full recovery and her active participation in the extracurricular activities at school were appreciated • The couple's contribution to their daughter's recovery was congratulated • Feedback from the family regarding their past experiences with the disorder and family treatment was gathered

Chapter 9
Breaking the Silence by Interdisciplinary Collaboration

INTRODUCTION

Home-based management is preferred to hospitalization for emaciated adolescent girls because it causes less disruption to their study, family life, and social activities. However, if the body weight drops so severely and drastically that there are damaging effects on health, hospitalization is the last resort to save her life.

A team approach is widely accepted for managing anorexia nervosa (AN) patients. However, how different team members actually collaborate may remain obscure to mental health professionals as well as to parents. Team members must fully understand the contributions of different mental health professionals (e.g., psychiatrist, clinical psychologist, psychiatric nurse) and the family therapists in providing holistic care. Such clarity of roles will also help the parents to seek help from appropriate professionals at the appropriate time.

Ideally, family therapists should be part of the multidisciplinary team. With expertise in family assessment and treatment, the family therapist can contribute to the holistic management by identifying the symptomatic cycle that maintains self-starvation, tapping into family strengths, and seeking parents' collaboration and cooperation with the multidisciplinary team in combating the disorder.

Patients and families must be seen as part of the team in combating self-starvation. The more actively they participate in treatment, the more promising the outcome will be.

This case illustrates how a family therapist, a multidisciplinary team, and the parents can cooperate and collaborate to break the symptomatic cycle that has maintained the disorder and how different measures can be adopted to empower the parents in healing, especially when the child is reluctant to relate to and to cooperate with the therapist.

BACKGROUND OF THE FAMILY

Ling, a 9-year-old girl, was a primary five pupil from a three-generational family. At the time of referral for family therapy, she was 32 kg, with a height of 146 cm, which was 85% of normal body weight; her BMI was 15. She had started dieting a year earlier when she was spending her holidays with her maternal grandparents at a resort in southern China. Both of her parents had finished high school. Her father worked in the service sector, while her mother was a junior administrator of a big company. Ling had a 6-year-old brother. Since both parents had to work during the day, they employed a Filipino maid to assist them in looking after the children. The maid had been looking after Ling since infancy, and her relationship with Ling was close. A very close maid (almost a surrogate mother in some cases) is an interesting "family" feature that deserves more exploration. The family was living with the maternal grandparents. Unsurprisingly, the grandparents had a very close relationship with the children. The grandparents helped look after the children as well.

Ling's body weight had dropped drastically from 37 kg to 26.5 kg, as reported at the first psychiatric consultation. As a result, she was immediately hospitalized. The patient had made no progress one and a half months after admission. She was bedridden during this entire period. Her eating was poor. She rejected the doctor in charge and all the nursing staff and refused to communicate with them. The only team member she was willing to relate to was the teacher of the Red Cross Hospital School, who taught her craft work while bedridden. All the hospital staff, especially the doctor in charge, had become very frustrated with Ling's rejection. The consultant psychiatrist had to provide emotional support to the doctor in charge as well as the nursing staff during Ling's early period of hospitalization. Ling often remained silent in front of the parents, who were very disappointed, anxious, and frustrated about their daughter's unsatisfactory progress in the hospital on the one hand and her refusal to talk with them on the other. Despite Ling's apathetic response toward her parents, they kept visiting Ling every day. Both the hospital staff and the parents depended on the maid to communicate with her. After more than a month of struggle with the hospital staff, Ling suddenly followed the medical advice and the prescribed diet. She told the teacher that the only way to be discharged was to restore her normal body weight.

The therapist and a doctoral student conducted a total of three family therapy sessions with this family. A mental health team comprising the psychiatrist, the psychiatric nurse, and the medical social worker observed the treatment behind a one-way mirror.

THE FIRST INTERVIEW

The therapist and the cotherapist ushered the family into the treatment room. Mr. and Mrs. N, Ling, the little brother, and the maternal grandmother attended the session. The parents sat together on the left side, the grandmother sat opposite the therapists, while the two children sat side by side opposite the parents. Ling made no attempt to greet the therapists. She avoided eye contact with the parents but whispered to her younger brother when he played with her.

Mrs. N was in tears when she talked about her present difficulty. Since hospitalization, Ling had chosen to be silent in front of her.

The mother said, "We sent her to hospital because of her declining health. She was angry about the forced hospitalization."

The therapist asked with concern, "What made you so sad?"

"I feel hurt as she didn't understand that we've done so much for her well-being."

The therapist asked, "Is she angry with the dad?"

Mr. N replied, "Yes, we sent her to consult the psychiatrist."

The therapist wished to explore if there was any difference in the parent–child relationship after the onset of self-starvation.

The therapist asked Mr. N, "How was your relationship with your daughter before her illness?"

Mr. N replied, "I used to chat and play with her before her illness. We do have fun together. Gradually we suspected that something had gone wrong with her health. She ate less and less. We consulted a family doctor, who referred us to a specialist. Ling felt that we were forcing her to seek medical advice. From that time onward, she refused to talk to us. She became mute and not a word was uttered in front of us."

The father worked as a service worker. He usually returned home around 8 p.m. As Mrs. N returned home earlier than her husband, she helped supervise the children's homework. However, Mr. N took part in a lot of leisure activities with the children during weekends.

The therapist felt the pain of the father from his facial expression. The therapist acknowledged his pain and wondered what he had done to fix the problem.

"Nothing. I feel extremely upset, sad, and helpless," sighed Mr. N.

Mrs. N was as helpless and upset as her husband. She had to rely on her younger son to persuade Ling to eat more during mealtimes. Ling was willing to talk only to the maternal grandmother, the maid, and the younger brother. The grandmother would play card games with Ling and learn from her about her life in hospital. The grandmother at first did not know that Ling was mute in front of her parents. She discovered it recently when her son-in-law was about to leave at the end of his visit. Ling hid herself behind the back of her grandmother and had no response when the grandmother suggested that she said "bye-bye" to her dad.

The therapist tried to engage Ling even though there was no confidence that Ling would respond; if the attempt failed, at least the therapist could personally experience Ling's rejection. The therapist turned to Ling and asked, "How old are you?"

Ling lowered her head, followed by a long silence.

The therapist repeated the question. Ling simply disregarded it. Silence was the most powerful weapon. Ling had learned to use silence so well. By turning her head against the therapist and fixing her gaze on the floor, her body posture showed that she was determined not to talk with the therapist.

The therapist retreated and turned to the parents, "Is your experience similar to mine?" Mr. and Mrs. N nodded.

The therapist attempted to positively reframe Ling's behavior: "She is a child with a strong will, isn't she?"

According to the grandmother, Ling had a strong will in comparison to her younger brother. Once she made up her mind to learn a life skill, she accomplished it as planned. Ling decided to master swimming during summer vacation. Her aunt, who was her coach, was amazed to find that she could swim quite well at the end of the holiday. Ling also studied well. Her parents did not need to supervise her schoolwork. She was studying in one of the top schools, and her academic performance was very good.

The therapist asked the son whether he agreed with the grandmother's view of them. The little boy replied with a sweet and shy smile, "Yes, I am less smart in studying than she."

The therapist turned to Ling and tried to engage her again, "Do you agree?"

Another long silence followed. The therapist waited for a few minutes and then said to Ling, "If you've decided not to express your view here, I'll respect your choice. I'll talk to you when you would like to tell your story."

The grandmother was the first to notice that something was wrong with Ling. Ling and the younger brother spent the summer holidays with the maternal grandparents in a resort in Mainland China. The grandmother found that there was a lot of Ling's hair on the floor while cleaning Ling's room. Ling had lost a lot of hair within a short period of time. The grandmother reported this to Ling's mother, who was aware of Ling's change too. Apart from the marked reduction in food intake, Ling insisted on going to the kitchen to prepare her own food. The mother shared her worry with one of her friends in church, who pointed her to a book. Upon reading it, the mother came to realize that her daughter was suffering from AN. She took her to consult a child psychiatrist, who admitted Ling immediately.

Listening to the parents' stories about Ling was different from experiencing the family drama. The parents' stories would at best reflect only how they perceived the problem, which might be different from a family drama emerging in the treatment session. The latter would reveal the family relationship topographically. Aiming to learn more about how the parents had actually interacted with Ling, the therapist planned to enact the family drama in the treatment room for assessment. It is crucial for the therapist to help the parents and the child perceive the need of talking to one another on a commonly concerned topic (Nichols & Fellenberg, 2000).

The therapist said to the parents, "So you have an impression that she was angry with you. Have you ever asked her why?"

"No. We just guessed."

The therapist suggested, "Would it be better for you to ask her now? You need to understand how she thinks and feels toward you."

On second thought, Mr. N took the courage to ask Ling, "What have we done that makes you decide not to talk to us? Is it because we have forced you to stay in the hospital?"

Ling was twisting her fingers, eyes fixed on her little fingers. A long silence again. Defeated, Mr. N sat back on the sofa and sighed while Mrs. N wept.

The grandmother came to the rescue. She said in a gentle and caring tone, "Tell your dad and mom what's on your mind. You would feel better after expressing your unhappiness to them."

Ling was as mute as a statue. The grandmother made the second attempt and said, "Let them know how you think and feel. They feel very hurt. If they have done something wrong, Prof. M [the therapist] may help your dad and mom to find the right way to help you." Ling showed no sign of changing her mind.

The therapist really felt for the parents and said empathetically to the parents, "It is indeed very difficult. You must feel hurt and defeated. For how long has it been like this?"

The father's tears began to fall. He said, "For at least 3 months." The therapist moved closer to the parents to express her support toward them.

The sadness spilled over to the grandmother. Initially she tried hard to control her emotion and appeared to be calm. Now she broke down and cried. She stammered, "I feel sorry for them. I feel sorry for them."

"Pardon me, for whom?" The therapist asked sympathetically.

"For my daughter and for Ling. If the situation persists, it'll become a big problem."

The therapist punctuated immediately, "What will be the problem?"

"My daughter cried every day after her hospital visit. I worried a lot. How can she supervise Ling to eat after Ling is discharged? She [Ling] will relapse." The grandmother continued, "Like a tree without water, it will dry up sooner or later. I am very, very worried that she will die one day. I told her repeatedly that a tree without water and soil would dehydrate and die."

The grandmother had said what the therapist had wished to say to Ling. Not long ago, mental health professionals believed that self-starvation was caused by bad parenting (Bruch, 1973). Based on this misconception, mental health professionals tended to blame the parents for the child's problem. In the past, a few therapists (e.g., Eisler, 1995) have acknowledged the suffering of the parents and appreciated their difficulties in facing this mysterious disorder.

Sympathetic with the impasse that the family was in, the therapist decided to express her compassion toward Ling by talking to the parents. "I find your daughter treated you like an enemy. Going against one's parents is quite an unpleasant experience. It also requires a lot of energy."

Facing Ling, the therapist talked to her, greatly puzzled: "If you are angry with them, you must hate staying in the hospital and prefer to be discharged as early as possible. You may not know that if you wish to be discharged soon, apart from the restoration of your body weight, you need the help of your parents and your grandparents. The doctor will seek their opinions. They can't help you even though they would like to, as they know nothing about what's on your mind. Your silence makes it difficult, if not impossible, for them to offer help."

Mr. N echoed with dismay, "Yes, totally impossible."

"Then you will get stuck in the hospital. It'll be fine if you wish to continue staying in the hospital. If you wish otherwise, your silence will defeat your wish."

The parents listened attentively. No sooner had the therapist left the treatment room than the father talked to his "deaf" daughter sincerely and asked her to think seriously what she wished to have, to continue staying in the hospital or to return home as soon as possible. Another long, dead silence. The therapists came back to the treatment room a few minutes later.

The therapist complimented the father for his patience, sincerity, and tolerance of his emaciated daughter.

The therapist asked, "Who understands her [Ling] most in this family?"

The father said, "Her mom."

"Only before her illness," Mrs. N elaborated further.

"I see. Who's next?"

"The maid. She has been looking after Ling since she was 6 months old. They are good friends. During her hospitalization, when she wished to get something from us, she would ask the maid to relay her request," said Mrs. N.

"So the maid has become the postman between you and your daughter." The therapist wondered if the maid had overtaken the parents' roles too.

"Yes," both parents agreed.

"Do you think it is appropriate for the maid to join the treatment?" asked the therapist since the maid had played such an important role in this family.

"Certainly."

The therapist wrapped up the session by highlighting the symptomatic cycle that had maintained the disorder in this family: "I feel for all of you. You are now at an impasse. Her silence has frustrated you; the silence has unwittingly become a power struggle between you and your daughter. It's very sad to see that both sides are the losers in the battle."

The therapist emphasized the following two messages: that they wished to help their self-starving daughter and that they must not feel culpable for her disorder.

"You wish to help her to be discharged as soon as possible but you don't know how she thinks and feels. I am glad that you have not blamed yourself for your daughter's illness. Some parents blame themselves; that doesn't help much."

The therapist turned to Ling and intensified the message: "I don't know what's on your mind. If you wish to return home soon, your silence will defeat your own wish."

"Do you want us to help break up this self-defeating pattern of interaction?" The therapist intended to seek their consent and elicit their collaboration in working on their difficulty. All family members nodded, except Ling, who was playing with her bracelet.

THE SECOND INTERVIEW

The whole family, including the maid and the grandfather, came to the second interview. Ling sat close to the maid and her younger brother, while the grandparents and the parents sat on two sides facing her. The cotherapist broke the ice by asking Ling to introduce her maid, but Ling simply ignored her and remained mute. Embarrassed, the mother introduced the maid to the therapists instead. The maid was 30 years old. Having worked for this family for a long time, she could understand some Chinese. However, the therapists communicated with her in English most of the time. The grandfather, with gray hair, was about 60 years old. He was gentle, kind, and caring with his two grandchildren.

The therapist asked the mother how she invited the grandfather to participate in family treatment; the mother said, "He's part of our family. He loves Ling very much. There is no need for me to persuade him to come. Last time he couldn't make it because he was in Mainland China."

The grandfather took the lead to tell us about Ling's problem; his story was similar to the grandmother's story. He had no idea why Ling began excessive dieting last summer. Ling had not rejected the grandfather. He learned a lot from Ling about her hospitalized life: "We are good friends. Yesterday during my visit, she showed me around the ward and the hospital. She was very willing to share her hospital life with me. Yesterday we took the elevator down to the hospital park. There was a man in the elevator who attempted to use the mobile phone but found it had no connection. A foreign doctor in the lift tried to explain to this man in English why the mobile phone couldn't work inside the elevator. The man failed to understand his English. Ling whispered to me and wondered why he was so ignorant of the fact that the mobile phone would be automatically cut off inside the elevator."

The therapist listened with great curiosity, "So your granddaughter has a lot of common sense. Do you know why she was self-starving?"

The grandfather replied, "I don't know. She was such a normal child before. She is intelligent and she picks up new skills fast. Last time she learned to ride the bicycle. Within a short time, she had already mastered the skill and enjoyed riding the bicycle very much while her little brother kept falling down from the bike."

The therapist asked once more, "Do you have any idea why she was on a vigorous diet?"

The grandparents said in unison, "We don't know."

Changing her posture slightly, the therapist turned to Mrs. N. and asked, "Would your maid know?"

The mother was very smart to pick up the therapist's message that she should discover the truth from the maid. She began to talk to the maid directly. The therapist had difficulty following the maid's story because of her heavy accent but was just able to catch it—there was a big fat boy in Mainland China who bullied Ling; he teased her and nicknamed her as "Miss Piggy."

The therapist asked curiously, "Who is the big boy?"

"He is our relative. Sometimes he attacked her verbally; sometimes he made use of his body to press against her. I had stopped him from bullying her several times. When he bullied her, she didn't know how to protect herself. She was too gentle and too kind. Ling never fought back. The boy continued bullying her because of her softness. He dared not bully other girls who were more aggressive," said the father.

"I see. I wonder if the big boy made any sexual advances on her."

The mother replied to the therapist with certainty, "No. that's quite certain. One of her teachers had asked her about that soon after her self-starvation and she replied, 'He wouldn't dare!'"

The therapist wanted to make use of this opportunity to help the parents and Ling break their symptomatic cycle of interaction—Ling's continued rejection of her parents through silence had crippled their ability to help and increased their sense of helplessness and failure. So she tried to identify an area of common concern for them to talk directly with one another.

"It seems to be better for you to ask her directly now. Would you like to try?" The therapist suggested tentatively and then sat back, sending a nonverbal signal to the parents that it was the time for them to take charge.

Mr. N took the courage to talk to his daughter: "You know Dad often protected you when Peter bullied you. Daddy wouldn't allow him to inflict any harm on you. Had he ever touched any part of your body?"

A long silence. Ling lowered her head more. She was fixing her gaze on the floor. The maid whispered to Ling and persuaded her to respond to her father. However, it proved unsuccessful.

Mr. N continued and said with frustration, "If you don't tell me about this, I'll ask Peter directly. Or you can talk to Nanny [the maid]."

The grandmother made a suggestion out of concern, "We can leave this room so that you can let Prof. M know about your story."

Ling shook her head strongly. As Ling was already so powerful, the therapist was cautious not to reinforce her powerful position. She turned to the family and said, "It's okay for her to stay silent. Maybe she didn't need your help and she didn't wish to be discharged from the hospital."

"That's not true. Ling told me that she is going to return home soon. Yesterday she had a day trip out from the hospital together with other patients. All of them were reluctant to go back to the hospital. She had already discussed with the doctor and the nurses regarding her wish to be discharged as soon as possible. She also negotiated with them and prepared the timetable primarily for this purpose," the grandfather said.

"Oh, thank you for letting me know about that. I must have misunderstood her." With a slight surprise, the therapist stated apologetically, "Expressing oneself is so important. Since I've not heard her voice, I've almost misunderstood her."

The grandparents and the parents were sympathetic with the therapist.

"She reiterated at the end of my hospital visit that she'll be home soon. She will have home leave during weekends. I clarified with her twice and she was quite certain about the arrangement."

"I never have the impression that she can have a day off. Perhaps I am wrong. Mr. X [grandfather], can you help to sort this out here?" Although the therapist did not wish to foster Ling's powerful position in this family by paying too much attention on her, she wanted to make use of this opportunity to help Ling to express her views to her parents.

"You asked me to let Mrs. C, the school bus driver, know that you are going to school next Saturday. I don't have her telephone number. It's better for you to ask your mom," said the grandfather. "Your mom has her phone number. Please ask your mom for her phone number. Otherwise we may fail to contact Mrs. C."

The grandfather was full of wisdom. He seemed to be reading the therapist's mind and had become the cotherapist by inviting Ling to resume direct dialogue with her parents. Ling declined his invitation with silence.

The therapist said to Mr. and Mrs. N, "I would like you to make use of the break to talk to her. The hospital staff will ask for my opinion after this session. I would really like to give my opinion but I need her help. I need to know if I could assist you [parents] in helping her to be discharged as soon as possible."

During the break, the grandparents and the maid stayed outside the room, leaving the parents and Ling together inside. Mr. N talked to Ling seriously, "Prof. M [the therapist] hopes to help you to go home as soon as possible. However, we are not sure if you like to be discharged or not. In the past you communicated with us through Nanny, the maid. That seems to work but that has its own limitation too. It's better for you to express your own view to us. If you refuse to do so, you are the one feeling lonely in the hospital." Another dead silence. Mr. N invited his wife to explain to Ling, but Mrs. N just shook her head.

The therapists discussed Ling's overall management plan with the multidisciplinary team members, including the psychiatrist, the medical social worker, and the nurses, who were behind the one-way mirror. The medical social worker told the therapist that something important had already occurred outside the treatment room. On her way to the washroom during the break, the medical social worker heard that Ling started telling her mother that she disliked coming to treatment. Such a delightful breakthrough had reinforced our treatment direction. There was a unanimous view that the formulated discharge plan should aim to continue to break the symptomatic cycle of interaction between Ling and her parents. Two specific goals were delineated, based on the family assessment: first, Ling would be encouraged to resume direct communication with her parents; second, an attempt would be made to heighten the parents' awareness of their tendency to depend on the maid in communicating with Ling and the fact that their parental roles must not be overtaken by the maid and the grandparents.

CONTRIBUTIONS OF THE MULTIDISCIPLINARY TEAM

Another multidisciplinary team meeting was held at the hospital. The following strategies were formulated to help break the symptomatic cycle of interaction between Ling and her parents. First, the teacher of the hospital-based school was assigned to explore with Ling if she had been sexually molested. Among the different multidisciplinary team members, Ling respected and trusted the teacher most. Second, the psychiatrist and the medical social worker would meet with Ling and discuss the discharge plan with her. Third, the hospital staff would restrict the visiting hours of the maid. Such a measure was meant to empower the parents in taking charge of their daughter's discharge and to discourage the maid from overtaking the parental roles in communicating with Ling. The medical social worker would explain to the parents the rationale behind the new policy.

Ling firmly denied that the big boy had sexually molested or abused her when the teacher explored the issue with her. She was silent during the family treatment because both therapists looked too serious and she was uncomfortable and uneasy relating to them.

Once the possibility of sexual abuse was ruled out, the psychiatrist and the medical social worker interviewed Ling to discuss with her the discharge plan. Playing the role of a bad guy, the psychiatrist conveyed a strong message to Ling that she had to achieve two goals, that is, to increase her food intake and to improve her relations with her parents, in order to be discharged. The psychiatrist stated sternly to Ling, "You have let us know your greatest wish of being discharged early, but I fail to see that you've done anything to achieve this goal. You chose to be silent in family therapy. You didn't communicate with your parents. Even if I discharge you tomorrow, are you sure that your parents would accept you back home since you are so difficult to relate to? A child should respect her parents. I'll take into account your parents' views in considering your discharge plan." The medical social worker took a relatively soft position by being empathetic and supportive of Ling. Ling finally broke her silence and told the medical social worker that she had no intention to be disrespectful to her parents. She remained silent most of the time simply because they had not been talking to one another for such a long time that she did not know how to begin. She wanted to have her hair cut during the weekend. The medical social worker supported her plan and suggested that she call her mother to get the doctor's approval. Ling followed her advice. The mother promised without hesitation.

The medical social worker interviewed the parents as well. She explained the plan of restricting the visiting hours of their maid. At first, the parents were afraid that this would jeopardize their relationship with Ling, as they had promised Ling that the maid would visit her every day. While acknowledging the parents' fear of offending Ling and their good intention to keep their promise, the medical social worker hinted to the parents, "Once there were these parents who promised their child a big treat at McDonald's. However, as they planned to go out, it was rainy and stormy. The parents finally broke the promise because of the awful weather, not because they were not trustworthy." The parents became more relaxed and smiled. Apparently the message was getting across.

The third interview was delayed on account of a serious community epidemic.[9] In the wake of crisis, the Child Psychiatric Ward was closed down

---

[9] Outbreak of severe acute respiratory syndrome (SARS) in 2003.

to minimize cross-infections. However, Ling had already achieved the weight target a week earlier. Her relation with the parents had improved, and direct communication between them had resumed.

THE THIRD INTERVIEW

Ling, her parents, and her little brother attended the third interview 2 months after the second interview. The epidemic was still spreading, and the family as well as the therapists were wearing masks. Ling's body weight had increased from 33 kg to 39 kg. Contrary to her previous attitude, Ling was friendly and polite to the therapists. She took the initiative to greet the therapists. Although the therapists failed to read Ling's facial expression behind the mask, her body gestures and her eyes showed that she was a different person.

The two children leaned on the father's legs, with Ling on one side and her little brother on the other side, while the mother sat separately in a corner of the room. The father was eager to share Ling's healing journey: "I am grateful to God. She [Ling] started eating better and better after the second interview. Her body weight increased steadily. Two weeks before the SARS crisis, physically she was fit for discharge. During the SARS crisis, the doctor strongly advised us to take her home. My wife and I saw the need too. Three days after the discharge, one of my neighbors was certified to be suffering from the SARS. We were very alarmed. Afraid of being infected, my boss even went abroad with his family. It was an unexpected delight that he granted me a long leave. Since we have a house in Guangzhou, we decided to move back to our summer house and stayed there till the SARS crisis was over."

The mother said, "Yes, we stayed there for over a month."

"We had an enjoyable life there. Our house's spacious," recalled the father. "The children liked riding bikes and we had barbecues in the garden. Ling had no eating problem. She said that she would never go back to the hospital."

The therapist congratulated them for their success in combating self-starvation and asked earnestly, "Who had helped Ling recover most?"

"Ling herself. She had done a lot for her own healing. She ate well and she had good relationship with us," said the father.

"We support her too," said the mother. The mother stayed with the children too, as she had incidentally left her job after the reorganization of her company.

"How did you repair your relationship with your daughter?" The therapist really wished to learn from them.

"Since meeting you, I talked more with her during the hospital visit," said the mother. "One day she showed me photos of the outing organized by the hospital school. On another day she shared with me how she related to different patients. From time to time she asked me to make some arrangements for her and I never say 'no' to her. It's a gradual process. There were no difficulties at all. Basically she is a talkative and expressive child." The mother continued, "She was slightly different. She would express her dislikes to me, rather than holding back and suppressing it before her illness."

It was at this point that the mother became very emotional. Tears started rolling down her cheeks. Her intense emotional response caught the therapist by surprise. It was impossible for the therapist to guess how she felt behind the mask.

While the therapist was wondering what should be done next, the cotherapist asked Mr. N, "Do you know why your wife is so emotional?"

"It's better for her to tell you personally. I can't speak on her behalf. Probably she had given so much in the past. Ling has finally recovered. She must feel deeply touched."

"Is it so?" Mr. N asked his wife with tenderness and compassion.

Mrs. N said no by shaking her head.

Mrs. N narrated, "I've cried several times in this treatment room. The first time I cried because I was deeply hurt. I didn't know what to do for her recovery. My husband and I prayed together. I prayed, prayed, and prayed even though I was not a Christian. I trusted that God would give us guidance. This time I cry because she has recovered."

Apparently religion had an influential part to play in helping the couple cope with Ling's self-starvation; it is also a source of hope for them.

"Your mom found that you're more expressive than before. Who taught you to be so expressive?" the therapist asked Ling in curiosity after acknowledging Mrs. N's mixed emotions.

"Someone in the hospital. I forget who she or he is," Ling replied vaguely.

"Is your mom different from the past?"

"No. She's still my mom." Her witty answer informed the therapist that Ling had a good sense of humor and could be playful. There was a burst of laughter.

"The greatest driving force for recovery came from Ling. The doctor once said to her that if she liked to be discharged, she must fulfill two expectations: first to eat well and restore the normal body weight; second to improve her relation with the parents. Ling achieved both with perseverance and determination. Besides, my two children know very well that we love them very much," explained the father.

"Is she adjusting well to school?"

"She gradually adjusted well to school. She was anxious in the first week of school. She had nightmares and woke up in the middle of the night. After my consolation, she would fall asleep again without any interruption."

Ling went on telling some of the interesting stories at school: how her classmates took off their masks without the teachers' permission and how they created their rituals while stepping on the hygienic mattress to disinfect their shoes, which was part of a special preventive measure adopted by all schools during the SARS crisis.

"As Ling has already recovered, there's no need for you to come back for treatment," said the therapist sincerely.

"Cheers. We can have a big buffet dinner tonight," Ling almost jumped up and shouted excitedly.

Mrs. N promised to give Ling a big treat upon the termination of the family treatment.

Table 9.1 summarizes the treatment principles employed for this family.

FEEDBACK FROM THE FAMILY

A posttreatment interview was conducted 3 months after the termination of family treatment. Ling's body weight had increased to 41.5 kg. The following was the family's subjective experience on family therapy.

As perceived by the parents, Ling's silence was the most difficult problem that they had ever faced. Mrs. N felt frustrated while Mr. N was very worried; neither knew how to help her recover. Ling confirmed that she was really angry with her parents for sending her to the hospital without any discussion with her.

Both Mr. and Mrs. N perceived family therapy as an important context where they could identify, understand, and discuss their problems and difficulties openly. Mr. N narrated, "Besides helping us examine our problem, we visualized the effect of self-starvation on Ling and different members of the family in treatment. Having a better understanding of the problem would help tackle part of the problem." Mrs. N elaborated, "We knew the negative consequences of AN but we dared not mention it at all at home. We avoided telling Ling that she would die if she continued self-starving. We denied that it's a possible outcome. With the therapist's facilitation, we faced the problem honestly."

Mrs. N treasured the experience of family therapy because she could express her worry, anxiety, and helplessness and share her mixed feelings with members of her family. Part of Mr. N's psychological burden was lifted after discussing the problem in the second session. The second session was useful to him in two ways. First, both his wife and he deepened their understanding of their problem. Second, it was crystal clear to Ling that she had to take up responsibility for her own recovery. Even though Ling remained silent, she heard hard and clear. Hence, upon the advice of the doctor, Ling started talking with her parents soon afterward.

Ling disliked the therapists and disliked family therapy. The treatment was boring and annoying. Mr. N and Mrs. N liked the therapists: The therapists were professional and knowledgeable, with good understanding of their needs and difficulties. The therapist employed two methods to help them: serving as a bridge and acting strategically. The mother recounted very well the therapist's message to Ling: "Your silence might suggest that you liked to continue to stay in hospital but your presence in the family therapy indicates otherwise; you hope to recover and return home as soon as possible. Whether Ling could be discharged or not depended on her own will. If she wished to be sick, there was not much other people could do to help." Actually Ling began to eat better and better after the second session. Their family relationship became closer after the treatment. The parents even recommended more government support for family therapy.

DISCUSSION

Research and anecdotal evidence have confirmed the association of AN with the peer subculture characterized by weight consciousness, fat phobia, and the adoption of the standard of beauty equivalent to thinness and slimness (Paxton, 1999). Acceptance and validation by peers are extremely important for children and adolescents. Peer pressure exerts enormous stress on teenage girls (Heaven, 1994). Teenage girls who are doubtful of their competence and personal effectiveness are vulnerable to using vigorous dieting as a means of pleasing their peers and winning friendships. Ling's self-starvation can be regarded as coping in response to the teasing and bullying from the big boy, Peter.

In hearing the grandparents' mention of Peter's pressing on Ling, the therapist had a suspicion of sexual molestation and sexual overtones. In the confused mind of a 9-year-old child, would she have interpreted this as molestation? Is it even possible she thought she could become pregnant? Was self-starvation a way to kill off menstruation that had started well before her peers? Was she ashamed of secondary sexual characteristics developing? The therapist has to seek help from the treatment team to assess carefully and to rule out the root cause, if any.

A self-starving child inevitably places the parents in a difficult position. Had the parents followed and respected the child's will, the child would have gradually withered, like a plant without nutrients, water, and sunlight, and would have eventually died. Most emaciated children and adolescents deny their self-starvation as problematic and are ambivalent or unmotivated in seeking help (Treasure, 1997). Faced with the declining health of their child, responsible and sensible parents must respond quickly and forcefully persuade the child to seek the necessary medical treatment and, in many cases, hospitalize the child upon medical advice, usually at the cost of violating the child's own will. In the eyes of the child, she is no longer the master of her own life. The child mistakes the parents' action as control rather than help. In this case illustration, the perceived "collusion" of the parents with mental health professionals reinforced Ling's belief that most of the adults, except the maid and the grandparents, were oppressive and overpowering. She was on the losing end of the power game.

Ling gradually learned that silence was an effective weapon over her parents and the mental health professionals in the hospital. She seemed to have the upper hand in the battle as her parents became increasingly frustrated, hopeless, helpless, and defeated. The doctor in charge and the nursing staff were equally frustrated and helpless. The power struggle continued to intensify and escalate. Nevertheless, Ling was unaware that by entrapping herself in the power struggle with the parents and her treatment team, she was the ultimate loser. She had driven away everyone around her, people who were most willing and conscientious to help but who had no way to do so simply because of her hostile and unapproachable attitude and her dead silence.

The foremost and crucial task undertaken by the therapists was to identify this self-defeating, interlocking symptomatic cycle between Ling and her parents and its linkage to Ling's relationship difficulties with the treatment team including the doctor in charge and the psychiatric nursing staff. As a prerequisite in effecting changes to the stifling relational pattern of interaction, the therapists needed to heighten the parents' awareness of the different parts played by different parties, including Ling, the parents, the grandparents, and the maid, in maintaining the problem. Changes could be possible only if each family member owned the problem and was ready to contribute to the process of change.

The treatment objectives were threefold: (a) to help Ling feel that she was the master of her own health and hence to feel responsible for her own healing and recovery, (b) to change Ling's perception that her parents were controlling her rather than helping her, and (c) to help the parents assist Ling to strive for full recovery rather than to exert control over her.

Due to various reasons (e.g., anger and hostility of the patient toward adults, personal constraints of the therapist), the therapist might be unable to obtain the patient's cooperation and develop a trustful relationship in the initial stages of treatment. As the treatment focus is on the symptomatic cycle consequent to self-starvation, the therapist has the freedom not to please the patient and not to build rapport with her as would usually be practiced in psychotherapy. It is more important to activate the mechanism of change on the afflicted individuals and families than to just change the symptom of self-starvation. While acknowledging the urgency of breaking through the escalating relational impasse, the importance of winning the confidence and trust of the emaciated child or adolescent should not be undermined. Therapeutic alliance has indeed been shown to be crucial in accounting for changes across different treatment models (Sprenkle & Blow, 2004). Nevertheless, a few hostile, angry, and uncooperative patients such as Ling might pose great challenges to the therapist and make it difficult, if not impossible, to develop the therapeutic alliance with them in the initial stage of treatment.

The therapists were as ineffective and impotent as the other team members in relating to Ling. The only person who could better relate to Ling was the hospital teacher whom Ling respected and trusted. The therapists were caught in a dilemma after experiencing Ling's rejection repeatedly in the first and second treatment sessions: Should they entrust the care of Ling to the hospital teacher who had rapport with Ling? Or should they continue the treatment strategically with the understanding that Ling's dislike of the therapist could be an impetus for her to combat self-starvation?

An indirect approach (Stierlin & Weber, 1989) was chosen because of the therapists' repeated experiences of being rejected in the treatment. The indirect approach assumes that all participants are able to act out of their own free will (Stierlin & Weber, 1989, p. 85). If Ling chose to be silent with her parents and the treatment team, she could also choose to resume direct communication with them. Options and choices were introduced to Ling through effective use of the "not-knowing" position and questioning techniques—Ling could choose to recover in order to defy the therapists and terminate the treatment, or she could remain unchanged and continue feeling miserable, lonely, and alienated as the sick patient in the hospital. Such an approach is empowering in nature, and it tactfully mitigated Ling's personal ineffectiveness by inviting her to take charge of her own life.

Teamwork pools the expertise and resources of different professionals, who together formulate and carry out a comprehensive treatment plan. Ideally, the family therapists should be an integral part of the team, as they possess the knowledge and skills in working with families of great diversity and heterogeneity. However, in reality family therapists have their own personal and professional limitations too. For instance, Ling perceived the therapists as unfriendly and too serious; she trusted the hospital teacher more.

The symptomatic cycle of interaction in Ling's family was unlocked only by the contributions of different team members and the different measures devised subsequently, for example, the intensification of the therapist's message by the psychiatrist and the medical social worker in the individual interview with Ling, the empowerment of the parents through restricting the visiting hours of the maid, and last but not least, the medical social worker's support of and encouragement to the parents. The outbreak of the SARS epidemic, though alarming and threatening in nature, unexpectedly perpetuated the positive changes and the transformation of the family. By moving back to Mainland China and living there for a month, the family reorganized their family life anew and drew closer together.

CONCLUSION

This case example illustrates the contribution of family therapy to the holistic management of the emaciated patient by identifying the symptomatic cycle of interactions between the self-starving patient and her parents. The family therapists succeeded in engaging each family member to examine the seemingly irresolvable problem created by Ling's silence and to identify the metaphoric meaning underneath the self-imposed silence. The treatment process heightened the awareness of the multidisciplinary team members to the isomorphism (resonance or parallel process) between Ling's power struggle with the treatment team members and her power struggle with her parents. Disrupting the symptomatic cycle of interaction hence became the shared agenda of the parents and the multidisciplinary team, without which parental supervision of meals at home would have been impossible. The triumph of Ling in restoring her health symbolizes success in teamwork and collaboration among the family therapists, the psychiatrist, the medical social worker, the hospital teacher, the nurses, and the parents.

The family therapist must collaborate with professionals in the hospital, but helping professionals in the community can contribute as well, especially in multiproblem cases.

Table 9.1: Treatment Steps and Principles Employed for the N Family

Treatment Session	Treatment Steps of the Model	Application for This Family
Session 1	• To briefly understand the history of the disorder and the patient's motivation for recovery • To explore and identify the constricting family process that has unfavorably affected the parents' collaboration in refeeding the emaciated daughter and, hence, maintained the symptoms • To negotiate a treatment contract by shifting the family focus from the symptom to the symptomatic cycle or the constricting family process that has maintained and escalated AN	• The therapist assessed Ling's history of onset and her motivation for recovery; assessment showed that Ling's awareness of her own problem was low and she had not yet engaged in any concrete action to strive for recovery; she was unfriendly to the therapist and had decided to remain silent throughout the session • The therapist shifted the assessment to the family context, which showed that the parents were highly motivated to help combat the disorder but Ling's persistent silence had disempowered them; the dysfunctional parent–child interaction seemed to be maintained by the role of the maternal grandparents and the maid as the "switchboard" of the family • Parents' difficulties and their sense of helplessness in relating to Ling were validated • The therapist discussed with the treatment team, who were watching behind the one-way mirror, the isomorphism (resonance and parallel process) between Ling's power struggle with her parents and her power struggle with the treatment team, except the hospital teacher

Table 9.1 (Cont'd)

Treatment Session	Treatment Steps of the Model	Application for This Family
		• Using an indirect approach, the therapist sent a strong message to Ling: she could choose to remain ill and continue to be hospitalized or to be discharged and recover with the assistance of her parents, who knew how to help only if she broke her silence and started to communicate with them • The therapist enabled the parents and the treatment team members to perceive the linkage of the constricting family structure to Ling's recovery; a shared contract to change the symptomatic cycle of interaction was accordingly made with the parents
Session 2	• To encourage parental collaboration by facilitating the parents to help the emaciated daughter rather than to control her	• With the participation of the maid and the maternal grandparents, the therapist enacted the family drama, which had confirmed the role of maid and the grandparents as the "switchboard" of the parent–child interaction • Further exploration had ruled out the possibility of Ling having been sexually molested during her vacation in Mainland China • The therapist dealt with Ling's continued rejection by reiterating her free will to choose between remaining ill and attaining recovery; the latter could be achieved only with the parents' cooperation • The therapist offered hope to the parents that they would be able to refeed their daughter at home should they change the current parent–daughter interaction

Table 9.1 (Cont'd)

Treatment Session	Treatment Steps of the Model	Application for This Family
Cross-Disciplinary Case Conference		Based on the above assessment, an overall management plan was developed: • The psychiatrist and the medical social worker reinforced the indirect approach by stressing to Ling her need to seek her parents' help if she wished to be discharged and recover • The frequent hospital visits of Ling's maid were discouraged • The medical social worker met the parents to explain the rationale of discouraging the maid from paying daily visits to Ling and to encourage them to assume active roles in parenting
Session 3	• To address unresolved conflicts and improved family relationships using culturally acceptable means • To handle relapses by preventing the reemergence of the symptomatic cycle and further enhancing the family relationships • To support individual development • To support the transformation	• Not applicable for this family as they had already resumed the old pattern of functional parent–child interaction • No need to do so as Ling had no relapse • The therapist appreciated the efforts of both Ling and the parents to drive away AN

Chapter 10
Anorexia Nervosa in a Poor Family

INTRODUCTION

In the West, anorexia nervosa (AN) is more prevalent in upper- and upper-middle-class families, with incidence among the lower social classes increasing only slightly in recent decades (Gard & Freeman, 1996; McClelland & Crisp, 2001). Thus, poverty is typically not seen as an important factor in AN—if anything, quite the opposite. The intertwining of poverty with AN has received little attention in the literature, even though poverty is known to correlate with family violence, inadequate parenting, single parenthood, and drug abuse—factors that may well have an impact on the incidence and severity of AN. A case report involving a family on welfare would therefore illuminate some of the linkages.[10]

It is believed that poverty has a moderating effect on a family's coping with AN via its impact on parenting. The low income leads to poor self-image and poor social skills on the part of the parents. They tend to employ punitive measures to discipline their children. Children of poor families, especially those with better education than their parents, might look down on their parents and tend to undermine them (Sampson & Laub, 1998). Self-starvation poses an additional challenge to parents of poor families. The problem is further aggravated for a new arrival family in which the mother single-handedly heads the family.

Imagine a family newly arrived from the countryside, the adults with low skills, low pay, and a limited social network; further imagine a divorce, leaving the mother single-handed. The story of an AN child in such a context powerfully illustrates the confluence of forces.

---

[10] Among 27 cases seen by the author's team in 7 years, there were 5 families on welfare, accounting for 18.5%.

BACKGROUND HISTORY OF THE FAMILY

The psychiatrist referred Ying to family treatment. Ying, a 14-year-old girl, had been suffering from AN for six months. Six months earlier, Ying went on a strict diet as she wished to be slim and to dance beautifully in her Chinese dancing class. Her body weight had dropped from 45 kg to 37 kg at the time of the referral; with a height 160 cm, her BMI was 14.

Her father, poorly educated, unskilled, and lowly paid and without marriage prospects in the city, had gone back to his home village to find a bride. It was a long-distance marriage, as he had to return to the city to work. Nevertheless, five children were born to the union. At the time of the interview, the eldest girl was 16 and Ying was 14, followed by two younger sisters aged 13 and 11 and a boy aged 9. The father was finally able to bring the family to the city, in two phases from 2 years earlier, and Ying arrived at age 13. The reallocation as well as her poor English caused Ying to drop behind in school—she was in Primary 6, where her classmates were 1 to 2 years younger. Paradoxically (though not unusually in these cases) the reunion was devastating to the family—in part because the much higher cost of maintaining the family in the city aggravated the sense of poverty and the confined living conditions escalated friction. The traditional, patriarchal, and dominating father abused the submissive, passive, and subservient mother—who then moved out with the children and filed for divorce. The mother and the children were placed on welfare and lived in one single rented room in a lower-middle-class community.

The therapist and the cotherapist, a doctoral student, provided a total of 11 family treatment sessions for this family.

THE FIRST INTERVIEW

The therapists ushered the family into the treatment room. The mother sat upright and rigidly facing the therapist; the five children sat side by side with the mother. The mother was tense and nervous. Ying and her siblings were polite to the therapist. The therapist found it hard to follow the mother's story relayed with a heavy village accent. The children expressed themselves well, indicating better adjustment. Ying was quite shy but friendly and mature. She explained her reason for dieting. She was learning Chinese dancing at school, liked it very much, and wished to be a slender and slim dancer. Her temper had become uncontrollable after she began dieting. She gradually found it hard to concentrate on her studies. The previously gentle girl had become fairly hostile and unreasonable in relating to her mother and siblings. Ying was perceived as the troublemaker in the family; hence, her mother and siblings were going against her.

Ying had gained 1 kg in 1 week since the pretreatment interview conducted by a research assistant, a trained registered nurse who was at the same time a doctoral student in social work. She had explained to Ying the detrimental effects of AN on health. Ying began to realize the serious consequences of self-starvation and was motivated for change and recovery.

Compared to Ying, the mother looked less healthy, more depressed, more miserable, and more preoccupied. She stared at the floor and avoided eye contact. Her anxiety and worry had abated slightly after Ying had resumed normal meals the week before. Conscious that this family came from a rural area, the therapist explored and assessed how the mother and children had adjusted to city life. After a few months of learning and adjustment, Ying and her siblings had gradually overcome the dialect barrier and had caught up in school. However, for the illiterate mother, adjustment was slow and painful. Relocation had been traumatic. She had been abused by her husband, she had been uprooted from her social network, and she no longer had the support of her own mother, who had previously helped to look after the children. She burst into tears when asked about her informal support system after reallocation.

The mother wept and said, "There is hardly any one I can turn to for help, except my mother. I want to phone her but the telephone bill is expensive. I don't know where I can seek help. One day a social worker from the center for new arrival families called to ask why I had not turn up for their activities; I told her about Ying's problem. She referred me to the specialist treatment center for eating disorders."

The therapist said, "I see. Do you receive any support from your ex-husband's family of origin?"

The mother shook her head and said, "No. They looked down on me and blamed me for the divorce."

Ying was the first to comfort her mother when she cried; strangely, the eldest daughter, PC, remained passive and aloof. The other children leaned forward to express their care and concern as well. Wishing to understand more about the mother's relationship with the children, the therapist turned to the eldest daughter, "Who is the best friend to your mother in the family?"

The eldest daughter, PC, whispered, "Ying."

The therapist asked, "How about you?"

PC replied, "I don't know."

According to the third and the fourth daughters, CC and KY, the mother spoiled the son the most. This was a common practice in families from Chuichow culture, well known for its patriarchal culture and its emphasis on the son and the male line. Ying helped to do most of the household chores while their eldest sister spent her time and effort on studying. Apparently Ying had been playing the role of the eldest daughter in the family. She was the confidante of the mother. Apart from helping with household chores, she also disciplined her younger sisters and brothers.

The children had no contact with their father and learned indirectly from their paternal aunt that their father had already remarried half a year ago. They felt for the mother and would do anything to cheer her up. They believed that their mother's unhappiness was partly related to Ying's self-starvation and her frequent temper tantrums at home and partly because of the mother's poor health.

Prior to the onset of Ying's self-starvation, this family had experienced several significant negative life events, namely relocation from the village to the city; the mutual adjustment among the father, the mother, and the children; the abuse and divorce; and, not least, family poverty. The onset of Ying's self-starvation was the last straw. Unsurprisingly, the mother felt incompetent, helpless, powerless, and desperate to refeed the emaciated daughter. She had no choice but to rely totally on the helping professionals. However, there were strengths to be found in this family. First, Ying was motivated for change and was responsive to professional guidance and support. Second, the children seemed to have a strong emotional attachment to the mother. Besides, the children adjusted quite well to the city and had become the mother's resources.

THE SECOND INTERVIEW

Ying's body weight had increased to 39 kg. The mother reported fewer conflicts with Ying during meals since Ying had less resistance to eating. While recognizing Ying's progress in gaining weight, the therapist sensed that there was a hidden conflict between the mother and Ying as they sat in unfriendly postures against each other. Further exploration revealed that Ying had refused to talk to her mother for a few days immediately after the first family treatment. She was angry with the mother for intruding on her privacy.

The mother explained to the therapist in a depressing mood, "Ying's temper tantrum was so great that I found it impossible to handle. I don't wish to ask my neighbor for help. I don't want them to have the impression that our family is full of problems. I have no one to turn to. I called her class teacher for help. She listened to my problem patiently but didn't give me any advice."

Ying replied assertively, "That is my personal matter and I don't want you to disclose it to my teacher."

The therapist validated Ying's anger and her need for personal privacy to be respected and at the same time appreciated that the mother must be very desperate. The third daughter, CC, agreed with the therapist that her mom had already tried every means.

The mother became very emotional; tears rolled down her cheeks. The mother perceived herself as incompetent and unable to look after the children properly. A good mother should be able to raise a healthy child rather than having an emaciated child like Ying. Apparently the mother was full of self-blame. She found herself equally ineffective in relating to the eldest daughter, PC.

The mother turned to the eldest daughter, PC, and said in a hostile voice, "I won't force you to live so unhappily with me. If you like to live with your father, please do so."

PC wept and replied to her mother rudely, "I don't know who is forcing whom. It is you who is pressing." She lowered her head with her gaze fixed on the floor.

After a long silence while the therapist was wondering what to do, Ying explained to the therapist why they had conflicts. PC, the mother, and CC came to Hong Kong 2 years ago. Within a month, the mother went back to the village to take care of Ying and the youngest son, leaving the eldest daughter, PC, and the third daughter, CC, under the care of the father. The relationship between the father and PC was good, as the father did take care of her. The youngest son was the father's favorite, followed by PC, CC, and KY, the fourth daughter. Ying was the least favorite child. PC was caught in a dilemma when the parents divorced. She suffered from split loyalty. Her mother wanted PC to leave her father and live with her and the siblings; such a decision was difficult to PC as she loved her father. PC had made a suicide attempt by cutting her wrist at school. Finally she chose to live with her mother. The father did not visit the children after the divorce. PC grieved for the loss of her father's love.

PC was crying while Ying told the story. The therapist looked at her empathetically and said, "You must have gone through a very difficult time. Would you like to share with us your story?" PC nodded and continued sobbing.

Without waiting for her daughter's response, the mother said in great pain and despair to PC, "If I were wrong, I would say sorry to you. If I had made a mistake, I am sorry for making you so miserable. You can join your father. You are free to do so."

The therapist encouraged PC to respond to her mother's anger but she refused to do so. PC remained silent for the rest of the session. The mother recalled her painful experience in relating to her aggressive and violent ex-husband. Every day he would give her HK$70 (less than US$10) to cover all of the family expenses. At night he would get drunk and beat her. She was living under constant fear and threats; so were the children. Moving out and separating from him was the only way to protect and save her life.

The therapist ended the session by addressing the mother's strong sense of self-blame. The same theme emerged repeatedly in this session: "I am not a good mother and I have failed to take care of you." The therapist reassured her that she could hardly have performed her mothering in a better way since she lacked experience in dealing with self-starvation, not to mention the relocation, the divorce, and single parenthood; the etiologies of AN were multiple, and she should not blame herself for causing her daughter's illness.

THE THIRD INTERVIEW

The family was in a lighter mood. Ying had gained 1 kg more in a week. Fighting during mealtime between the mother and Ying had stopped. Both Ying and the mother were pleased with the progress.

The mother liked to make use of this session to resolve her conflict with PC. She said to the therapist that since PC had already been living with her, they should both put aside the past misery and try to adjust to each other. PC had to face the constant fighting and quarreling of her parents and had to live with her aunt for 6 months. The mother learned little about how she coped during that period but guessed that she must have suffered.

The therapist praised the mother for her courage and initiative to deal with the conflict directly. She encouraged the mother to talk directly to PC. PC sat next to Ying and her brother, wearing an awkward smile. CC and KY were giggling and whispering to each other. The therapist suggested that CC and KY move closer to the therapist, leaving more space for the mother to talk directly to PC.

The mother changed her seat and faced her eldest daughter, PC, directly. Using a warm and nurturing voice, she said, "Let's forget the past and try to relate to each other in a better way. Both of us have already been suffering a lot. Your father didn't give us a good life. We should try to work it out ourselves. Do you like the idea? If Mom had used nasty words to scold you, please forgive me. I didn't mean that. I couldn't help it."

The therapist was deeply touched by the mother's sincerity and genuineness. Asking for forgiveness is never easy, especially for a woman who has gone through so much pain and suffering. PC was frozen to her seat, indicating no sign of responding to her mother.

The therapist said encouragingly to PC, "Can you respond to your mother? It is not easy for her to plead for your forgiveness."

CC, KY, Ying, and the little brother laughed at PC and said, "She [PC] wouldn't talk to Mom. She's too shy."

The therapist replied to them seriously, "Please don't laugh at her. Let's give her time to sort it out." The therapist sat back and waited.

PC finally uttered, "I have not thought of our conflicts for a long time."

The mother was very pleased with PC's reply, and she talked for a while on how they should relate to each other differently in future. For instance, PC should let her know her difficulty at school, and she would try her best to facilitate her study. Since one of PC's greatest wishes was to improve her English and to be a top student in class, the mother allowed PC to take private school, despite the tight family budget.

To the amazement of the therapist, when the mother finished talking, all the children, except PC, clapped their hands in applause. The therapist walked straight up to the mother, shook hands with her forcefully, and said, "I am proud of you. You impress the children and me so much." The mother was filled with joy and confidence.

THE FOURTH SESSION

The patient had gained 1.5 kg within 2 weeks. The children chatted and giggled happily among themselves while sitting on the sofa. Ying's drawing had won the third prize in an art contest, and the drawing was displayed at the Central Park in the community. In order to give her mother a pleasant surprise, Ying and her two younger sisters lied to the mother that they wished to visit the park with her. Her mother at first turned down their request and preferred staying at home to prepare the meal. They insisted, and the mother finally went with them and saw Ying's drawing. Caught by surprise, the mother felt totally unprepared but joyous. Ying won a bronze award and HK$300 (US$36) in this contest.

As Ying had made steady progress in the past 2 weeks, the therapist asked the mother and Ying how they had achieved it. Apart from resuming normal meals, Ying drank a glass of nutritious milk every day. Ying liked the milk, but the family could hardly afford more since it was quite expensive. It cost HK$60 (US$8) per can, which amounted to 60% of their daily food budget, as welfare provided only HK$100 (US$13) per day for food. Part of the poor family's difficulty in coping with self-starvation came from the stringent family finances. The therapist suggested that Ying and her mother seek help from the psychiatrist as well as the medical social worker in the hospital. The former could prescribe the milk to them as a pharmaceutical supplement at a lower price and the latter could help the family to apply for an additional welfare subsidy. Ying responded to the therapist's suggestion with silence, suggesting that she was hesitant. The therapist assumed that her hesitation might be related to the shame associated with help seeking. Further inquiry revealed otherwise. Ying feared that the psychiatrist might not be able to afford the nutritious milk; her request would place an additional financial burden on him. Such an unexpected and considerate answer from Ying was beyond the therapist's expectations. The therapist suddenly realized that as a newcomer to the city, the family knew little about the health care service, which was heavily subsidized by public funding. The therapist praised Ying for her thoughtfulness toward the psychiatrist, gave a brief explanation of the health care system, and then invited Ying and the mother to do a role-play, through which an assessment would be made if they could present their financial difficulty to the psychiatrist and the medical social worker. They showed sufficient skills to achieve the task in the role-play.

During the Christmas holidays, the mother's 19-year-old nephew died suddenly because of acute hepatitis. Fearful of infection, the mother decided on comprehensive medical check-ups for her children. As she was poorly informed about local resources, she went back to their homeland for this purpose. The results showed that all her children were healthy. However, the sudden death of the nephew had increased the mother's anxiety and heightened her sense of mortality toward Ying's self-starvation. Although Ying had progressed steadily, the mother remained as worried as before; she was fearful of relapse. The therapist showed empathy toward the mother's anxiety and encouraged her to have a direct dialogue with Ying.

The mother said tearfully to Ying, "I don't want you to die suddenly like Fai [the nephew] did."

Feeling slightly uncomfortable and embarrassed, Ying replied reassuringly, "Mom, don't worry. I am eating normally. I'm fine. I understand that your stomachache is related to my illness. I'll have a speedy recovery soon. I promise you but please promise us that you'll eat too."

Confused in hearing this, the therapist punctuated and asked what exactly Ying meant by saying that the mother needed to eat too. The third and the fourth daughters, CC and KY, though appearing to be self-absorbed in reading throughout the treatment session, raised their eyes from the book and said, "Mom usually takes little food during meals, leaving most of the food for us." The eldest daughter, PC, and the youngest son agreed too. The mother could not eat well because she had been suffering from an ulcer since relocation to the city. There was severe pain in her right hand too. Her health condition deteriorated in facing the tremendous stresses arising from Ying's AN. She went to Guangzhou to seek medical treatment for herself. Aside from her health problems, the meager family budget left the mother with no choice but to save the good food for the children, hoping that they could grow healthily.

Apparently the mother was sacrificing her health for her children. The therapist was deeply touched and could hardly find words to express her respect for the mother's sacrifice.

The therapist leaned forward, held the mother's hands, and said softly and slowly, "I have met many mothers in the past. You are indeed the most caring mother I've ever met."

The mother's eyes reddened and turned watery. Her body shook, and she cried for a while. When she calmed down, the therapist rounded up the session and said, "It's not hard to imagine that you must have gone through a lot of bad experiences in the past 2 years. I am impressed by your capability as a good mother. Your children's clothes are always clean and tidy. They're healthy and happy. Your four daughters like reading. You've already done a lot for your children. With the steady progress of Ying's health, it's time for you to take care of your own health. Without good health, your children will be unable to reciprocate your love with filial piety in future. So your children grow, your future is full of hope."

After the treatment, the therapist contacted the psychiatrist and the medical social workers by phone to solicit their help to tackle the financial problems of the family. They both promised to help.

THE FIFTH AND SIXTH SESSIONS

Ying continued gaining weight. Her body weight was 45 kg 3 months after the commencement of family treatment. The medical social worker applied for a financial subsidy for Ying's extra diet; an extra HK$500 (US$64) was provided each month for food.

Ying's mother had gone through hand surgery. Her left hand was bandaged. She looked tired and pale. In responding to the cotherapist's concern for her health, the mother spent a few minutes talking about the hand surgery and the doctor's assessment of the functioning of her left hand. The doctor advised her to stop doing all household chores. In the past week, her children had helped with the household chores. However, Ying was very unhappy that she had to take up the major share, especially preparing the meals, while the other siblings contributed little. She had insufficient time to do her homework. The third sister, CC, helped with the laundry. The fourth sister, KY, and the youngest brother, SY, refused to help at all. The eldest sister, PC, participated only minimally because she had to prepare for her examination.

Ying protested and said, "This arrangement is unfair. I need to study for my lessons too."

The therapist acknowledged her feeling of unfairness. The therapist said to the mother, "Do you agree that such an arrangement is unfair?"

The mother replied, "Yes. The rest of them are not as filial as Ying. They are selfish."

The therapist followed up and asked, "As you are the family head, can you tell your children how each of them should share the household chores?"

The therapist sat back and let the mother take charge, intending to let the mother feel empowered and recognized as a competent mother. The mother discussed with KY and asked her if she could help more. KY negotiated with her mother that she would help only if the youngest brother, SK, shared in the work. KY blamed the mother for spoiling her son too much. He spent plenty of time playing computer games throughout the day. KY also failed to accept that the eldest sister, PC, was excused from her duty because of the examination. Feeling upset and slightly angry, the mother tried to control her mood and explain calmly why allowance was given to the eldest daughter. PC had expressed twice to the mother that she hoped to have better examination results. The mother demanded the youngest son, SK, to contribute too.

Immediately after the enactment, the therapist congratulated the mother for the wonderful performance. The mother reciprocated with a broad smile, her eyes shining with hope and disbelief.

THE SEVENTH AND EIGHTH SESSIONS

As soon as the family settled down in the treatment room, Ying and the mother began to quarrel. Ying shouted at her mother in an irritated mood that she had already listened to the mother's advice and stopped overeating this morning. She felt bad that her mother had often scolded her in the past 2 weeks. She was the only one in the family whom the mother was angry with. Strangely enough, although the mother was angry with Ying, she apologized to her daughter repeatedly. The mother's apology was incongruent with her anger and frustration as well as with the mother–daughter conflict that had emerged.

The therapist gently stopped their destructive interaction and attempted to explore what had been bothering them at home. Overeating was not the main issue. A week ago, the conflict occurred in the evening because Ying refused to do the household chores. The mother asked her to go to the nearby shopping mall to phone the therapist, with the hope that the therapist could help Ying to see the mother's difficulty.[11] Ying did phone the therapist, but to her disappointment the therapist was not in the office.

Ying's anger was in part attributable to the mother blaming her for not helping and in part attributable to her recent row with the third sister, CC. After the row, CC began a cold war with her and did not talk with her at all. The therapist asked Ying which problem she wished to tackle in this session, the conflict with her mother or the conflict with her sister, CC. Ying preferred resolving the latter. The therapist then invited the mother to move her seat and sit next to her, in the belief that the children had the ability to iron out their row.

Under the therapist's encouragement, Ying said to CC, "I've almost recovered. I don't like you to insult me as abnormal. I've self-starved myself in the past few months but I am normal now."

CC whispered to her sister, KY, her good friend in the family, rather than replying to Ying directly. As their voices were too soft, the therapist could not pick up any words. Using her body language, the therapist urged CC to respond to Ying.

CC said reluctantly, "Usually after quarrelling, I would immediately forget our quarrel." Ying asserted her views emphatically to CC and KY that she was no longer ill.

---

[11] The mother asked the daughter to call the therapist outside because she wanted the daughter to have more privacy to talk to the therapist.

Indeed Ying was right. She had already resumed her normal body weight of 48 kg. Despite their recovery, it was not uncommon for patients suffering from AN to have family members still treating them as sick, which would definitely be unpleasant to the recovered young person.

Ying accused CC of being impolite to the mother, while CC attacked Ying for her frequent tantrums in front of the mother.

The mother was saddened by their quarrel. She wept quietly. The therapist was concerned about the mother and invited her to tell her story. The mother felt disappointed toward the children. In the past 2 weeks, the doctor advised her to stop doing any household chores. She had no alternative but to seek their help to share the household chores. However, they refused to do so because they had to prepare for their examinations. Previously Ying was most willing to help. In the past 2 weeks Ying disappointed her too. Perhaps she had spoiled the children too much and had seldom made demands on them. What hurt her most was that the children had no mercy toward her poor health conditions and continued fighting one another. Her children did not respect her and they simply refused to listen to her.

While the mother expressed her hurt, anger, and frustration, the children remained silent. The eldest daughter PC and Ying lowered their heads and gazed upon the ground; CC, KY, and SK, the youngest son, shifted restlessly. The therapist moved closer to the mother to give her more support.

The therapist asked the mother softly, "What is your expectation toward your children after the surgery?"

The mother turned to the children and said firmly, "Your cooperation and your understanding. Please stop fighting. I only need your help while I am sick. Once recovered, I will be your full-time servant again."

THE NINTH SESSION

Ying told the therapist shyly that her menstruation had come back during Chinese Lunar New Year. Contrary to the therapist's expectation, Ying was unhappy with the therapist's congratulations. Ying looked embarrassed, slightly uneasy, and confused while replying to the therapist, suggesting that there might be a problem, but she was hesitant to disclose it. The therapist supported and encouraged her to tell her difficulty but in vain. Ying remained silent. While the therapist had no idea what to do next, the mother asked Ying if she would like to talk about this problem in the presence of her siblings. Ying replied, "No." The therapist had been insensitive and had not realized that to Ying menstruation was a private matter and should not be openly discussed in the family, especially in the presence of her brother.

Thanks to the mother's help, the therapist finally understood why she was stuck in the session. Ying would discuss the problem with the mother and the therapist only in the siblings' absence. The siblings were only too happy to leave the treatment room and to wait outside. Once they left, Ying started talking to her mother and the therapist: She was worried that her health had not yet fully recovered because the menstrual flow was light. She had decreased the intake of food in the past few days as her constipation had worsened. The mother had already accompanied her to consult the Chinese herbalist as well as a medical practitioner in the community. The latter had prescribed orange fibers, at least twice a day. The mother was angry that Ying did not follow the doctor's prescription simply because it did not taste good.

After listening to Ying's story, the therapist shared the mother's worry. She began to realize why Ying had responded to the therapist's congratulations coldly at the beginning of the session. Ying had reduced the intake of food to tackle her constipation. She would easily fall into another vicious cycle: reducing food intake and suffering from constipation, followed by more vigorous dieting and more serious constipation. Ying would relapse if she failed to identify other alternatives in resolving the problem of constipation.

Aware that she was not in a position to offer medical advice, the therapist intervened through an enactment, aiming to help them to engage in a joint effort of problem solving.

During the negotiation, Ying stressed that it was her private matter and she liked her mother to keep her promise. In return, her mother promised not to openly discuss her problem of constipation and menstruation at home. Her protest sent a strong message not only to the mother but also to the therapist. Upon the persistent request of the mother, Ying finally agreed to take the orange fibers twice per day. If the prescription failed, she would consult the doctor immediately.

THE TENTH SESSION

Ying had successfully maintained her normal body weight. But her two sisters CC and KY told the mother that Ying was on a diet again. Alarmed and exasperated, the mother became watchful of Ying's eating during mealtime. Ying protested against the surveillance. The old pattern of the mother–daughter conflict reemerged. Ying had strong grounds to justify her protest, as her body weight had not dropped. She reassured her mother that she only tried to avoid obesity rather than going through a vigorous dieting regimen as before. But to her mother, Ying had recovered physically, but psychologically she continued to be preoccupied with recurrent thoughts of dieting. Besides, her temper tantrums had increased at home. The previous nightmare still haunted the mother.

Before this session, the therapist had planned to terminate the treatment because Ying had succeeded in maintaining her body weight over the past 2 months. Her menstruation had returned too. All these were positive indicators of recovery. The emergence of the mother–daughter conflict in the session changed the therapist's mind. If the therapist did not intervene; the symptomatic cycle of interaction would be escalated. Under the self-fulfilling prophecy, Ying might starve again according to the mother's fear or as a way of punishing her.

The therapist stopped their destructive pattern of interaction and engaged Ying in the joint review of her current stresses. Part of Ying's trouble came from the mother's surveillance and the study stress. It took Ying a long time to do her mathematics homework. In the past week, she often finished her homework around midnight. Like most kids growing up in a poor family, Ying knew too well that education was the means to escape poverty and climb the social ladder. Studying well was not only the fulfillment of a personal dream but also an advancement of the family's welfare.

Her third sister, CC, interrupted the dialogue between the therapist and Ying. She was willing to tutor Ying. She could do so as she was already in junior secondary school. She had come to the city a year earlier and adjusted well to school. Ying preferred solving the problems on her own, rather than relying on her younger sister, CC, as she believed that she learned more when being self-reliant. As she spent more time and effort on her homework, she felt distressed for being unable to finish the household chores assigned to her. She had no way out except to throw a temper tantrum. The review helped to alleviate the mother's anger. She suggested reducing Ying's household chores. Ying's academic problems remained unresolved, but her mother became more empathetic and supportive of her.

THE ELEVENTH SESSION

It was a hot sunny day. The children and the mother were all sweating while greeting the therapist. In order to save the bus fare, they had walked a long way from the train station to the treatment room. All the children including Ying looked bright and pleasant. It was also the first time the mother greeted the therapist with a smile. As they were in such a good mood, the therapist anticipated that the conflict between Ying and the mother had been resolved.

Ying had consulted the Chinese herbalist in the past 2 weeks, and the herbalist advised her to take less "hot" food to restore the balance between the yin and the yang, the two body energies.[12] Her body was too "hot," which accounted for her frequent temper tantrums and her problem of constipation. The diet therapy proved effective, as Ying threw fewer temper tantrums the week before and her problem of constipation was resolved.

Not knowing where to go, the therapist asked the family openly, "How are you going to make use of today's session?"

Ying was, as always, the first person to speak. She complained, "We need your help to fix my little brother's problem. He behaves like a monster at home. He kicked and bit us like a mad dog when we stopped him from playing computer games. He even threw a chair at us while quarrelling with us [the sisters]. We couldn't control him; neither could my mom. Mom once said that if he remained unmanageable, she would call the police for help."

PC, CC, and KY echoed Ying's story. They said in unison to the little brother, "Playing computer games is not good for your study, nor for your eyes. The eye doctor has already warned you about it. Mom is worried of your poor eyesight."

Their little brother grumbled vaguely. He looked fragile, but his facial expression unveiled his uncompromising thought. He was prepared to fight fiercely with his sisters. The mother reasoned with the son that his behavior was totally unacceptable, in the hope that he could better behave himself in future. The son fought back, declaring that he was not going to compromise with anyone in the family; they were intrusive and disrespectful of what he was doing.

Finding it difficult to parent her son, the mother turned to the therapist and explained what had happened at home. Owing to tight finances, the family could afford having only one computer at home. However, all the children needed the computer for the Internet searches for their school projects. The youngest son occupied the computer most of the time to play computer games. This enraged his sisters because they were unable to finish their school assignments. The therapist explored with the family if

---

[12] According to Chinese medicine, food is classified as hot or cold on the basis of the effects on the body.

alternatives (e.g., computer facilities in the public library or in the youth center) were available in the community. It was discovered that they had already made use of these community resources, but these resources were inaccessible at night. To the sisters, the little brother was playing and not studying. He should be the one to give in, but the youngest brother asserted that he had the right to use the computer. Neither party had indicated any readiness to compromise. The situation was really difficult for the mother. It was a hard nut for the therapist to crack too.

The easy way to go around was to explore and assess the needs of this 9-year-old boy. The therapist, showing curiosity, asked the boy, "What game do you like most, the *Age of Empires*?" The boy shook his head and replied, "It's a new game on the Internet." The therapist invited him to explain more about the game. With enthusiasm, the boy explained briefly how he played the game. The greatest fun was that he could pair up with his good friend to beat the enemy. Having lowered the boy's defense mechanism, the therapist turned tactfully to inquire about his conflicts with his sisters. He said that the conflict could be avoided and he would be able to discipline himself if his sisters and his mother were less intrusive. He was a big boy, and he knew when to stop playing the computer game. The therapist complimented him for his readiness to assume responsibility for his own behavior while suggesting alternative ways for his sister to relate to him differently.

When the therapist finished complimenting the little boy, the mother smiled and said in a very nurturing voice to his son, "Maybe I have been too restrictive in not allowing you to go out to play basketball with your classmates after school. I am fearful that there'll be some bad guys bullying you around. I can't protect you."

The boy replied, "I know who is a bad guy and who is not. You've got to trust me. Staying home is boring me to death."

Negotiating for a while, the mother and the son came to a compromise that the mother would allow him to go out for an hour after school; in return, the son would shorten his time on the computer games.

The mother had indeed done a marvelous job. She had acknowledged the boy's need for fun and leisure while meeting the needs of her four daughters. Placing her hands on the mother's shoulders, the therapist congratulated her for her effective parenting.

CC and KY expressed their worry when the therapist shared her view that it should be a golden opportunity to end the therapy. They found that Ying was still thinking about dieting. Ying explained that she was simply avoiding obesity. She could hardly tolerate having a belly. The therapist joked with her that her belly was invisible to others, including the therapist. She gave a brief explanation to Ying that her belly reserved fatty tissues that would give her a good body shape. Ying listened attentively but with great puzzlement. Growing up is never easy for an adolescent girl when society puts such emphasis on thinness and slimness as the standard of beauty.

Three months after the termination of the treatment, Ying's body weighed 50 kg; her menstruation had returned. Ying and her third sister were enrolled in a top secondary school in the community. They were adjusting well academically and socially in school. With the assistance of the medical social worker, a public housing unit of 400 sq. ft. was allocated to the family on compassionate grounds. The family moved to the new apartment, large enough to be partitioned into three rooms. The day-to-day conflicts between the youngest brother and his sisters were drastically reduced, given the increased space. The mother had successfully gone through a second hand surgery. The mother and the children were healthy, happy, and relaxed.

Table 10.1 summarizes the treatment principles employed for this family.

DISCUSSION

In comparison with the other emaciated young people, Ying was motivated for change and had assumed responsibility for recovery. Several reasons might account for this. First, the history of the disorder was short. Its effects on the patient's psychosocial functioning were less serious than for chronic patients; the disorder had not yet fully controlled her life as well as the family life. Second, the secondary psychological gains arising from self-starvation such as a false sense of control were not predominant for Ying. Third, Ying's mother had identified her self-starvation earlier and sought help from the social worker in the community, with further referral within a short period of time. Fourth, the brief health education given by the research assistant, who has solid medical and nursing knowledge in this area, had positive effects on Ying.

The management of this patient and her family was different from that of other patients since Ying had initiated her journey of healing right after the pretreatment interview. Unsurprisingly, the symptomatic cycle of interaction that had maintained the symptoms gradually dissolved and disappeared soon after the first interview, without much assistance from the therapist. Transformation of the problem was easy for this family too since the mother and Ying's siblings were already concerned and worried about Ying's health. They perceived themselves to be playing an active part in helping Ying to restore her health.

However, the symptomatic cycle of interaction between the mother and the emaciated daughter emerged in the ninth and tenth sessions when Ying was on a diet again since she wished to deal with constipation and to avoid obesity. Fearful of relapse, the mother became watchful of Ying's eating during mealtime. The mother–daughter entanglement might have precipitated the relapse. The critical task of the therapist was to prevent relapse by shifting the focus from working on the symptom to unlocking the symptomatic cycle of interaction, as suggested by Micucci (1998). The therapist assisted the mother and Ying in unlocking their symptomatic cycle of interaction through deepening the mother's understanding of Ying's stresses, supporting Ying to express her discontents and anger toward the mother and the siblings, and encouraging Ying to take on responsibility for her own health.

AN had triggered the mother's self-blame and increased her sense of powerlessness and helplessness as a single parent in a new homeland. Such feelings were understandable since she lacked knowledge and skills in handling the health crisis of her beloved daughter. She was ill informed on readily available and accessible community resources in the city. All these cumulative stresses had undesirable effects on her health. The worsening of her ulcer and the increasing pain in her hand were indicators of her distress and her need for professional support and guidance.

The treatment goals for this family were twofold: (a) to empower the mother as an effective parent in helping Ying's recovery by mitigating the mother's self-blame and by restoring her sense of competence in parenting and (b) to continue effecting positive changes for Ying's recovery.

These two treatment goals could be achieved only if the family was helped to deal with its poverty and the unresolved problems arising from the legacy of the parents' divorce. Family poverty and the accompanying stresses resulting from the economic deprivation had cumulative effects on parent–child relationships and the sibling relationship (Sampson & Laub, 1998), which in turn affected the family's coping with self-starvation.

Disagreement is part of family life for families with AN. In addition to conflicts directly arising from the disorder, the hidden and open conflicts of this family were multiple. They were partly brought about by the unresolved issues arising from the separation and divorce of the parents, as typified by the conflict between the mother and her eldest daughter, PC, and partly due to the inadequate family resources, as typified by the argument over the use of the computer and not being able to buy the nutritious milk for Ying. There was conflict over the division of household chores because the family had to reorganize itself subsequent to the mother's poor health and her physical inability to take up her habitual roles and functions in the family.

Such families burdened with past miseries often present themselves as weaker than they are in reality (Minuchin, Colapinto, & Minuchin, 1998). The therapist should look beyond the problem of self-starvation and elicit the family strengths and competence. In this case, the resources were the children, as they had better adjusted to city life, the love and care of the mother toward the children, and the strong emotional ties between Ying and her mother.

The therapist had employed treatment strategies of actively involving the mother and the children in the treatment process as well as creating new experiences for them to learn new ways of relating to one another. Experiential in nature, the process of empowering the mother was predominantly around the identification and resolution of hidden and open conflicts in this family. In enactment, family members are encouraged to talk with one another on the commonly identified topic (Nichols & Fellenberg, 2000), and the therapist is then able to assess the nature and the process of the family conflicts and utilize them to achieve the therapeutic goal of empowering the mother. For instance, in the 3rd session, the mother was assisted in resolving the conflict with her eldest daughter, PC; in the 11th session, the mother was encouraged to handle the conflicts between the son and his four sisters. All these positive experiences helped to bolster the mother's confidence and restore her competence in parenting, which in turn increased the children's respect and appreciation toward the previously lonely, depressed, and desperate mother. Besides enactment, positive reframing of the problem, appropriate punctuation, boundary setting, consistent delivery of positive feedback, and facilitation of the family's joint effort in problem solving were also used, all with good results.

Societal resources should be mobilized, and the family should be linked to accessible social services. Economically disadvantaged families are inevitably involved with multiple social systems, including health care services, the education system, and welfare services, all of which could have potential effects on family treatment.

The therapist, in this case also a social worker, was able to assess the service needs of the family and to collaborate with different helping professionals, namely the psychiatrist and the medical social worker, in marshalling different services for the family. Other therapists would need to work closely with a social worker who can play an active role as the case manager for the family and whose professional practice is family oriented. Otherwise, inappropriate services might even weaken the family functioning and dilute the family process, and at its worst might even replace the parental functions (Minuchin et al., 1998). For instance, a placement of a child in foster care service for poor parents with inadequate parenting skills may shatter parental confidence and deprive the child an opportunity to grow up at home.

A culturally sensitive lens would be extremely useful in working with an immigrant family. The therapist should be perceptive enough to recognize the differences in cultural beliefs and values between the therapist and the family. The mother's rigid sitting posture in the first and second sessions was an expression of her respect for a university professor, easily misread as a sign of nervousness and anxiety.

As indicated by the results of the posttreatment interview, the family found that family therapy had helped them in the following areas: (a) Ying's recovery from the disorder, (b) a more equitable arrangement of the house hold chores, (c) reduction in the frequency of family conflicts, and (d) cultivation of harmonious relationships between the mother and the children and among the siblings. In brief, family therapy had effected changes at both the individual and the family levels, in addition to restoring Ying's health. Although the therapist perceived that she had succeeded in empowering the mother, the family had not reported this in their posttreatment interview. The disparate views between the therapist and the family suggest that it may be premature to arrive at any conclusions regarding the treatment effectiveness in this area.

CONCLUSION

This case study has demonstrated the interplay of AN and family poverty. Specifically, family poverty inhibited the family's coping with AN through two possible paths: first, through its direct effect on family resources; second, through its mediating effect on family relationships. This case provides anecdotal evidence that poor families suffering from AN can benefit from family therapy if the problem is identified and treated early. Resource mobilization and provision of tangible social services must be part and parcel of the management; such can be ensured through close collaboration with a social worker, preferably with a family-based orientation in practice, who would take up the role as the case manager of the family.

Table 10.1: Treatment Steps and Principles for Ying and Her Family

Treatment Session	Treatment Steps of the Model	Applications for This Family
Session 1	• To briefly understand the history of the disorder and the patient's motivation for recovery • To explore and identify the constricting family process that has unfavorably affected the parents' collaboration to refeed the emaciated daughter and, hence, has maintained the symptom • To negotiate the treatment contract by shifting the family focus from the symptom to the symptomatic cycle or the constricting family process that has maintained and escalated AN	• The therapist assessed Ying's history of onset and her motivation of recovery; assessment showed that Ying was aware of the serious consequences of the disorder and had already made efforts to gain weight; hence, the fight between Ying and her mother at mealtime had stopped soon after the pretreatment interview • The therapist acknowledged Ying's effort of helping herself and encouraged her to resume normal eating • A family assessment revealed that the mother and the children emigrated from a rural area 2 years ago, experienced difficulties in family reunion with the husband, suffered from spouse abuse, and subsequently separated from the abusive husband and lived apart on the welfare subsidy with weak social support; however, the children adjusted quite well in the city and had become important resources of the illiterate mother • The therapist provided emotional support to the helpless and powerless mother, who was full of self-blame

Table 10.1 (Cont'd)

Treatment Session	Treatment Steps of the Model	Applications for This Family
Session 2	• To continue exploring and identifying the constricting family process that has unfavorably affected the parents' collaboration to refeed the emaciated daughter and, hence, has maintained the symptom • To address unresolved conflicts and improved family relationships using culturally acceptable means	• The therapist made use of the conflict between Ying and her mother to understand more about the mother's self-blame and helplessness in parenting Ying and the four children • Exploration had shown that the mother was insensitive to Ying's need for privacy; her relationship with the eldest daughter was full of tension and conflicts due to the eldest daughter's emotional attachment to the father and her reluctance to move out to live with the mother during the parents' separation • The therapist helped the mother and the eldest daughter to resolve their conflicts by allowing each of their stories to be heard in treatment
Session 3	• To help to work on the constricting family process that maintained anorexia nervosa • To address unresolved conflicts and improved family relationships using culturally acceptable means	• To empower the mother by encouraging her to talk to the eldest daughter directly to resolve their conflicts and to identify a better way of relating to each other; the mother had performed her role well, and her children applauded spontaneously to express their appreciation of the mother's effort

Table 10.1 (Cont'd)

Treatment Session	Treatment Steps of the Model	Applications for This Family
Session 4	• To encourage parental collaboration by facilitating the parents to help the emaciated daughter, rather than to control her • To address unresolved conflicts and improved family relationships using culturally acceptable means	• Ying was progressing satisfactorily; review of her progress had shown that she had taken a glass of nutritious milk every day according to professional advice • The therapist explored whether the family could afford the expensive milk; it was found that neither Ying nor her mother had sought help from the psychiatrist, the medical social worker, or the therapists because of their insufficient understanding of the health care services in the city; brief information on health care services was provided and the therapist helped to present their needs for financial assistance to the psychiatrist and the medical social work • The therapist handled the mother's anxiety and fear of Ying's sudden death by inviting Ying to reassure the mother that she had already resumed normal eating during mealtime • The therapists continued to recognize the mother's effort by giving all the good food to the children at the risk of her own health
Sessions 5 and 6	• To encourage parental collaboration by facilitating the parents to help the emaciated daughter, rather than to control her • To address unresolved conflicts and improved family relationship using culturally acceptable means	• Aiming to continue empowering the mother, the therapists helped the mother to listen to Ying's protest of being overloaded by the household chores and toward the unfair arrangement of the household chores among the siblings and to invite the mother to take charge of the situation • The therapists set up a context for the mother to solve the problem jointly with the children and to demand each child to share in the household chores

Table 10.1 (Cont'd)

Treatment Session	Treatment Steps of the Model	Applications for This Family
Sessions 7 and 8	• To address unresolved conflicts and improved family relationship using culturally acceptable means	• In these two sessions, the therapists created a context for Ying to resolve the conflicts with her third sister, CC, who kept treating her as if she were still sick despite her gradual recovery; the therapists supported Ying to voice her discontent and invited Ying and her third sister to discuss this directly
Session 9	• To handle relapses by preventing the reemergence of the symptomatic cycle and further enhancing the family relationships	• In this session, the therapists helped Ying to deal with her anxiety and worry arising from the constipation and menstruation, which resumed with the steady gain in weight • This treatment step was necessary to prevent relapse, since Ying had started to reduce food intake to tackle constipation • The therapists and the mother learned to respect Ying's sense of boundary and privacy in discussing her menstruation and constipation only in her siblings' absence
Session 10	• To handle relapses by preventing the reemergence of the symptomatic cycle and further enhancing the family relationships	• The mother had become watchful of Ying's eating during mealtime and Ying fought back against the mother's surveillance; the old pattern of mother–daughter conflicts reemerged • The therapists helped to unlock the self-defeating interaction pattern through a joint review with Ying, aiming to understand the stresses that she was currently facing; the review had released the mother's worry and hostility and deepened her understanding of the meaning of Ying's dieting at home

Table 10.1 (Cont'd)

Treatment Session	Treatment Steps of the Model	Applications for This Family
Session 11	• To further enhance the family relationships to prevent relapses	• Ying continued to gain weight and her health condition was improving; her efforts of taking charge of her own health and recovering were complimented • Ying and her sisters brought out their conflicts with the youngest brother and the mother's failure to iron out their conflicts; the therapists created the context for Ying and her sisters to deal with the conflicts with the youngest brother, who had promised to reduce his hours of playing computer games so that his sisters could use the computer for homework
Follow-up sessions	• To support individual development • To support the transformation	• The therapists provided support and gave compliments to Ying for her active participation in school

Part IV

Perceived Treatment
Effectiveness and
Treatment Efficacy
of Family Therapy

Chapter 11
Perceived Treatment Effectiveness of Family Therapy

INTRODUCTION

In using family therapy to help emaciated young people, one faces several burning questions. In the eyes of young people and their families, to what extent is family therapy helping to resolve their symptoms, to foster parents' coping, and to improve family relationships? As perceived by the youth and their families, which areas should be improved in family treatment? The best way to answer these questions is through a systematic study into the emaciated young people's and their families' views after the completion of family treatment.

This chapter reports one such study, based on the author's practice. Like almost all practices, the sample is necessarily restricted to one cultural group, and an attempt is made both to elicit conclusions that might have general applicability and to point to factors that might have cultural specificity in Chinese populations, the latter as far as possible contrasted with parallel studies and conclusions from studies in the West.

METHOD OF STUDY

Research Design

Qualitative research is able to identify people's experiences and understand the meaning of their experiences within their immediate social context (Cole, 2005). The research design consists of multiple case studies (Yin, 1994), which refer to "an empirical inquiry that investigates a contemporary phenomenon within its real-life context, especially when the boundaries between phenomenon and context are not clearly evident" (Yin, 1994, p. 13).

A total of 30 young people suffering from anorexia nervosa (AN) were referred for family therapy in this study, with 27 children and adolescents and 7 adults. Of these, 4 children and adolescents dropped out from treatment, for a 14.8% dropout rate in this group; 22 patients and families completed the family treatment, while one patient's treatment was unsuccessful. The overall completion rate of family treatment for the children and adolescent group was 81.46%. The results of this study indicate that these patients fully recovered, as indicated by their change in body weight, resumption of menstruation, reduced severity in the symptoms associated with eating disorders and level of psychological distress, and improvement of perceived family functioning (Ma & Lai, 2009). Seven adult patients and their families recovered after family treatment as well.

Upon the completion of the family treatment, the families were invited to attend a posttreatment interview on a voluntary basis. A total of 25 families participated in the in-depth posttreatment interview, with 18 from the adolescent group (total = 23) and 7 from the adult group (total = 8).

The mean age at onset for the adolescents was 13 (SD = 1.78); the mean age at referral was 14 (SD = 1.59). All these patients were female and had been diagnosed with AN. In each case, the duration of illness was less than 3 years. The mean body mass index (BMI) for the adolescents at referral was 15.17 (SD = 1.81) and had increased to 19.37 (SD = 2.2) after treatment, which was within the norm for children and adolescents in the community (Leung, Cole, Tse, & Lau, 1998). Three were studying in Grade 6, ten were in junior secondary, nine were in senior secondary, and one was in college.

For the young adult women, the mean age of onset was 18.5 (SD = 2.1) and the mean age at referral was 23.4 (SD = 7.7). Five patients were college students while one was in Grade 12–13. The mean BMI at referral was 14.51 (SD = 7.7). After family treatment, the mean BMI had increased to 17.54 (SD = 2.50).

Lower-middle-class families were overrepresented, in contrast to Western clinical samples (e.g., Krautter & Lock, 2004; van Furth et al., 1996). The family types included nuclear families (n = 17), single-parent families (n = 6), an extended family (n = 1), and a blended family (n = 1).

Data Collection

The posttreatment interviews were conducted by a doctoral candidate who was also a qualified and registered nurse, using an interview guideline (appendix 4). The treatment interview elicited the families' responses in the following areas: helpfulness of the treatment in resolving the symptoms and in improving family relations (e.g., marital relations, parent–child relations, and sibling relations), factors conducive to or hindering recovery, functions and roles of the therapist, areas for improvement in clinical practice, willingness of the families to refer other families in need to the research project, and ways of explaining the services to other families in need. The research assistant followed the natural flow of the families' stories and made use of the interview guideline only when necessary.

With written consent from the young people and families, all these interviews were audiotaped for verbatim transcription and identification of categories. Another research assistant, a master's student in social work who had no involvement in treatment, was invited to transcribe the posttreatment interviews verbatim, and the therapist translated these transcriptions into English.

Data Analysis

Content analysis (Krippendorff, 1980) was adopted to identify the types of perceived treatment effectiveness in different areas. The therapist developed the coding system in the following way: The therapist went through the transcripts many times, marked off units that were related to the same topic (e.g., perceived helpfulness in resolution of symptoms, perceived helpfulness in conflict resolution), and then divided them into topics (e.g., resolution of mother–daughter conflicts, resolution of father–daughter conflicts) and subtopics (e.g., resolution of mother–daughter conflicts at mealtime, resolution of father–daughter conflicts at mealtime) at different levels of analysis (Miles & Huberman, 1994). The linkage of one category to another was closely examined, and the differences across these categories, if any, were identified. The results of the analysis were repeatedly reviewed to ensure accuracy.

This chapter reports some conclusions drawn from the posttreatment interviews, which focus on the perceived treatment effectiveness of family therapy. Individuals are labeled as participant, father, or mother, followed by a numeral (1–25) to indicate the family.

RESULTS OF THE STUDY

From the perspectives of the participants, the changes they had experienced were multidimensional, including restoration of body weight, resumption of physical and psychological well-being, reduced family conflicts, and increased mutual understanding in the family. The recovered young people's sense of personal effectiveness and confidence were enhanced, and they no longer suffered from severe mood swings. The helpless and desperate parents had become less distressed and upset, more hopeful and empowered; their coping was enhanced. They had regained parental competence to assist the recovering daughter, to resolve the intergenerational family conflicts, and to foster mutual understanding in the family.

Two unexpected outcomes were reported. First, the depression of a father was uplifted after treatment. Second, the results of this study illuminated the coping process of these parents. Like building a jigsaw puzzle by organizing all these bits and pieces together, effective coping as subjectively defined and experienced by these parents comprised three processes: (a) the process of being understood and supported; (b) the process of cognitive reappraisal of the problem encountered, specifically the part that a parent can play in rescuing the emaciated daughter and the part that the young person should be responsible for in her own recovery; and (c) the behavioral change in parenting.

The changes brought about by family treatment were complex, with changes in one area spilling over to other aspects of family relationships. The dynamics of these changes were far more complex than the lineal presentation of the results of the study might suggest.

Perceived Helpfulness on the Symptoms

To the majority of families interviewed, the emaciated young person in each family had resumed normal intake of food after treatment.[13]

Father 2 (adolescent) narrated, "I think her eating problem has been almost resolved. About 90% of the problem has been tackled but she still has some psychological difficulties."

Mother 7 (adolescent) narrated, "In these six sessions, we could discuss her problem (AN). We have tackled the problem. Most importantly, she would like to recover and live as a normal person. After treatment, she felt happy. She is no longer worried about eating and eats as much as she wishes. She hopes to recover and to begin further studies."

Father 8 (adolescent) narrated, "It [family therapy] has helped a lot. Before that, Participant 8 was stubborn. She refused to listen to her mom and me. During the treatment, the therapist explained to her the negative effects

---

[13] Part of the data of this study have been reported in Ma and Lai (2006).

of self-starvation on her health and her brain. Her brain would become less functional; there would be an imbalance of hormones and she would have hairy limbs. She listened and took the professional advice seriously. She began to eat more. Now she has resumed her menstruation. She looks healthy."

The parents' views were consistent with those of the self-starving daughters regarding the effectiveness of family therapy in recovery. The recovered daughters agreed with the parents' view by nodding their heads immediately following their parents' sharing or by replying "Yeah" in response to the parents' views.

Participant 22 (adult) was perceptive enough to differentiate the role played by the family in facilitating her recovery from its role in causing the disorder: "My problem does not lie with my family. There are problems in my family but the main cause of my disorder was unrelated to my family or my family problems. However, through this treatment and the collective action of my family, I am able to resolve the problem leading to my illness." Participant 22's food refusal problem was related to her peers' denigration and repeated verbal sexual harassment during her first year of study in college. She narrated, "Before treatment, I was very angry and locked myself up in the dormitory. In treatment, I learned to look at my schoolmates from different angles. I don't mind whether they are idiots or not. I don't care how they treat me, even if they are ruthless toward me, especially after I feel the concern of my family."

Another family reported that reduced family conflicts had resulted in a change of the eating problem. The second younger sister of Participant 21 (adult) narrated, "We began to be less stubborn in defending each of our viewpoints. It ended up there were fewer conflicts in the family. My eldest sister's [Participant 21] eating problem started to improve. In the past she never had any snacks. Once we ate ice cream bars together. I feel that she has become more open."

For two families, the parents found that family therapy could partially resolve the problem of emaciation, while the afflicted young people held different views regarding the recovery.

Mother 11 (adolescent) said, "About 60% to 70% of her problem was resolved. Compared to her previous eating, she ate more and had a greater variety of foods but she has not yet recovered." Participant 11 protested and said, "90% of my self-starvation was cured." In reply to how she would rate herself on a scale of 0 to 10, with 10 indicating recovery and 0 indicating still remaining sick, Participant 21 answered without any hesitation, "8. I am still stubborn about food." Her father was less optimistic: "I don't think there is any change regarding her eating. Many of her psychological problems remain unresolved."

Two young people perceived family therapy as unhelpful to drive away the disorder. While family therapy was effective to improve family relations, it was ineffective in addressing their psychological issues.

Participant 16 (adolescent) narrated, "I felt that you need to rely on yourself. It's your body. My family could be very supportive but if I choose to vomit, they couldn't do anything. My recovery depends on my own will." Her mother elaborated: "Her hospitalization helped to take care of her body weight. [The treatment] here helped to look after her psychological need."

Participant 20 (adult) said, "It [family therapy] couldn't help me nor has it had any effects on my problem. Family therapy can't stop you from vomiting. It can help your family to analyze the problem. Having no problem in your own family doesn't mean you have no problem. There are problems of my career, of my friends and of my dating." Participant 20 explained, "I recovered because I wish to be beautiful. I still vomit from time to time. Probably it symbolizes something that I wish to ventilate." Her mother said, "Yes, only of slight help [referring to family therapy]. She vomits less than before."

Perceived Helpfulness on Psychological Well-Being

Emaciated young people are characterized by a strong sense of personal ineffectiveness, poor self-image, and poor self-esteem (Bruch, 1973). As revealed by the family stories, family therapy had positive effects on their self-esteem and sense of mastery

Mother 21 (adult) narrated, "After treatment, her mood improved. She was willing to listen. Her confidence was greatly enhanced." The father agreed, "What drove us to continue to receive treatment, despite the slow progress in the middle phase, is that family therapy has given a lot of confidence to my daughter."

Mother 12 (adolescent) narrated, "The therapist asked me to stand up and compare my height with my children. She told me that they have grown up and I should let them try their ways, let them do whatever they like to do." Participant 12 said later, "Yes, she [therapist] asked my mom to let me try my own ideas; that's very good. Nobody in my life has ever trusted me."

These young people regained their confidence and a sense of mastery partly from the therapist's validation and concern (Participant 21 and Participant 22) and partly from the change of the parents' ways of handling their problem (Participant 24).

Participant 21 narrated, "At that time I had no confidence. I was frightened and desperate. But the therapist's warmth and her smiling concern gave me tremendous confidence and encouragement. Once she said affirmatively that she had confidence that I would make it."

The youngest brother of Participant 22 commented, "The most useful part of family therapy for my elder sister [Participant 22] is that she would have a person to turn to. She [Participant 22] felt that we were attacking her. During treatment, she no longer felt lonely because the therapist was always on her side." Participant 22 narrated later, "Why did I trust her [the therapist]? It's because she's genuine and concerned about me very much."

The father of Participant 24 narrated, "In the treatment, we communicated with one another. We learned about each other's viewpoint, had mutual understanding and mutual support. For instance, once my daughter asked her mom not to force her to eat this and drink that. Afterward, her mom was less rigid and uncompromising."

Family therapy was found to be effective in reducing the parents' distress, anxiety, and worry that had arisen directly from their daughters' self-starvation. After treatment, the parents' psychological well-being was greatly improved, as revealed by the following narratives.

Father 6 narrated, "She [his wife] has more energy. She goes shopping more. I feel relieved after I saw that there were many ways to deal with the problem. I am more relaxed, have more to say at home; life has become more interesting."

Mother 8 narrated, "During her illness, I was very upset when I saw that she [her emaciated daughter] was unhappy. I was afraid and worried in facing her vomiting. She's emotional from time to time. I gradually become less frightened. I just ignore her when she is moody." The eldest sister said: "Besides helping T [the inflicted sister], she [the therapist] has helped my mom to become happier. She often smiles now."

Father 14 (adolescent) narrated, "My mood improved a lot after treatment. I scolded her (the emaciated daughter) less. We express our concern and feel better."

Mother 23 (adult) said, "I no longer feel gloomy; at least there is hope. X [the emaciated daughter] should be able to recover."

For Father 18 (adolescent), the therapist had helped to identify and unintentionally treated his depression, caused by his business bankruptcy after the Asian financial crisis. Father 18 narrated, "We have our own problem. I'd no chance of meeting helping professionals in the past. After disclosing my misery and my business failure to my children, 80% of my depression that has been lingering on for a few years has been lifted."

In short, in the eyes of these families, family therapy was helpful in reducing the psychological distress and enhancing the psychological well-being of both the parents and the young person.

Perceived Effectiveness on Empowering Parents' Coping

The process of empowering the parents' coping varied from parent to parent. Woven through the data were the parents' voices recounting, in bits and pieces, what they perceived to be useful in coping with the disorder. To Father 1, talking the problem over in the session was sufficient in lifting up his psychological burden; once relieved, he could better understand the problem.

Father 1 said, "After talking over all these problems, I feel less heavy and more relaxed. Our family is willing to face her illness and I've already tried my best to change our communication." Father 1 continued, "In the second session, the situation that we faced had become crystal clear to me and to her [Participant 1]. I worked even harder to let her know that if she wished to be discharged from the hospital, she needed to work hard for recovery."

To another parent, the therapeutic context that permitted them to share their pain and suffering with the emaciated daughter attenuated stress, and they were enlightened by having their attention shifted from the young person's eating problem to different developmental needs.

Mother 7 said, "Here she [Participant 7] learned that she was not the only sacrifice and victim in the family; we [the parents] are too." The mother continued in the latter part of the interview, "We began to know that it's a family affair; not an individual affair in fighting AN. The therapist didn't talk much about her eating problem. She helped us to discuss her friends [Participant 7's], her unique way of shopping, and the bright side of her personality." The father supplemented, "Although we interact with young people every day, we know little about our children. We learned from her [the therapist] how to view the growing up of my two children from a different angle, like allowing them to loiter around the shopping mall. We've been looking after them too much and too well. We helped them do everything and plan everything. We should be more distant and let go."

To the parents of Participant 16, for the therapist to side with them by verbalizing the unacceptability of the emaciated daughter's temper tantrum was very supportive and empowering, while another father appreciated the therapist's direct advice and suggestions.

Mother 16 (adolescent) recalled, "The first time I met the therapist, I had a strong feeling that there's hope for my daughter's recovery." The mother continued later, "The most memorable moment in treatment was when, after my daughter blew up in the session, the therapist uttered that if the patient was her daughter, she could not but feel very angry and out of control, since she was so annoying and unreasonable. I felt that she [the therapist] really understood my difficulty as her mother." The father joined in the conversation and corrected the mother: "Not just for the mother but for the parents."

Father 7 (adolescent) narrated, "Her illness came about partly because while growing up, she felt that she couldn't control and master life; so she controlled herself, the amount of food to be eaten and controlled others' eating too. That's her way of mastering life. We [he and his wife] committed the same mistake. We controlled her to do this and to do that. Now we can let go and be relaxed. Let her manage her own difficulties. The effects of doing so are positive." Participant 7 replied, "Yes, to a great extent this is good but I need their guidance if I make a mistake."

Perceived Effects on Family Relationships

Some of the primary aims of family therapy are to help reduce family conflicts, foster family cohesion, and cultivate a culture of hope. To what extent is family therapy effective in helping to reduce the family conflicts, foster family cohesion, and improve family relations?

Reduced family conflicts. Emerging from the data was a marked contrast of the family situations experienced by these families before, during, and after the treatment.

Before treatment, the family conflicts of these families were frequent and intense, to the extent that it was like "a time bomb," a metaphor used by one mother. The fights usually occurred between the mother or the father and the afflicted adolescent over eating and food; both parties refused to compromise. Family treatment brought positive changes, first and foremost the reduction of family conflicts in terms of both intensity and frequency.

Participant 5 (adolescent) narrated, "My conflicts with my mother and my sister had reduced a lot. It's better than before." Her brother said, "To put it simply, our home is quieter than before. In the past there were frequent fights every day; all these fights arose from trivial things around eating and food. The family atmosphere was tense, which in turn had affected our mood badly." Participant 7 narrated, "Before treatment, we [she and her mom] often fought because of food. I forced her to eat. After treatment, there's no more fighting. We chatted like good friends." Mother 7 narrated, "All our family happiness was gone. We were in a state as if a time bomb would explode anytime. During therapy, I started to think differently. I asked what had been missing in our family. Our family lacked communication. After treatment, she [the patient] changed. She has become the center of happiness in the family. She plays and jokes with us."

Father 8 (adolescent) narrated, "Our family relation was extremely poor mainly because she [Participant 8] refused to eat and her mom forced her to eat. She [patient] wouldn't listen and they fought. During treatment, the therapist suggested that I offer help to my wife. We [he and his daughter] went out for meals. I lectured less, gave her [patient] more time and space to take care of her health. Their conflicts lessened and vanished." The father continued, "She [patient] used to argue fiercely with me. Now she is more compromising."

Participant 17 (adolescent) narrated, "Apparently our family relations had improved. At least no more fighting and no more cold war have occurred." The father echoed, "Our family has become more cohesive."

The fourth sister of Participant 19 said, "With bad temper, she often fought with mom and with us. She didn't want food and my mother was very upset. We were unhappy and our family was in a mess. Now our family life's very good."

These passages illustrate graphically how changes occur and that two-way interpersonal relationships improved. The change could be initiated by an individual family member (Father 8 and Participant 7), by the mother and daughter as in the case of Participant 5, or by the whole family (Participant 17), and there would be rippling effects on other family members.

Increased family cohesion. According to the families' descriptions, the therapeutic context created in treatment allowed each of their voices to be heard. Most importantly, family members were able to share and contradict each other's viewpoint over an issue that was addressed. The process of sharing and contradiction was also a process of eliciting multiple realities held by different family members. This process had unexpectedly deepened the family members' mutual understanding and fostered their mutual concern. The family narratives have indicated the therapeutic power of family therapy in this area.

The brother of Participant 5 (adolescent) said, "She [the therapist] would seldom focus only on their problem [the mother–daughter conflict]. She would ask for my view while they were fighting. She would invite my youngest sister to express her opinion even though she was quite young. Hearing how other family members perceive the same event is memorable. We can contribute to problem-solving by giving our views on the problem. In the end not only she [Participant 5] benefited from the discussion; the whole family benefited too."

Participant 7 said, "Before treatment, I often thought that I was the only one suffering in this family. I suffered most. After attending the treatment, I found that my mom and my dad were as pained as I was."

Participant 12 narrated, "After listening to their views, I started to feel that they [her mom, eldest brother, and sister] are very concerned about me. When I have conflicts with them, I wonder if I had gone too far, to the extent that I was hurting them." Her mother nodded and said, "Previously she [Participant 12] often thought that we owed her a lot. After treatment, she began to wonder if she was wrong."

Participant 16 said, "Our life is better and we know how to relate to each other better." The mother said, "When she [Participant 16] failed to meet my expectations, I began to understand her by tuning in to her perspective. You [therapist] took care of our psychological needs by letting us understand more and communicate more."

Mother 16 narrated, "At home we knew that we were unhappy with one another but we wouldn't discuss it. Here there were fewer barriers. We communicate. We talk. We let others know our views. Previously we hid our financial difficulty from our children, as we didn't wish to put a psychological burden on them. After disclosing our difficulty to them honestly, they understood why we expect them to study harder. They understood that we had given them a lot." The mother continued, "She [the therapist] had deepened our understanding toward one another."

Besides helping the families overcome their barriers for mutual concern and mutual understanding, the therapist had successfully helped the families to develop a sense of togetherness and cohesion by shifting their overfocus on the pathology of the emaciated young person to the need for a team building to combat the disorder.

Participant 7 said, "I gradually found that she [the therapist] didn't focus on me and blame me for the disorder. She focused on helping us to work as a team. That's good."

Father 8 narrated, "My deepest impression is that we helped one another to move on. Once I wanted to give her up witnessing that she was starving to death. We haven't done so. We supported and encouraged one another in facing her illness. Family cohesion is very important."

Areas for Improvement

The participants of this study made several constructive and useful suggestions to improving the clinical practice, which included (a) provision of individual therapy for the emaciated young people, (b) extension of the treatment time from one and a half hours to two hours per session, (c) increasing the frequency of family treatment from a fortnightly to a weekly basis, (d) offering more active and direct guidance and advice for the less educated parents, (e) recommending useful readings on management of AN for parents with higher education, (f) providing home-based rather than centered-based family therapy service, and (g) providing flexible arrangements for family members to meet the therapist separately with explanation given on ways of conducting family therapy.

DISCUSSION

This study makes several contributions. It generated lots of conclusions, most of which echo those from the West, and confirmed the generality of the issues, despite the different concept of *jia*, family. As the family is the unit of study, the perspectives of both the emaciated young people as well as their family members provided useful insights that have enriched our understanding of their diverse subjective experiences in treatment. However, this inquiry is only exploratory, with a small sample size that may restrict the generalizability of the conclusions; also, there may have been memory loss or even selective memory in the posttreatment interviews, not to mention selective response among those treated.

From the perspectives of the participants, all except two participants reported that family therapy had been effective in helping to restore body weight and resume normal eating. The therapeutic process enhanced the psychological well-being of the afflicted young people and their parents, reduced the frequency and intensity of family conflicts (in particular conflicts arising from eating and food), and increased mutual concern and mutual understanding among family members on the basis of which family cohesion was fostered.

The suggestions made by the participants on ways to improve the clinical practice confirmed the therapist's beliefs that families in the face of the disorder have diverse needs and difficulties. The therapist has to be versatile and flexible in providing treatment in terms of the time, frequency, format, and intervention strategies.

For the better educated and more resourceful families, support and broadening their perspectives in appraising their problems and family situations seem to work well. For families with less education and fewer resources, active advice and health education are more useful. Families with different circumstantial needs call for the therapist to be flexible in assuming different roles: as a facilitator, an advisor, and an educator.

The collective voices of these parents tell us that empowerment is not a unitary concept: Different approaches are necessary in responding to their different needs. Nevertheless, empowerment always starts with the parents feeling supported, which would help to lift their worry, anxiety, and hopelessness and reduce their strong sense of culpability. Besides support and advice, parents also appreciated the opportunity to share their pain and suffering with the emaciated daughter. On hearing this, the daughter would begin to realize that she was not the only victim; her parents' suffering could be just as intense and unbearable. This would serve as common ground for them to join hands in fighting AN.

This study provides preliminary evidence to support the effectiveness of the selected family treatment model to drive away the disorder, to restore the well-being of the emaciated young people and the parents, to empower the parents' coping, and to improve family relationships. More empirical work is needed to assess its effectiveness and efficacy.

Perceived Treatment Efficacy of Family Therapy From the Perspective of the Therapist and the Families and Concluding Remarks

INTRODUCTION

The clients' voices and reports of their subjective experience provide invaluable information for improving clinical practice, but the therapist's own reflections are important as well. Synthesis from the clinical experience can provide answers to the following questions: How did family therapy effect changes for the emaciated young people and the families? Which skills and techniques were more useful? Who had benefited most from family treatment? Who did not respond to treatment?

Family therapy is a matter of choices rather than a matter of truth (Minuchin, Nichols, & Lee, 2007). It calls for the therapist to choose among different alternatives in the use of language, metaphors, knowledge, skills, and techniques. Such a choice must be guided by theory, and the theoretical knowledge as reported in the literature is predominantly based on experience in Western societies. Given that family therapy is inevitably intertwined with the culturally specific concept of family and its actual manifestation (in aspects such as the typical composition of those living under one roof and their expected roles), it is all the more important to draw from this study insights that may have specific relevance to Chinese societies—whether in confirming the generalities of conclusions in the Western literature or in pointing to significant differences.

This concluding chapter examines the treatment efficacy of family therapy based on client feedback gathered from the posttreatment interviews,[14]

---

[14] The details of the clients' feedback are presented in Ma (2008).

with the details of the study described in chapter 11 and the therapist's reappraisal of her past clinical experiences.

PERCEIVED CHARACTERISTICS OF FAMILY THERAPY

The Clients' Voice

According to the perspective of the young people and the families, the therapeutic power of family therapy lies in its emphasis on the family as a unit of care. Conventional psychiatric treatment often comprises medical treatment and supportive work for individual patients. In contrast, family therapy takes care of the needs of the whole family. The shifted focus of care relieves the afflicted young person's sense of guilt and shame and addresses the psychosocial needs of different family members, including the young person, her parents, and her siblings.

One of the fathers narrated, "We dared not talk at home. She [the patient] is dying, but we dared not utter a word; nor were we courageous enough to bring up the subject at home. Here we can talk about our fears, our worries, and our helplessness. By bringing out the problem, we know where we were stunted."

The treatment provided them with a context to identify family problems, bring out hidden family conflicts, and utilize their own resources in conflict resolution.

The Therapist's Voice

The participants' perceptions of family therapy are interestingly compatible with the fundamental assumptions of the treatment model, specifically beliefs on family self-healing abilities, reciprocal interaction between the symptoms of the disorder and family relationships, and the context-based treatment focus.

The advantage of family therapy is that it requires the therapist to meet the whole family and work hand in hand with them. Generally speaking, Chinese families are reserved to seek help from mental health services (Tseng, Lin, & Yeh, 1995). They prefer keeping their family affairs behind closed doors. The Chinese translation of *family therapy* (家庭治療) can unfortunately imply that the family is pathological and unfortunately reinforces their ambivalence in seeking help. Once they understand that family therapy is to help them resolve their own problem rather than to fix their pathology, most of them would attend treatment regularly and actively. Besides the life-threatening nature of the disorder, family members have their need to share the pain and suffering too. Family treatment provides such a venue for them to fulfill such a need.

WHAT MADE CHANGES POSSIBLE

The Clients' Voices

The participants described graphically how the therapist had facilitated changes, through both indirect and direct maneuvers.

Indirect therapeutic maneuvers included (a) creating a holding and secure therapeutic context for problem solving in the family, (b) encouraging voices of different family members to be heard and allowing for multiple realities to emerge for an identified event, and (c) developing a therapeutic context conducive to change for the youth and the family, such as enacting the family drama and suggesting reenacting the family drama in a constructive way.

Direct interventions consisted of teaching, guidance, advice, and suggestions. For instance, the therapist provided guidance for the parents on the developmental needs of a growing child, especially her need for greater psychological space and autonomy; the therapist suggested stopping the destructive pattern of interaction and firmly requested that they respond to one another differently.

Among all these treatment strategies, the young people and the families found that the environment that allows expression of different views was very useful. Different voices provide enlightenment and inspiration and highlight the multiple perspectives in real life. They had better understanding of each other and could identify new possibilities to resolve their difficulties. They gradually perceived their active role in problem solving.

Both the afflicted young person and the family members indicated that the therapist's empathy, care, acceptance, and sincerity were crucial to motivating the ambivalent young person to participate actively in treatment and to attain recovery. Feeling understood, supported, and trusted, the emaciated young person began to be more cooperative and permitted the therapist to reach her inner resources and strengths.

The Therapist's Voice

Therapeutic beliefs. Three therapeutic beliefs are clinically instrumental in engagement and treatment. First is the therapist's nonblaming attitude toward the afflicted young person and her family. Second, while acknowledging the power of sociocultural forces in shaping an individual, the therapist believes that each human being is in turn also an active agent shaping himself or herself and also society. He or she has the free will to change or remain unchanged. Third, the therapeutic belief that there is a healthy side of the patient that will ultimately defeat the pathology is extremely powerful. These beliefs offer hope to young person and her family and make it easier for the therapist to deal with the therapeutic impasse, to face resistance and rejection, and to stay with the emotional intensity arising from the family conflicts.

Therapeutic skills and techniques. Among the different therapeutic skills and techniques, the arts of questioning, enactment, and reframing are most pertinent to effective assessment and treatment. Asking the right questions at the right time on the basis of the information given by the young person and the family would gradually help to shift their perspective of the problem from an individual frame to a relational frame.

Two types of questions are useful for assessment, namely circular questions (Penn, 1982) and hypothetical questions (Stierlin & Weber, 1989). The former, developed by the Milan School (Cecchin, 1987), aim at mapping out the family relations without intrusion and disrespect, while the latter open options and alternatives for future action. Examples of circular questions include the following: Who is the first one to discover the young person's disorder? Who is her best friend in this family? What would dad do when Ling threw temper? Examples of hypothetical questions include the following: Suppose you (the patient) have recovered, how should your sister behave to make you believe that she no longer treats you as a crazy person? Suppose you are now stronger than before, how are you going to face sexual harassment from your classmates? Suppose you had already defeated AN, what would be your life goal?

Besides letting the therapist understand the crux of the problem, effective use of questioning would assist the young person and the family to examine their problems in a new light, thereby increasing their possibilities in making changes. Questioning is not only a process of exploration but also a process of reframing, through which the same event or person can be understood from a different perspective.

Unlike the classical structural family approach, it was not a standardized treatment protocol for the therapist to arrange a lunch session (Fishman, 2006; Minuchin, Rosman, & Baker, 1978) to elicit the family drama evolving around eating during mealtime. Some of the young people disliked having meals with the therapist present. The therapist usually respects their wishes, but if the body weight were to continue to drop, the therapist would insist on arranging a lunch session, but with an explanation: She needs to assess why the parents fail to refeed the young person. With adequate explanation, the young person and the family would follow the professional advice without great resistance. To the young person and the family, a lunch session can be profoundly intense, threatening, and unpleasant. Nevertheless, it is a golden opportunity for the therapist to induce a crisis for change and to identify a potential healer, if any, in the family; both are essential ingredients for change.

There is a caveat in conducting the lunch session: While one wishes to induce a strong sense of crisis, it is equally important to be supportive and empathetic. If not handled with care and genuine understanding, the lunch session can reinforce and escalate the power struggle between the parents and the young person. When they realize that food is the only medicine for the young person, the parents may become more forceful, which may be interpreted as parental control rather than as parental care.

In order to be effective, the therapist has to send dual messages persistently in the lunch session. To the young person, the therapist would say, "You may not realize how resistant your disorder is and you may not agree with my observation. You are definitely in need of your parents' help and assistance to defeat the disorder. Your parents need your consent before they can exercise the parental authority effectively." To the parents, the therapist would say, "I can see how difficult the situation you have to face. You too need to join hands to face it together. You need to explain to your daughter why both of you have to lend additional power and energy to her to fight with the disorder."

WHO BENEFITS MOST FROM FAMILY THERAPY?

The profiles of the recovered young people in our study show that family treatment benefits those young people with a shorter history of the illness and with supportive and high-functioning parents who have not much difficulty in career, marriage, health, or mental health.

Family treatment was also timely and a relief for those emaciated young people who had begun to experience the frightening effects of malnourishment, such as repeated and sudden coma or gross weakness of the limbs. An emaciated young person told the therapist, "I come to therapy because I don't want to die so young." Another young person was so weak that her father had to carry her on his back to meet the therapist. She narrated, "I have no choice but to follow your advice to stay home and eat and eat." The physical condition of this young person was the worst among all cases handled. However, she carried out what she promised and recovered steadily after 10 sessions because of her determination to recover and unconditional parental support.

Those emaciated young people failing to respond to family therapy have the following characteristics: They have a lot of psychological gain (e.g., false sense of achievement and peer recognition) from the disorder. They sense something went wrong with their health but are not unduly frightened or worried, as their physical weakness does not seem to them to be severe. If their parents also have personal difficulties in midlife such as facing job loss, a marital crisis, or poor health or mental health, then the task of engagement becomes even harder.

CHANGING SOCIETAL NORMS

One can see AN at two levels: first, the issue of beauty as defined by society standards and, second, underlying stresses that cause particular individual to succumb.

Social norms and expectations obviously play a significant part in the etiology and management of AN (MacSween, 1993). Some of these norms may be ridiculous when seen in the cold light of rationality, but this would not be apparent to the players enmeshed in drama itself. The story of women in China with bound feet (which is a horrible disfigurement) illustrates this point.

In the early twentieth century, China underwent a significant social reform. A group of liberal social reformers led by Kang Youwei (康有為) and Western missionaries strongly advocated abolishing foot binding in society, but the reform was met with fierce resistance. Unexpectedly, the strongest resistance came from women with bound feet, supposedly the victims of foot binding. They argued that their right to have bound feet had been violated. Foot binding was their individual choice, and the reformers should leave them alone (Ko, 2005).

This sentiment was well depicted by Feng Jicai (2002) in his novel *Three-Inch Golden Lotus* (三寸金蓮) when Xiang Lian (香蓮), the protagonist, together with other women with bound feet went on strike on the street, for the first time in their lives, against the free feet movement. Xiang Lian's strong response seemed to be understandable because she was able to become the fourth concubine of a rich merchant and gradually gained power in the family, predominantly because of her beautiful three-inch feet.

History tells of the difficulties involved in changing the beauty norms of society. Those educated and raised in modern society would expect that women with bound feet must have welcomed the free feet movement as liberation and emancipation. There would be no more pain and suffering for their daughters, who could walk, run, jump, and dance freely with normal and healthy feet. They themselves would no longer need to take care of their tiny feet to ensure that they looked as tender and erotic as a lotus. However, subjectively these women with bound feet perceived it differently. The bound feet symbolized beauty, status, and power in their family and society. For over five dynasties, Chinese women had learned since childhood that only young girls from rich and upper-class families could have the exclusive privilege of binding feet; the tiny lotus feet promised a good marriage and would win the approval of the in-laws and relatives after marriage.

The current norms of beauty, especially feminine beauty, are in many ways similar if taken to the extreme: (Excessive) thinness is valued and promoted, can be harmful, but is embraced by the victims themselves. The therapist's experience in working with the emaciated young people is similar to experiences of the liberal and humanistic Chinese social reformers and Western missionaries whose beliefs and advocacy were at odds with the societal norm toward beauty at that time. The greatest difficulty experienced is the resistance and ambivalence of the emaciated young people toward recovery. Their rationale for remaining emaciated is persuasive and powerful—*our society cherishes fragility and thinness as the standard of beauty*. One adolescent girl once challenged the therapist and said, "No girl in this society likes to be fat and ugly. You are wasting your time."

It may well be that changes to social norms and values are better sought through social reforms at policy and institutional levels rather than through family therapy. In helping these young people, a family therapist has to be backed by a strong conviction that the current standard of beauty, that is, "thin is beautiful," is as toxic as the beauty standard imposed by those fetishistic kings, members of the gentry, and rich merchants in ancient China. The therapist needs to believe in the diversity and variability of beauty, which is subjectively defined and varies according to different body shapes, heights, ages, and ethnic groups; such a belief could be shared with the afflicted young person honestly, if asked. The therapist's response is, "I would join hands with you in pursuing beauty—which can take different forms—but not at the expense of jeopardizing your health and endangering your life." The young person would initially respond to such honest sharing with puzzlement, bewilderment and disbelief, followed later by relief and a warm welcome. As recalled by a young person, "At least there is a common goal between us, namely the pursuit of beauty."

One needs to go beyond therapy to understand whether society has provided sufficient opportunities for young people to develop their sense of personal effectiveness, to enhance their self-esteem, and to develop competence in different aspects of life. Like peeling an onion layer by layer, the pursuit of beauty is usually the most frequently cited reason for self-starvation at the beginning of treatment. Further exploration reveals that these emaciated young people have been suffering from a strong sense of personal ineffectiveness, a lower sense of mastery, and poor self-esteem. They are also under multiple stresses arising from ingrained family conflicts, study pressures, and relationship difficulty with peers. Excessive dieting and reduced body weight have unfortunately provided them with a false sense of achievement, mastery, power, and status; hence any therapeutic endeavor in helping them recover is bound to meet with ambivalence, resistance, and, at its worst, even apathy.

CONCLUDING REMARKS

The therapist's experiences of helping young people suffering from AN and at the same time engaging in cross-disciplinary research are highly facilitative and mutually beneficial. Clients are indeed the best authors of their life experience. A client-driven approach (Moustakas, 1994) was adopted for this study, which allowed the emergence of the clients' subjective experiences and life stories in different stages of treatment.

The results of the pretreatment qualitative interviews assisted the therapist to understand problems and needs of the emaciated young people and their families. As the themes of control, power struggle, maturity, and fear repeatedly emerged from narratives of different emaciated young people, the therapist's sensitivity in picking up these psychological issues gradually heightened; this helped in establishing an emotional connection with the young person quickly and perceptively. Even though from time to time the therapist was lost in treatment, she could muddle through for a while, tolerate the uncertainty and ambiguity, and finally go back to work on the core issues. Involving the three postgraduate students as cotherapists in treatment was a very fruitful experience; their fresh mind and their sharp observation enriched my understanding of the young person and her family.

Despite the limitations of the study, the preliminary findings of this study are encouraging and promising, suggesting that family therapy should be incorporated as an integral part of services for Chinese emaciated young people and their families. We have no excuse to deprive them of such a good service.

Appendices

Appendix 1
Voices of the Chinese Emaciated Young People

INTRODUCTION

In working with the Chinese emaciated youth, the author was struck by their relentless pursuit of thinness, to paraphrase what Hilde Bruch (1973) typically described, and their stubborn resistance to change despite the anguish they were suffering from, their highly restrictive social life, and the turmoil that the whole family experienced. As uttered by a 21-year-old young adult woman in a pretreatment interview, "My eating is grossly pathological. Normal people would not eat like this. However, another side of me does not wish to become normal. I don't know why." The harder the parents pressed her to take in food, the more obstinate she felt in going on a diet. Repeated persuasion and threats were futile. Family conflicts were escalating, and nothing seemed to work for the patient and the family. They all got trapped in an interlocking helpless and hopeless situation.

While recognizing the function of psychiatric diagnosis to identify, classify, and categorize different disordered eating, one has to be cautious of its limitation as a therapeutic tool. A psychiatric diagnosis informs us of nothing about the patient as a "person" in his or her immediate sociocultural context or of his or her individual experiences. For instance, how does the patient experience anorexia nervosa (AN) existentially? In the eyes of the patient, what are the pain and suffering brought about by food refusal? Despite the pain and suffering, why does the patient refuse to change and choose to continue self-starving? What are the forces, both intrapsychic and interpersonal, maintaining self-starvation?

In comparison to the biomedical-based disorders such as schizophrenia, the therapeutic purpose of psychiatric diagnosis is less significant in psychogenic disorders such as AN because drug treatment has little use in curing

(Devlin & Walsh, 1995; Lock, Le Grange, Agras, & Dare, 2001; Palazzoli, 1985). The therapeutic purpose of understanding the subjective experience of the patients and their families is greater than prescribing a psychiatric label. A psychiatric label, if exercised inappropriately, can be a dehumanizing experience. The stigmatization of mental illnesses may reinforce the patients' sense of inadequacy and increase their sense of deviancy. An understanding of the patients' subjective experience would help the therapist to appreciate the difficulties and struggles faced by these young people and to learn about their needs and concerns, which in turn may open up possibilities and shed light on the formulation of treatment goals and strategies.

In contrast to the biomedical model and its empirical epistemology, social constructionists denounce the existence of universal truth and reality in human behavior, which to a great extent is shaped by the history, culture, and values of a society. Knowledge is subjective and inductive rather than objective and reductionistic in nature; knowledge is the result of social interactions, created and recreated through languaging (Laird, 1995). Realities are multiple. There is a shift of concern from discovering the facts as such to understanding the subjective experiences of individuals and families and from playing an expert role to adopting a role of an anthropologist whose genuine curiosity and openness allow him or her to listen to the stories and experiences expressed.

In view of the cultural difference between the East and the West, documenting the subjective experience of the emaciated young people is important, as it provides us with rich information on how self-starvation may be shaped and reinforced by the unique family context as well as by the sociocultural forces of society.

In this appendix, the author reports on the subjective experiences, both positive and negative, of 35 Chinese patients diagnosed with AN, and those of their families, based on the narratives that emerged from the pretreatment in-depth interviews. Implications for clinical practice are discussed at the end of this appendix.

LITERATURE REVIEW

Western Studies

Until the late 1980s, Western researchers had seldom paid serious attention to the patients' subjective views of self-starvation. There are six studies identified in this area, with two on perceived causes (Beresin, Gordon, & Herzog,

1989; Tozzi, Sullivan, Fear, McKenzie, & Bulik, 2003), five on factors relating to recovery (Beresin et al., 1989; Garrett, 1996; Hsu, Crisp, & Callender, 1992; Rorty, Yager, & Rossotto, 1993; Tozzi et al., 2003), and one on patients' attitudes toward the illness (Serpell, Treasure, Teasdale, & Sullivan, 1999). Investigators of all these studies believed that patients were experts of their illness and would be in the best position to inform mental health professionals about their experiences. Participants in all these studies, except one (Serpell et al., 1999), had recovered from this disorder. The number of patients participating in these studies ranged from 13 (Beresin et al., 1989) to 69 (Tozzi et al., 2003). Five studies (Beresin et al., 1989; Garrett, 1996; Hsu et al., 1992; Rorty et al., 1993; Tozzi et al., 2003) made use of in-depth interviews in data collection, while Serpell et al. (1999) invited patients ($n = 18$) to write a letter to their disorder as a friend and then as the enemy.

As indicated by the results of two studies (Beresin et al., 1989; Tozzi et al., 2003), the patients' perceptions of their family were quite negative. Family conflicts and family dysfunction were perceived as major factors contributing to the onset of self-starvation, while weight loss, dieting, pressures, and stresses were frequently cited as the perceived causes as well. Before the onset of the illness, patients had experienced life transitions such as change of school, loss of good friends, or separation from family.

In Beresin et al.'s (1989) study, participants perceived the process of recovering as a process of self-acceptance, while patients of Garrett's (1996) study viewed it as a form of spiritual quest that required connection with oneself, connection with others, and connection with the natural worlds or the cosmos. Having accepted themselves, the patients found it more capable to tolerate anger and resentment, particularly toward the mother. Patients in Rorty et al.'s (1993) study were determined to drive away the illness when they were too fed up with the disorder and desired a better life. Empathic and caring relationships with others (whether therapists, peers, or important persons in the young woman's life) were facilitative to the patients' recovery. Participants in Tozzi et al.'s (2003) study also listed a supportive relationship or a partner, maturation, and therapy as three essential factors accounting for recovery, suggesting the promising role played by interpersonal relationships in the cure of self-starvation.

Patients' sense of loss subsequent to the recovery as AN had functioned as "protective armor" for not growing up and being independent (Beresin et al., 1989). The results of Serpell et al. (1999) had shown that patients had positive and negative views of the disorder. Patients perceived it as helping them to feel safe, being looked after, and being protected; making them feel more attractive; allowing them to feel in control or giving structure to their lives; increasing their confidence; allowing them to avoid uncomfortable emotions; and finally giving them a feeling of being different, special, or even superior to others. However, patients were constantly upset by the thought of food or feeling controlled by food. They lost friends and relationships and experienced a sense of being taken over by the illness.

All the above studies have made significant contributions to the field as they have attempted to understand patients' subjective experiences of the disorder and recovery. Being sensitive to the power disparity between patients and the researcher, these researchers employed different means such as letter writing, autobiographic accounts, and in-depth interviews to elicit the patients' stories as nonintrusively as possible. However, despite their contributions, these studies' focus was patient centered. The views of the afflicted family were overlooked. As supportive family relationships play a significant role in recovery, hearing the families' voices and attempting to understand their experiences are important too. With the exception of one study (Serpell et al., 1999), the participants were recovered patients recalling their past experiences. The retrospective effects due to memory loss might bias the data of these studies.

Local Studies

Local studies on AN can be roughly grouped into four types. The first type focuses on the diagnosis and symptoms of AN (e.g., Lee, 1993; Lee, Ho, & Hsu, 1993). For instance, Lee pointed out in his study that Chinese patients might not necessarily suffer from fat phobia, whilst nonfat phobia was as common as fat phobia in the clinical presentation. The second type focuses on the study of the public attitude toward body satisfaction and body shape (e.g., Lee, 1997; Lee, Leung, Lee, Leung & Yu, 1995). For example, an attempt was made to compare secondary school students' perception of body satisfaction and body shape among three Chinese societies, namely Hong Kong, Shenzhen, and rural Hunan (Lee & Lee, 2000). The results of this study indicated that eating disorders were related to the degree of Western acculturation in society. The third type focuses on assessing the psychometric properties of measures developed in the West, such as the Eating Disorder Inventory, for their reliability and validity in Chinese societies (e.g., Lee, Lee, Leung, & Yu, 1997). The fourth type was undertaken by our research team to explore and identify the meanings of self-starvation and food in Chinese societies (e.g., Ma & Chan, 2003; Ma, Chow, Lee, & Lai, 2002). Despite these contributions, there has been insufficient attention given to identifying the subjective experiences of the patients and their families.

SOCIOCULTURAL CONTEXT OF HONG KONG

Since the 1950s, Hong Kong, a former British colony, has been transformed from a small fishing village into an economically affluent and modernized city with a population of approximately 7 million, of which 97% are Chinese. The overall GDP per capita in 2002 was US$24,460 (Hung, 2001, p. 37), which is the highest compared with other major cities in Mainland China.

At the beginning of the 1980s, Hong Kong was affected by political uncertainty brought about by the resumption of sovereignty by the People's Republic of China in 1997, by the economic downturn due to the Asian financial crisis in 1989, and by the economic restructuring after the Open Door Policy on the Mainland. Following the economic downturn was a surge in unemployment. The unemployment rate increased from 2.2% in 1997 to 8.8% in July 2003 and dropped to 5.4% in October 2005, while underemployment climbed from 1.1% in 1997 to 4.2% in July 2003 (Hong Kong SAR Government, 2005).

In the midst of all this, social change has also led to a reduced birth rate and a decrease in family size. According to the 2001 census, the average household size dropped from 3.4 in 1991 to 3.3 in 1996 and then to 3.1 in 2001; a typical family comprises the parents and one or two children (Hong Kong SAR Government, 2001).

Parents in Hong Kong have become more child centered than the previous generation, spending more time and effort in looking after their children, paying special attention to their academic performance that symbolizes achievement and success. The increasing educational opportunities and a powerful influence of the mass media have exposed our younger generation to the Westernized lifestyle and values of individualism, independence, and autonomy. Unsurprisingly, they have also embraced the Western standard of beauty, that is, slimness and thinness, as an ideal body shape and body image. Current local studies (Lee, 1993; Leung, Lam, & Chan, 2001) have shown that body dissatisfaction is common among university students and secondary school students. This may partly account for the rising number of eating disorders in adolescent girls and young adults.

To search for more culture-specific factors, however, a closer look at the characteristics of the Chinese family and the stresses and tensions that have surfaced in the past decade is necessary.

CHARACTERISTICS OF CHINESE FAMILIES
AND THEIR LINKAGE TO AN

The family is the fundamental social unit in the Chinese society. It is of paramount concern for Chinese families to maintain harmonious interpersonal relationships and to establish social order in society—a cardinal value embedded in the Chinese mind from the teachings of Confucianism and Taoism (Chen, 2002). Apart from the use of nonconfrontational language, a harmonious relationship is promoted and conflict can be avoided through coping strategies such as self-restraint and self-discipline, indirect expression of disapproval, saving face for counterparts, reciprocity, and an emphasis on particularistic relationships (Chen, 2002, p. 14). It is a norm rather than an exception for Chinese families to sweep their conflicts under the carpet and to attribute the misgivings, accusations, and social or personal faults to the patient and the presenting symptoms, in this instance self-starvation. As compliance and conformity constitute the rule, adolescent rebellious behaviors and individuation are perceived as threats to the parents' authority and as chaos upsetting the family harmony.

Filial piety is another governing ethical principle being passed on from one generation to another. Chinese children and adolescents are familiar with the first cardinal rule from *Xiao Jing*, the Classic of Filial Piety: "Your body with your hair and your skin is a gift from your parents. You must treasure this gift to be filial" (*Xiao Jing*, first chapter, trans. James Legge, retrieved April 1, 2004, from http://members.tripod.com/wckfc_library/xiaojing. htm). To the self-starving Chinese adolescents, this teaching can be a cultural resource in treatment and would be an impetus driving them to recover; yet it can also be a legitimate excuse for parents to tighten their control over their emaciated child.

In the traditional Chinese patriarchal culture, individuation of adolescent girls from the family is constrained structurally and culturally. Women in Chinese societies are expected to be submissive and subordinate and to subjugate to the will of the father, the husband, and the son in their three different life stages as an unmarried daughter, as a wife, and as a widowed mother, respectively (Pearson & Leung, 1995). Salaff (1998) found in her qualitative study that daughters of lower-class Chinese families would give up their educational opportunities and work instead in order to support the family and their brother's education. With increasing educational attainment and participation in employment, however, young people in modern Hong Kong have become better educated and have more freedom in the pursuit of their careers in comparison to those of their mothers' generation (Westwood, Mehrain, & Cheung, 1995). Nevertheless, their personal development and identity are subtly tied down by the ideal womanhood and motherhood socially constructed by Chinese culture. Adolescent girls may be torn between two opposing cultural forces from the East and the West being submissive, loyal, and self-sacrificing to the family interest on the one hand and being independent, autonomous, and individualistic on the other. This often leads to a sense of anomie or alienation, not knowing where to turn in the process of growth and development.

OUR RESEARCH

Partly influenced by a belief that AN is context dependent and is better understood when examined within its sociocultural context and partly driven by the author's curiosity to know whether family treatment is equally effective for Chinese AN patients and their families, we started a research project titled "Evaluation of the Effectiveness of Structural Family Therapy for Chinese Patients Suffering from Anorexia Nervosa in Hong Kong" 4 years ago, in collaboration with an adult psychiatrist and a child psychiatrist of the Department of Psychiatry of our university, with the aim to evaluate the treatment effectiveness of the selected family treatment approach in helping Chinese AN patients and their families.

Data Collection

As part of the study, intensive pretreatment interviews were conducted to identify family expectations toward treatment and their needs and difficulties. The entire family was interviewed in the pretreatment interview to elicit the family experiences. A Ph.D. candidate with training in nursing and social work helped to conduct the pre- and posttreatment interviews, using interview guides (see appendices 3 and 4). We advised the research assistant to follow the flow of the families' narratives and stories closely rather than following the interview guide rigidly, in the belief that patients and families are the best authors of their life experiences.

Sociodemographic Profiles of the Participants

A total of 35 patients and their families participated in this part of the study, with 27 adolescents and 8 young adults, all suffering from AN. The family was taken as the unit of study.

The mean age at onset for the adolescent girls ($n = 27$) was 13 ($SD = 1.7$). The mean age at referral was 14 ($SD = 1.5$). For the young adults ($n = 8$), the mean age of onset was 18.5 ($SD = 2.1$). The mean age at referral was 23.4 ($SD = 7.7$). The mean body mass index (BMI) of the adolescent girls at referral was 14.9 ($SD = 2.2$), while the BMI of the young adults at referral was 13.9 ($SD = 1.8$). Out of the 27 adolescent girls, 3 studied in Grade 6 in primary school, 13 studied in junior secondary, 10 studied in senior secondary, and 1 studied in college. Of the adult group, 5 patients (62.5%) from were college students, while 3 (37.5%) were students at the matriculation level.

The mean family size of the adolescent girls was 4.1, while the mean family size of young adults was 2.8. A total of 6 adolescents came from single-parent families, as a result of either the death of the father or the divorce of their parents; 1 patient was brought up in a three-generation family, while 20 others came from nuclear families. As for the young adults, 7 came from nuclear families and 1 from a blended family with a stepfather. The monthly family income of these families (mean of adolescent girls = HK$26,372.00; mean of young adults = HK$30,250.00) was higher than the general average household income of HK$18,705.00 in Hong Kong (Hong Kong SAR Government, 2001). Among the 27 adolescent girls and their families, 4 (14.8%) relied on a welfare subsidy provided by the Hong Kong SAR Government.

Data Analysis

A research assistant, who was a master's student in social work and had no direct involvement in treatment, helped to transcribe the pretreatment interviews verbatim in Chinese, and the author translated the Chinese script into English, going through the English version many times to ensure accuracy in translation. The author coded the transcripts of the pretreatment interviews and grouped them into a number of categories for comparison and for extraction of major themes for analysis. The author developed the codes by (a) going through the transcripts of the family interviews and marking units that were related to the same topic (e.g., effects of AN on the patient), (b) dividing them into topics (e.g., positive and negative effects of AN on physical health, psychological well-being and schooling), and (c) dividing them into subtopics (e.g., mother–daughter conflicts around eating and developmental issues, father–daughter conflicts around eating, developmental issues) (Miles & Huberman, 1994).

The following paragraphs describe the effects of AN on these young people's health, schooling, and psychological well-being. Its effects on family relations are described in appendix 2. In order to protect the privacy of these patients and their families, all their identifiable personal data have been either modified or deleted. The author uses pseudonyms in the presentation of the results of this qualitative study.

SUBJECTIVE EXPERIENCE OF THE PARTICIPANTS

Negative Consequences of AN

AN has negatively affected different aspects of the patient's life: (a) the body, (b) schooling, (c) psychological well-being, and (d) family relations.

Effects on the body. Rebecca, a 19-year-old adolescent girl who started dieting after constipation, narrated, "I dared not eat much as I feared that it would worsen my constipation. After dieting, whenever I took in food, I felt my stomach bloating. The more severe my stomach bloated, the less food I dared to take in. The problem of my constipation worsened and my menstruation stopped two years ago. Gradually I didn't feel hungry at all."

Nearly all of the patients reported that they had no appetite or feelings of hunger. However, their eating could be out of control at other times. A 17-year-old adolescent girl reported, "I have a fruit for lunch. I don't have appetite at lunch. When I return home, it is different. I eat a lot. I could eat 10 pieces of breads ceaselessly. I could hardly control myself and my head is full of the images of food. Sometimes, I get out of bed to search for food during the middle of the night."

A few patients practiced bingeing and purging. Stephanie, a 20-year-old young woman, said, "Sometimes after eating, I can't control myself. I continue eating and eating. I can't stop even though I am already very full. I don't know if it is purging. However, I can manage it without eating for a whole day. I don't feel hungry."

Patients suffered from loss of hair, which was brought about by nutritional deficits. In response to her 16-year-old sister Anna's fear of losing more hair, the second elder sister said, "I told her that her hair had become thinner and thinner. She argued back that my hair was as thin as hers." The eldest brother echoed, "The floor was full of her hair." Her mother had divorced her husband 10 years ago. Being a dual-career mother, she had to work and take care of the family and her three children single-handedly. The involvement of her ex-husband in child care was minimal. He visited them only twice per month, usually on weekends.

Most of these patients found they lacked energy and had concentration and mobility difficulties. They would easily fall asleep in class and could not follow what had been taught. A 14-year-old adolescent with a body weight of 39 kg at a height of 162 cm, Ann, narrated, "I can't run around as much as I wish. Walking up a few more steps on the stairs is impossible. It's impossible to sleep late. I feel tired easily. I can't stay out for long shopping. I don't have energy even though I wish to do it well. But I am unhappy when I begin to gain weight."

The mobility of a 17-year-old patient, Josephine, was greatly affected by the severe drop of her body weight. She had been self-starving for 4 years after being teased by a close relative for being fat. At referral, the body weight of Josephine had dropped from 47 kg to 25 kg at a height of 145 cm. Her father had to carry her on his back to the pretreatment interview, as she was physically too weak to walk up five flights of stairs to the university treatment center to meet the research assistant.

Lily was a 14-year-old adolescent who had a severe drop of body weight from 50 kg at a height of 162 cm to 29.6 kg after being rejected by her peers at summer school. Her mother recalled, "She broke her leg during a trip to the Mainland. We consulted the bonesetter. He refused to treat her and strongly advised us to send her to the hospital. The medical staff admitted her immediately. On the second day of her hospitalization, she was suddenly in a coma and needed complete bed rest." Lily's story indicated that AN in its serious form can be critical and fatal. Crisis intervention in terms of hospitalization, despite its drawbacks, is the only alternative for patients like Lily whose body weight has dropped quickly and severely within a short period of time.

Effects on schooling. Before the onset of AN, these young people were achievers at school. The performance of a few patients was exceptionally outstanding. Their academic performance deteriorated after emaciation, and their concentration was affected. Their energy level was low.

Winnie told her story: "I changed to a new school in F 6. It is a new school and I don't like it. I slept in class. I felt tired and slept on the desk. I couldn't follow what the teacher said in class." Winnie had already stopped studying at the time of referral. Another adolescent girl said, "My academic record dropped 200 marks last term. I can't concentrate at all. I am thinking of food and there's only food on my mind. I can't listen to any word uttered by my teacher in class."

Repeated hospitalizations interrupted schooling for these adolescents and young adults. Five adolescents had been hospitalized three times before being referred to the author for family treatment. Parents of a 12-year-old adolescent girl, Mary, were strongly advised by the psychiatrist to seek family treatment on her third relapse. Mary suffered from AN at the age of 10 when she was a Primary 4 pupil. Her body weight dropped to 29 kg at a height of 145 cm. When she was admitted, she was forced to stop school. Although Mary continued her education at a hospital-based school, the service was not equivalent to the learning experiences provided by her own school. As in the case of Lily, the repeated hospitalizations forced her to repeat her study. This had become totally unacceptable to Lily and her parents as she was one of the best students in class. Lily viewed that the worst part of her illness was that she could not study in school.

Tension and stress in studying contributed to the onset of AN. Jane's mother narrated, "She [Jane] ate less and less during her second year at university. She spent all her time and energy studying. She kept saying that she had no time for meals."

Besides the academic pressure, relationship problems with peers in school was another perceived cause of self-starvation. Stephanie, a 20-year-old adolescent girl who moved into the university dormitory in her first year at university narrated, "My roommate rejected me. She didn't chat with me. She turned her back against me when she came back from class. I felt very unhappy and lonely on campus." In replying to whether this related to her food refusal problem, the patient replied, "Yes."

A mother of a 14-year-old adolescent girl, Lily, recalled, "She started having eating problem last May. She didn't get along well with her classmates. She expressed her anger by not eating. In July she spent her summer holidays overseas in a summer school. At the end of her trip, I picked her up from the airport. I was shocked in meeting her. She was thin and pale. She told me that her classmates rejected her in summer school and she lost her appetite there." The research assistant asked, "Can you tell me what had made you so unhappy in summer school?" Lily explained, "I have friends in summer school. Five of us are good friends. However, my four friends often played together and left me alone in the school."

Psychological distress. As described by most of the parents, the previously obedient, nice daughter had become a "monster" after emaciation, characterized by unpredictable outbursts of temper tantrum and fluctuating moods. Parents were frightened, angry, worried, and helpless. These adolescents and young adults were confused and felt strange about such change.

A mother of a 20-year-old young adult woman, Nancy, said, "As a matter of fact, Nancy was a good girl. The problem was her emotions. When she threw her temper tantrums, I couldn't stand it. She banged her head on the walls. She hit herself. Being a mother, I felt extremely bad to see my little daughter keep injuring herself."

Ann's mother narrated, "Ann can be very scary. A week ago after taking in a whole plate of food, she said that she felt anguish. She dashed straight out onto the road. We were alarmed and shivered."

Patients started to suspect that something must have gone wrong psychologically with their sudden temper outbursts. Winnie was one of them. She narrated, "I feel that something must be wrong with me. I threw temper tantrums frequently. I must have suffered from a psychiatric problem and I asked the doctor to refer me to see a psychologist." She explained further, "I came into conflict with my family easily. After quarreling, I would blow up. I couldn't stop at all. I threw away things that were lying around. I banged against the wall. I hit the table hard. I couldn't calm down. I was very upset. I couldn't breathe. I was out of control."

May, a 20-year-old college student with a food refusal problem, and her parents stated that their main concern was not May's own health but the health of her eldest sister who had a 2-year history of self-starvation before May's onset. May said her eldest sister's emaciation was more serious than her disorder and was in greater need of professional help. May said, "Her [the eldest sister's] temper was the worst in our family. Last night she threw away the rubbish bin. There were a few small decorations on top of the piano. She threw them all away." In the past, May's parents were hesitant to seek professional help because they feared that in doing so it would affect their eldest daughter's career. The most urgent problem of the family was the psychological distress of the eldest daughter. They wished that the therapist could help to resolve this urgent problem. If resolved, May's problem could be tackled as she modeled herself after her eldest sister.

These young people were reported to have depressive moods, negative self-perceptions, and distorted worldviews. The mother of a 21-year-old young adult woman with a 7-year history of the illness said, "She [her daughter] needs help to lift up her mood and to change her distorted thought. There is something wrong with her way of thinking. She tends to think negatively."

A 12-year-old adolescent whose body weight had dropped to 31 kg at a height of 143 cm cut her wrist to relieve her misery after family conflicts. She jumped up and yelled at other family members when they talked loudly. She misinterpreted, thinking that they were scolding her.

In appearance, these young people impressed the author as obstinate, rigid, and narrow-minded. They were resistant to hearing views that were in contrast to their own views. Beneath their hostility was the persistent self-doubt about their own judgment and value. They were passive and timid in defending their own interests and voicing their own needs.

Jane admitted that she did care about how other people see her, especially the perceptions of her parents. She said in tears, "Yes, I do mind very much. I am not good at anything. Yes, in every aspect. It is a feeling. I feel that they look down on me. I can't do anything well. Yes, almost everything." Jane repeated "everything" three times in the pretreatment interview. Her self-doubt and her lack of self-confidence did not match with her past excellent academic performance at the university. Even though Jane could feel the love of her parents, she was unsure if she had fulfilled their expectations and had done her best to please them.

Psychological Gains of AN

Despite the negative effects, these young people and their families reported psychological gains from this disorder, namely a false sense of control and increasing parental concern.

Ann's father narrated, "Dr. X [the psychiatrist] said that she [Ann] wished to accomplish a lot. But she found that in reality she couldn't control what would be happening. Not many people can have full mastery of life. She wished to get full marks on her studies and that's impossible. She can't control that. What she can control is only her body weight." Ann replied, "That's partially true. I can't control my studies. That's true. My academic performance generally is very good but I'm weak in a few subjects. I do mind performing poorly in these few subjects." Keeping fit and having a slim body shape were other reasons for Ann's dieting.

Lily's father said, "She's still quite resistant to increasing her body weight. Although she wishes to recover, she is caught in a conflict. Like fighting in a battle, on the one hand she likes being healthy. She treasures us and doesn't like to place an additional burden on us. On the other hand she has a psychological blockage. She is fearful of an increase of her body weight." Her mother said, "She told me that she wishes to have good health but she was in a dilemma. Her ambivalence is, she has experienced a lot of hardship in order to achieve her goal of losing weight. She has attained that. She doesn't want to give it up." Lily confessed at the end of the interview, "The most difficult part is that I succeeded with my strong will to lose weight in the past. I need to double my efforts to increase my body weight." Lily honestly admitted that she had not yet made up her mind to drive away AN.

Apart from the false sense of control, four adolescents (Lily, Jane, Stephanie, and Helen) reported feeling loved by their parents more after the onset of AN. They were pleased about the improvements to the mother–daughter relationship as well as the father–daughter relationship. These positive changes are described in chapter 5.

SUMMARY

From the perspective of the emaciated young people, with the onset of the AN they lost their sense of hunger, suffered from constipation, lost their menstruation, lost their hair, and had limited mobility. Paradoxically, when they took in food, they felt the stomach bloating, a body signal that had unfortunately reinforced their fear of resuming normal eating. The malnourishment brought with it the negative consequences of low energy level, poor concentration, and falling asleep easily, which in turn had seriously affected their study and their school performance. As most of these young people were achievers at school, their self-confidence and sense of competence were shattered or eroded with the deterioration of their academic performance. They were depressive and unpredictable, with great fluctuations in mood, sudden outbursts and temper tantrums, coupled with destructive behaviors such as banging one's head against the wall and hitting the table hard. One of the young people had already suspected she might be suffering from a mental disorder. Contrary to our expectations, a few vocal and expressive adolescent girls and young adult women viewed AN as their friend because they experienced a sense of false control and a sense of achievement in life, which undoubtedly explained their low motivation to seek recovery.

Finally, also revealed in the narratives were the perceived causes of excessive dieting that included constipation, academic pressure, poor peer relations, and pursuit of thinness; all these provided additional anecdotal evidence to support the fact that the etiology of AN is multifactorial.

Appendix 2
Voices of the Afflicted Families

INTRODUCTION

Jane's mother said, "The disorder not only affects her [Jane] but also our whole family. It affects our family badly." Another father moaned, "Yes, she suffers but our suffering is by no means less than her suffering." Ling's father said, "Her illness is the greatest blow that we've ever faced since our marriage. It is also the most difficult event we have to deal with in life." The voices of these three parents have illuminated the fact that our scope of understanding anorexia nervosa (AN) should be enlarged to include the family as a unit of attention and care.

The stories told by these families have demonstrated that AN affects the family atmosphere, increases family conflicts, worsens sibling relationships, changes parent–child relationships, and induces marital distress. However, the positive side of the disorder is that after its onset, parent–child and marital relations in these families improved. Four "absent" fathers, who had been fully occupied with work previously, adjusted their priorities in life and spent more time at home to share the problems with the spouse. Among all the family members, the well being of the mother was greatly affected.

FAMILY TENSION AND FAMILY CONFLICTS

The effects of AN on the family were most apparent during meals.[15] The family atmosphere was tense and unpleasant. The 5-year-old little brother of Mary, a 12-year-old girl who started dieting at the age of 10, said, "We usually quarreled during meals. She [his sister] kept scolding my mom and

---

[15] Some of the results of this qualitative study were published in Ma (2005).

dad. When I ate slowly, she scolded me too." The father agreed and said, "Yes, it's very tense." The mother added, "She stood next to me and closely monitored me when I put rice into her bowl. She scolded me when I put more. She scolded everyone in the family including the paternal grandma for cooking delicious food for her." As far as the mother could recall, Mary had never behaved like that. She changed only after emaciation.

Mealtime became a battlefield for these families. In Anna's family, the fight would usually start 20 minutes after dinner. Anna's mother described, "Usually my son would protest in silence, followed by me." The son explained, "I was too angry to eat." Anna protested and said, "You [the mom] were angry when I ate. You scolded me when I didn't eat. It's better for me not to eat." Anna's mother was a single parent who had been divorced from her husband for 10 years. As a custodial parent, she had to care for the three children without any assistance from her divorced husband. The father usually visited the children twice per month during weekends. Working on a full-time basis as a junior administrator, she had already stretched herself to the limit psychologically and physically, balancing the demands of parenting and work. She had no confidante to turn to for help. Anna's problem could be regarded as the straw that broke the camel's back. She not only worried about Anna's health but also felt for her eldest son and daughter. Anna forced them to eat more than they needed during mealtime. She blew up when they refused to follow suit.

May's eldest sister, a young professional who suffered from AN 2 years longer than May, deliberately came home late in order to avoid facing the family conflicts during dinner. She would wander around the shopping mall until 9:00 in the evening. May's mother narrated, "She doesn't wish to come home early. Having meals with May would usually end up having fights with her. Both of them only like vegetables. When she found out that May had taken her portion of food, she couldn't control herself." Her conflicts with the parents and May had been escalating since she lost approximately 14 kg after a rigorous diet in a short period of time. A physician had advised her to go on a diet because of her obesity and its detrimental effects on her health. She had taken the advice to the extreme.

Avoidance of family conflicts can create a situation as bad as what happened in Miranda's blended family. Miranda had been suffering from AN for 3 years at the time of referral. She had multiple records of shoplifting and had almost been committed to custodial care by court order, had her psychiatrist not rescued her. Miranda described her family situation: "We seldom talk among us. In the past we chatted with one another. After my mother married Uncle X, she became quiet and didn't like talking. Like Uncle X, she changed completely. We don't have fun together. We don't have any family day. I don't think our family looks like a family. Each of us takes care of our own business. When I returned home from school, I locked myself in my room. When Uncle X came home, he read the newspaper or watched TV, and so did mom." It was uncertain if this change was brought about by AN or by the remarriage of the mother. However, one could hardly dispute the fact that the communication blockage in her family was quite serious.

EFFECTS ON SIBLING RELATIONS

As revealed by the family stories of Mary, Anna, and May, AN unfavorably affected sibling relations. Previously good relationships had become strained, while unsatisfactory relationships got worse. The case of Stephanie throws light on this.

Stephanie's eldest sister narrated, "Our relationship was fine until she had this problem. I would tell her [Stephanie] my troubles. She seldom did so to me. She became impossible to relate to. Partly because she refused to talk to me and partly because I had my own concerns, I've given up chatting with her. She didn't respect me and she shouted at me. She didn't like going out with me." Stephanie's relationship with her eldest sister was competitive in nature. The eldest sister was the top student in school, and her academic performance was better than Stephanie's. Stephanie often felt like she was living under the shadow of her eldest sister. She was jealous of her eldest sister because she was the favorite child of the parents as well as the teachers. Stephanie's relationship with her youngest brother was even worse. Being the only son in a conservative Chinese family, her youngest brother was the spoiled child. Tearful and upset, Stephanie told her story: "He [her youngest brother] is violent. He beat me hard several times. He strangled my throat with his strong arms. I almost suffocated to death." The mother explained apologetically that her son was fed up and could not tolerate seeing Stephanie throw a temper tantrum in front of the parents for trivial things anymore. He wished to control himself but in vain. The mother was torn between the two when they fought with each other.

The healthy siblings felt left out by the parents who spent most of their time and energy on the afflicted adolescent.

Mrs. Y, the mother of a 14-year-old adolescent who had dropped her body weight to 39 kg at a height of 162 cm, said, "My youngest son had a problem too. He had a poor temper. Last Sunday he went to my room and talked to me. He told me that he was unhappy because I neglected him."

EFFECTS ON PARENT–CHILD RELATIONS

Negative Effects of AN on Parent–Child Relations

The young people's relationships with the parents and especially with the mother deteriorated, characterized by constant fights and quarrels. Their fights were usually around food and eating.

Miranda said, "I hate the food that my mom prepared. I don't like the way she prepares it. It's repulsive. Yes, very repulsive. When I was not around, she would deliberately put more oil into the food. I felt bad that she cooked only for me. Because of this, I chose not to take any meal prepared by her. I didn't eat at all and did it intentionally." The mother said, "Relating to her [Miranda] is difficult." Miranda explained enthusiastically, "My mom seemed to fail to see our problem. I feel that my mom doesn't know how to be a mother. Well, maybe because she has never been a daughter. She doesn't know the feeling of being a daughter. She doesn't try to understand my feelings, the feelings of her daughter."

Similar mother–daughter conflicts had occurred in Jane's family too. Jane's mother went to the market, bought a basket of Jane's favorite food, and prepared it for her. To her disappointment, Jane refused to take any. Jane said, "She [her mom] gave me a big scolding." The mother replied, "You are exaggerating but I really was very angry. She [Jane] once asked me not to force her to eat. I followed her suggestion but she didn't carry out her promise. The only way that works is to force her to eat." Jane said, "She [mom] has tried her best to help me. Yet I don't think she understands my illness, and I cannot accept her way of helping. My dad's way of treating me is better."

Ling, a 14-year-old adolescent whose body weight was 37 kg at a height of 160 cm at the time of referral, declared war on both parents after hospitalization by refusing to talk to them for almost 3 months. Ling's mother said, "Ever since we took her to consult the doctor, she refused to talk to us. She talked to every one in the family: the maid, her little brother, her grandma, and her grandpa, except to us." As interpreted by the mother, Ling felt that her parents no longer loved her and had dumped her in the hospital. Before the illness, Ling's relationship with both parents was good, especially her relationship with the father. The father recalled, "I played with her and her youngest brother. We all played together. Every night I told them bedside stories. Sometimes we behaved as children and fought for food together." The mother said, "When we were aware that she had become thinner and thinner, I asked her to eat more. From that time onward, we sensed the distance between us. She tended to avoid chatting with us." Ling's silence was extremely powerful. Her silence had maddened her parents and made them feel defeated, with a strong sense of powerlessness, helplessness, and hopelessness. Frustrated by Ling's apathy and deliberate silence, the couple kept paying hospital visits to their beloved daughter every day after work, hoping that a miracle would occur and Ling would break the ice and talk to them one day.

Josephine perceived her mother as her best friend in the family. Interestingly, in replying to a question on how many marks she would give to her mother–daughter relationship on a scale of 0 to 10, with 0 indicating the relationship as not good and 10 indicating the best, Josephine gave only 4. She explained, "I give 4 marks to describe our relationship because I force her to eat." Her mother was her only target. The mother's feelings came to light at the end of the pretreatment interview when she talked to her husband: "You [the husband] never know how horrible that 'monster' is. She forces me to eat." The mother used the metaphor of monster to describe Josephine's AN.

Positive Effects of AN on Parent–Child Relations

Four adolescents (Ann, Helen, Stephanie, Lily) reported improved mother–daughter relationships after the onset of the disorder. To the delight of these patients, their parents had become more concerned for them.

Ann said smilingly, "My mom loves me more because of the illness even though that's bad to win her love by being sick."

Helen narrated, "I feel that my mom loves me very much. She is generous and she knows how to analyze problems. After I had this illness, I had no friends. I often stayed at home. When I was unhappy, she taught me to cheer up. Of course, sometimes her view was different from mine. We argued and had bad times. Like most of the traditional mothers, she is nagging." Helen had been sick for 7 years and was repeatedly hospitalized. She stopped schooling and was socially isolated from her peers. It was sad that her mother had become her only "peer" in her life.

As disclosed by Stephanie, her relationship with her mother improved when her mother became aware of her problem. She was more willing to spend time with her and was more tolerant of her temper.

Lily's 19-year-old brother narrated, "She lost many things from this illness. She lost her learning opportunity, her friends, and her health. Yet she gained our love, our parents' love, and my love." The brother explained, "In the past we were not so concerned and worried less about her. Now we love and understand her more."

The same was applicable to the father–daughter relationship. Stephanie,

Jane, Lily, and Kelly reported positive changes in the father–daughter relationship.

Stephanie said that her father scolded her less, while Jane appreciated her father's increasing concern and love.

Jane's mother vividly described the change in the father–daughter relationship: "It [AN] made her dad concerned about her more. In the past, Papa only concentrated on work because the children had no problem. He felt relieved. Now both of them [Jane and her dad] are very close, both emotionally and communication-wise. This has never happened before." Jane's dad went to Jane's bedroom every night to see if she slept well. He usually returned home late before her illness because of his increased commitment to his business. He also accompanied her more, talked with her more patiently, tried to understand her problems, and suggested solutions to her. Instead of thinking of them as intrusive, Jane liked her father's regular visits and perceived them as an expression of love and concern.

Lily's father said, "I had a good relationship with Lily in the past. As I became busier with my work, I felt the distance between us. After she was sick, I felt that this was not good. I tried my best to spare more time to keep her company. I wish to accompany her to overcome the illness."

Kelly said, "I can only give 5 to 6 marks [on the scale of 0 to 10 with 0 denoting the poorest relationship and 10 the best relationship] for my relationship with Papa beforehand. After I was sick, it became 8 marks. He chatted with me more and was concerned with me more."

While welcoming the growing concern of their parents with delight, paradoxically Ann, Jane, and Margaret viewed that the excessive parental love was suffocating to them and unhelpful to their recovery. Ann commented that their exclusive concern over her was unfair to her brother and sisters.

Margaret, a 13-year-old adolescent girl whose body weight had dropped from 44 kg at a height of 160 cm to 36 kg at the time of referral, narrated, "I don't like that they're [her parents] too concerned. Their concern was horrible. I mean both of them [her dad and mom]. They often stared at me. Even though when my dad watched television, he would secretly gaze at me. It's horrible. They constantly gazed at you. They've become calculative with my eating."

EFFECTS ON THE PARENTS'
MARITAL RELATIONSHIP

Negative Effects of AN on the Couple's Relationship

The family narratives revealed that couples had different views on AN and subsequently dealt with the problem in different ways, which in turn created tensions and distresses on the marital relationship.

Jane's mother said, "Besides leading to a disparity of views, we became stuck sometimes in our interpersonal relationships." The couple had different views of the problem. The mother said, "I watch the videotapes and read magazines. I understand self-starvation can be very dangerous and fatal. I fear that it will affect different parts of her body. My husband had insufficient knowledge on this. He didn't think that her food refusal was a grave problem. I am sort of a straightforward person. I had no patience to play with her. I forced her to have a medical examination and I forced her to see different professionals. My husband felt that I was too nervous." The couple argued and quarreled every day over what was the appropriate way of handling Jane's food refusal problem. Jane's dad was liberal and lenient. He treated her like a little child and coaxed her to eat. Jane's mother pressed her daughter by force. The more lenient her husband was, the more pressing Jane's mother was toward Jane. The mother said, "He begged her to eat. If she didn't take any meal, he let her be. So we quarreled every day at the dinner table. I told her dad, 'You follow her wishes; you stand on her side; she will continue indulging in self-starvation.'" The fight between Jane and her mother at mealtime had shifted to a fight between the couple; they had been defeating each other in refeeding Jane.

A mother of a 15-year-old adolescent, Terry, said, "Sometimes I would blame him [her husband] for not standing on my side. He didn't perceive her problem as I perceived it. He often said that I was too nervous. I have only two daughters. Who will take care of them if I don't do so? I feel I am a loner in fighting this battle." The father expressed his view: "Basically I trust them all. My wife's too close to my two daughters. She pays all her attention on them. She tends to become nervous over petty things. She's too involved." This couple had given birth to twins soon after their marriage. The mother became a full-time housewife to look after the twins. Their marital relationship was satisfactory before the onset of their daughter's AN. The wife described her husband as responsible and reliable. She never doubted his commitment to the family. Despite his long working hours, he helped his wife to look after the twins during their babyhood.

Josephine's mother told her story: "We [she and her husband] didn't fight but we did have arguments. I saw the crisis. But his emphasis was on ensuring that she sit for the public examination. I realized that when she studied, she couldn't concentrate. I started a row with him. I gave in and let him carry her to the examination. As a matter of fact, I would not accept such a student sitting for the public examination if I were the examiner. If I were the teacher, I would ask the student not to take the exam." Josephine's parents were well educated and successful in their careers. They actively sought treatment for her daughter only after the public examination was over.

Not infrequently the husband blamed the wife for creating the trouble. Mrs. H's story typically reflected this. Mrs. H was a new immigrant to Hong Kong from the Mainland. Partly because of her low education and partly because of her rural background, she felt that her husband and her mother-in-law discriminated against and rejected her soon after the family reunion. Before her daughter's onset of the disorder, she had left home twice when quarrelling with her husband. She returned home a week later as she missed her two children very much. Mrs. H said, "During mealtime, he wore a long face. He didn't utter a word. But reading from his facial expression, I knew that he blamed me for causing all the trouble at the dining table, and I shouldn't force my daughter to eat. I told him that either he could take charge of the family and my daughter's health or I would make my own decision to take her to see the doctor. He refused to communicate with me and threw his own temper tantrum."

Positive Effects of AN on the Couple's Relationship

AN's effects on the relationship of Mr. and Mrs. N. were positive rather than negative. Mrs. N viewed that her husband had offered emotional support to her throughout the course of the daughter's illness. As a Christian, the father prayed every night, while the mother sought support from her own parents as well as her colleagues. Both of them shared the common goal of rescuing their emaciated daughter. This couple enjoyed a satisfactory marital relationship before Kelly was ill. Their marital relationship had not changed much even after the onset of their daughter's AN.

To Mary's parents, after the onset of their daughter's AN, their marital relationship improved; they had better cooperation with each other to face this life-threatening disorder. They spent more time together to discuss Mary's problem.

Which Family Member Was Most Affected?

From the perspective of these families, besides the patient, the disorder affected the mother exceedingly.

Lily's brother said, "My mom and my sister [Lily] suffer tremendously. She was often worried. My mom's health is okay but emotionally she is not okay. My mom suffers a lot psychologically."

Rebecca, the 17-year-old adolescent whose father was deceased, said, "After the illness, I only threw temper tantrum in front of my mother. I never did that to my eldest brother and my eldest sister. I only quarreled with my mother and I never listened to her."

Terry's father said, "Because of her deep involvement with the two daughters, she is easily upset by anything that happens to them, including trivial matters."

Tammy, a 14-year-old adolescent with a body weight of 28 kg, in reply to whom she would miss most if she died of self-starvation, said, "My mom, followed by my papa and my eldest brother." In reply to the question of whom she worried most in the family, Tammy replied, "My mom."

In Jane's family, different members had different answers. Jane's mother thought that AN had affected Jane's younger sister the most, followed by herself, while it had affected her husband the least. Her husband disagreed and said, "I feel that it affects my wife the most, not my youngest daughter. There was no doubt that she was concerned for her sister at the beginning of her illness. But when Jane forced her to eat more, she became upset and felt that her sister was too overbearing to her. She would complain to us." Jane said, "She was okay after complaining to us."

Nevertheless, the effect of the disorder on the father was by no means lesser than that on the mother.

Jane's father said, "Frankly speaking, when she [Jane] was not well, I couldn't sleep well. I felt tense. I woke up from time to time and went to check on her." The father continued, "I wish to elaborate more. I closely monitor her health, her psychological condition, and her daily behavior. I often estimate the risk of her health and the severity of the crisis to see if immediate treatment is necessary."

Tammy's father said, "I think of her [Tammy] while working. I keep urging my wife to bring Tammy to see the doctor."

DISCUSSION

Our study is a step forward from previous Western studies (e.g., Beresin, Gordon, & Herzog, 1989; Tozzi, Sullivan, Fear, McKenzie, & Bulik, 2003) in two aspects. First, the unit of analysis in this study was the family. Our participants were the patients and their family members. We were able to hear their voices collectively and learn about their different perceptions toward the disorder as well as its differential effects on family relations. Second, in contrast to previous studies that were conducted after the patients had recovered for some time and that depended on the patients' recall in telling their stories, the patients in our study were seeking treatment from our family treatment center. Their narratives reflected their thinking and feelings in the present. What we have heard would not be biased by the retrospective effects of memory loss.

Despite these contributions, there are also limitations to this study. First, given the limited time and the presence of the whole family in the interview, the views of individual family members and the adolescent or young woman might not have been fully expressed. Second, in qualitative study, the researcher is an important research instrument in data analysis and interpretation of the findings; hence, the personal and professional experiences of the author might bias the data analysis and data interpretation in this study (Scott, 1997).

The patients' stories have illuminated the fact that the emaciated young people suffered from multiple losses. They lost their health. Their normal schooling was interrupted by repeated hospitalization; their studies were adversely affected. Their temper became unpredictable with severe mood swings. In the eyes of the parents and the siblings, the patient changed from a nice little girl into a "monster" that was beyond their comprehension and coping. Both the patient and the family members were struck by the self-defeating symptomatic cycle of interaction. Consequently, these young people felt increasingly isolated, lonely, ineffective, and incompetent in managing their lives while their parents became more depressed, desperate, helpless, hopeless, and exhausted.

As revealed in the last appendix, these emaciated young people lost their feelings of hunger and suffered from stomach bloating after they ate; these physiological responses impaired their ability to assume responsibility for recovery. The bodily responses sent them incorrect signals that their physical condition was not as bad as the parents and the professionals had perceived. Besides multiple losses, patients derived secondary psychological gains from AN, albeit an increased false sense of control and parental concern and love.

This explains why young people in the face of AN usually fight the disorder with ambivalence and resistance. In the initial stage of treatment, it became a challenge for the therapist to motivate the young person to take charge of her own health and be responsible for her own recovery.

The subjective experiences of the young people and their families have pointed the way for mental health professionals to manage young people suffering from AN at the individual and family levels. At the individual level, the therapist needs to help motivate the young person to participate actively in treatment and to be responsible for her own recovery. On the basis of our participants' stories, there are three directions that the therapist may take in motivational work: (a) to heighten the awareness of the young person on the gravity of the negative consequences of the disorder and to support her in facing any physiological pain arising from resumption of normal eating in the early stage of treatment; (b) to increase her sense of control, mastery, and effectiveness in areas other than dieting and body weight; and (c) to facilitate her in realizing that parental love is by no means conditional.

Nevertheless, the parental love received was too excessive and too controlling to the patients; they needed more psychological space for personal struggle and growth. It is crucial for the parents to learn to let go of the emaciated child when her health allows them to do so.

As AN becomes intertwined with family relations and dominates family life, it is necessary to involve the whole family in treatment, with the aim of helping families find ways to solve their problems (Eisler, 1996, 2005). According to family therapy, the family holds the key to the solution. The families' problem-solving ability was damaged by the stifling family contexts, and their ability to change was paralyzed accordingly.

Consistent with the results of the Western studies (e.g., Beresin et al., 1989; Tozzi et al., 2003), the family narratives have indicated that the afflicted families were full of family conflicts. Family conflicts frequently occurred during mealtimes, usually resulting in huge arguments and tense family atmospheres. Apart from the power struggle between the parent and the afflicted young person over eating versus not eating, family conflicts arose from sibling rivalries and marital conflict owing to the disparity between the parents in their conceptualization and management of the disorder.

The family narratives have challenged two myths commonly held by local mental health professionals working with Chinese families. First, family conflicts are uncommon in Chinese families as Chinese people are reserved in expressing their feelings and tend to avoid open displays of emotions to maintain social harmony (Cheung, 1995). Second, even with the presence of family conflicts, Chinese families tend to sweep their conflicts under the rug and refuse to disclose them to outsiders for fear of losing *mianzi*, face. The family narratives suggested otherwise. These families never hesitated to disclose their difficulties to us at the pretreatment interview. Perhaps the tensions and stresses arising from self-starvation were indeed too tremendous. Parents cried out for professional help because their family life had already become organized around the disorder and in a few cases had even become controlled by the disorder.

The family conflicts provided the family therapist with rich and graphic information for assessment: the area of conflict, the actors involved (who and with whom), the process of conflict, the presence of a mediator, and the possibility of conflict resolution. Most importantly, the family therapist was given ample opportunity to understand the pattern of family interaction, which may have maintained or escalated the symptoms of AN.

AN brings devastating consequences not only to the patients but also to individual family members and the family as a whole. Among different family members, the disorder greatly affects the mother's psychological well-being, but the effects on the father are by no means lesser. Their pain and suffering are as great as those experienced by the emaciated young people. The mother's psychological distress can be partly attributable to the division of labor between women and men in families and society; a mother is still the primary caregiver for her children in Chinese societies such as Hong Kong. Paradoxically, by taking up the major share of the child care responsibility at home, the mother is blamed by her spouse, her relatives, her friends, and even mental health professionals when a child has a problem. The mother-blaming or parent-blaming attitude is absolutely unfair and demoralizing to the mother or father. Their needs for professional care and concern are indeed imminent.

These narratives suggested that AN induced negative as well as positive changes on family roles and family relationships. For instance, the previously peripheral father was more willing to share parenting with his spouse; the father–daughter relationship was strengthened and improved. The narratives suggested that the family therapist must be strategic to minimize the negative effects of the disorder on the family on the one hand and to maximize the positive impact to achieve the goal of helping on the other hand. Strength-oriented Western family therapists (e.g., Eisler, 2005) have argued that activating family resilience in the face of life-threatening illnesses such as AN is helpful.

Appendix 3
Interview Guide for Pretreatment Interview

1. Please tell me why your family is seeking help from our family treatment center? To what extent is it because of your daughter's anorexia nervosa?
2. How serious is your daughter's illness? Besides anorexia nervosa, are there other problems in your family that need our assistance and help?
3. Why did anorexia nervosa occur?
4. Have there been any changes in life since the onset of the disorder? How did anorexia nervosa affect you (the patient)? How did it affect your health? How did it affect your study? How did it affect your family relations? How did it affect your mood? How did it affect your relationships with your peers?
5. Have there been any changes in your family since the onset of the disorder? How did anorexia nervosa affect your family? How did it affect parent–child relations? How did it affect sibling relations? How did it affect the parents' marital relationship?

Appendix 4
Interview Guide for Posttreatment Interview

1. Is family therapy helpful in resolving anorexia nervosa for your daughter?
2. Is family therapy helpful in improving family relations (e.g., marital relations, parent–child relations, and sibling relations)?
3. What are the factors accounting for the emaciated young person's recovery?
4. What are the factors hindering the emaciated young person's recovery?
5. How do you perceive the roles and functions of the therapist in healing? (researcher trying to invite each of the family members to express their views)
6. Are there any areas for improvement in our clinical practice?
7. Are you willing to introduce our services to other families in need? If yes, how are you going to introduce our services to them?

References

Chapter 1

American Psychiatric Association. (1994). *Diagnostic and statistical manual of mental disorders* (4th ed.). Washington, DC: Author.

American Psychiatric Association. (2000). Practice guideline for the treatment of patients with eating disorders (Revision). *American Journal of Psychiatry, 157*(1, Suppl.), 1–39.

Beresin, E. V., Gordon, C., & Herzog, D. B. (1989). The process of recovering from anorexia nervosa. *American Academy of Psychoanalysis, 17,* 103–130.

Bronfenbrenner, U. (1989). Ecological systems theory. *Annals of Child Development, 6,* 187–249.

Churven, P. (2008). Hunger strike or medical disorder? Is anorexia caught in our flawed dichotomy between body and mind. *Australian and New Zealand Journal of Family Therapy, 4,* 184–190.

D'Abundo, M., & Chally, P. (2004). Struggling with recovery: Participant perspectives on battling an eating disorder. *Qualitative Health Research, 14,* 1094–1106.

Dare, C., Eisler, I., Russell, G. F. M., & Szmukler, G. (1990). Family therapy for anorexia nervosa: Implications from the results of a controlled trial of family and individual therapy. *Journal of Marital and Family Therapy, 16,* 39–57.

Eisler, I. (1995). Family models of eating disorders. In G. Szmukler, C. Dare, & J. Treasure (Eds.), *Handbook of eating disorders: Theory, treatment and research* (pp. 155–176). Chichester, UK: John Wiley.

Eisler, I. (2005). The empirical and theoretical base of family therapy and multiple family day therapy for adolescent anorexia nervosa. *Journal of Family Therapy, 27*, 104–131.

Elkaim, M. (1997). *If you love me, don't love me: Undoing reciprocal double binds and other methods of change in couple & family therapy* (H. Chubb, Trans.). Northvale, NJ: Jason Aronson.

Fishman, H. C. (1996). Structural family therapy. In J. Werne & I. D. Yalom (Eds.), *Treating eating disorders* (pp. 187–215). San Francisco: Jossey-Bass.

Friedan, B. (1963). *The feminine mystique.* London: Penguin.

Ko, D. (2001). *Every step a lotus: Shoes for bound feet.* Berkeley: University of California Press.

Lock, J., Le Grange, D., Agras, W. S., & Dare, C. (2001). *Treatment manual for anorexia nervosa: A family-based approach.* New York: Guilford.

Luepnitz, D. A. (1988). *The family interpreted.* New York: Basic Books.

MacSween, M. (1993). *Anorexic bodies:* A feminist and sociological perspective on anorexia nervosa. New York: Routledge.

Micucci, J. A. (1998). *The adolescent in family therapy.* New York: Guilford.

Minuchin, S. (1974). *Family and family therapy.* Cambridge, MA: Harvard University Press.

Minuchin, S., Rosman, B. L., & Baker, L. (1978). *Psychosomatic families: Anorexia nervosa in context.* Cambridge, MA: Harvard University Press.

Nichols, M. P., & Schwartz, R. C. (2007). *The essentials of family therapy* (3rd ed.). Boston: Pearson/Allyn & Bacon.

Rhodes, P. (2003). The Maudsley model of family therapy for children and adolescents with anorexia nervosa: Theory, clinical practice, and empirical support. *Australian and New Zealand Journal of Family Therapy, 24,* 191–198.

Russell, G. F. M., Dare, C., Eisler, I., & Le Grange, P. D. F. (1992). Controlled trials of family treatment in anorexia nervosa. In G. F. M. Russell, C. Dare, I. Eisler, & P. D. F. Le Grange (Eds.), *Psychobiology and treatment of anorexia nervosa and bulimia* (pp. 237–261). New York: American Psychiatric Press.

Selvini Palazzoli, M. (1985). *Self-starvation.* Northvale, NJ: Jason Aronson.

Sprenkle, D. H., & Blow, A. J. (2004). Common factors and our sacred models. *Journal of Marital and Family Therapy, 30,* 113–129.

Tozzi, F., Sullivan, P. F., Fear, J. L., McKenzie, J., & Bulik, C. M. (2003). Causes and recovery in anorexia nervosa: The patient's perspective. *International Journal of Eating Disorders, 33,* 143–154.

Treasure, J. (1997). *Anorexia nervosa: A survival guide for families, friends and sufferers.* Hove, UK: Psychology Press.

Walsh, F. (1998). *Strengthening family resilience.* New York: Guilford.

Ward, A., Troop, N., Todd, G., & Treasure, J. (1996). To change or not to change—"How" is the question? *British Journal of Medical Psychology, 69,* 139–146.

Weaver, K., Wuest, J., & Ciliska, D. (2005). Understanding women's journey of recovering from anorexia nervosa. *Qualitative Health Research, 15,* 188–206.

White, M. (1983). Anorexia nervosa: A transgenerational system perspective. *Family Process, 22,* 255–273.

Wang, P. (2000). *Aching for beauty: Footbinding in China.* New York: Anchor Books.

Chapter 2

Abou-Saleh, M. T., Younis, Y., & Karim, L. (1998). Anorexia nervosa in an Arab culture. *International Journal of Eating Disorders, 23,* 207–212.

American Psychiatric Association. (1994). *Diagnostic and statistical manual of mental disorders* (4th ed.). Washington, DC: Author.

Birmingham, C. L., Su, J., Hlynsky, J. A., Goldner, E. M., & Gao, M. (2005). The mortality rate from anorexia nervosa. *International Journal of Eating Disorders, 38,* 143–146.

Bowlby, J. (1969). *Attachment and loss, vol. 1: Attachment.* New York: Basic Books.

Bruch, H. (1973). *Eating disorders: Obesity, anorexia and the person within.* New York: Basic Books.

Bruch, H. (1978). *The golden cage: The enigma of anorexia nervosa.* Cambridge, MA: Harvard University Press.

Crisp, A. (1995). *Anorexia nervosa—Let me be.* Hove, UK: Lawrence Erlbaum.

Fairburn, C. G., Cooper, Z., Doll, H., & Welch, S. L. (1999). Risk factors for anorexia nervosa: Three integrated case-control comparisons. *Archives of General Psychiatry, 56,* 468–476.

Fosson, A., Knibbs, J., Bryant-Waugh, R., & Lask, B. (1987). Early onset anorexia nervosa. *Archives of Disease in Childhood, 62,* 114–118.

Franko, D. L., Keel, P. K., Dorer, D. J., Blais, M. A., Delinsky, S. S., Eddy, K. T., et al. (2004). What predicts suicide attempts in woman with eating disorders? *Psychological Medicine, 34,* 843–853.

Fung, M. S. C., & Yuen, M. (2003). Body image and eating attitudes among adolescent Chinese girls in Hong Kong. *Perceptual and Motor Skills, 96,* 57–66.

Geist, R., Davis, R., & Heinman, M. (1998). Binge/purge symptoms and comorbidity in adolescents with eating disorders. *Canadian Journal of Psychiatry, 43,* 507–512.

Godart, N. T., Flament, M. F., Perdereau, F., & Jeammet, P. (2002). Comorbidity between eating disorders and anxiety disorders: A review. *International Journal Eating Disorders, 32,* 253–270.

Grinspoon, S., Thomas, E., Pitts, S., Gross, E., Mickley, D., Miller, K., et al. (2000). Prevalence and predictive factors for regional osteopenia in women with anorexia nervosa. *Annals of Internal Medicine, 133,* 790–794.

Halvorsen, I., Andersen, A., & Heyerdahl, S. (2004). Good outcome of adolescent onset anorexia nervosa after systematic treatment: Intermediate to long-term follow-up of a representative county-sample. *European Child & Adolescent Psychiatry, 13,* 295–306.

Hay, P. (2004). Australian and New Zealand clinical practice guidelines for the treatment of anorexia nervosa. *Australian and New Zealand Journal of Psychiatry, 38,* 659–670.

Hebebrand, J., Himmelmann, G. W., Heseker, H., Schäfer, H., & Remschmidt, H. (1996). Use of percentiles for the body mass index in anorexia nervosa: Diagnostic, epidemiological, and therapeutic considerations. *International Journal of Eating Disorders, 19,* 359–369.

Herpertz-Dahlmann, B., Muller, B., Herpertz, S., Heussen, N., Hebebrand, J., & Remschmidt, H. (2001). Prospective 10-year follow-up in adolescent anorexia nervosa—Course, outcome, psychiatric comorbidity, and psychosocial adaptation. *Journal of Child Psychological Psychiatry, 42,* 603–612.

Herzog, D. B., Greenwood, D. N., Dorer, D. J., Flores, A. T., Ekeblad, E. R., Richards, A., et al. (2000). Mortality in eating disorders: A descriptive study. *International Journal of Eating Disorders, 28,* 20–26.

Hoek, H. W., & van Hoeken, D. (2003). Review of the prevalence and incidence of eating disorders. *International Journal of Eating Disorders, 34,* 383–396.

Hsu, L. K. G. (1991). Outcome studies in patients with eating disorders. In S. M. Miren, J. T. Gossett, & M. C. Grob (Eds.), *Psychiatric treatment: advances in outcome research* (pp. 159–180). Washington, DC: American Psychiatric Press.

Jacobi, C., Paul, T., de Zwaan, M., Nutzinger, D. O., & Dahme, B. (2004). Specificity of self-concept disturbances in eating disorders. *International Journal of Eating Disorders*, *35*, 204–210.

Kaye, W. H., Bulik, C. M., Thornton, L., Barbarich, N., Masters, K., & Price Foundation Collaborative Group. (2004). Comorbidity of anxiety disorders with anorexia and bulimia nervosa. *American Journal of Psychiatry*, *161*, 2215–2221.

Keel, P. K., Dorer, D. J., Eddy, K. T., Franko, D., Charatan, D. L., & Herzog, D. B. (2003). Predictors of mortality in eating disorders. *Archives of General Psychiatry*, *60*, 179–183.

Keel, P. K., Klump, K. L., Miller, K. B., McGue, M., & Iacono, W. G. (2005). Shared transmission of eating disorders and anxiety disorders. *International Journal of Eating Disorders*, *38*, 99–105.

Key, A., Mason, H., Allan, R., & Lask, B. (2002). Restoration of ovarian and uterine maturity in adolescents with anorexia nervosa. *International Journal of Eating Disorders*, *32*, 319–325.

King, E. A., Gordon, P. A., Wheeler, M., & Russell, G. F. M. (1985). Cystic ovaries: A phase of anorexia nervosa. *Lancet*, *326*, 1379–1382.

Klump, K. L., & Gobrogge, K. L. (2005). A review and primer of molecular genetic studies of anorexia nervosa. *International Journal of Eating Disorders*, *37*, s43–s48.

Lai, K. Y. C. (2000). Anorexia nervosa in Chinese adolescents—Does culture make a difference? *Journal of Adolescence*, *23*, 561–568.

Lai, K. Y. C., de Bruyn, R., Lask, B., Bryant-Waugh, R., & Hankins, M. (1994). Use of pelvic ultrasound to monitor ovarian and uterine maturity in childhood onset anorexia nervosa. *Archives of Disease in Childhood*, *71*, 228–231.

Lantzouni, E., Frank, G. R., Golden, N. H., & Shenker, R. I. (2002). Reversibility of growth stunting in early onset anorexia nervosa: A prospective study. *Journal of Adolescent Health*, *31*, 162–165.

Lask, B., & Bryant-Waugh, R. (Eds.). (2000). *Anorexia nervosa and related eating disorders in childhood and adolescence* (2nd ed.). Hove, UK: Psychology Press.

Lee, S., Chan, Y. Y. L., & Hsu, G. (2003). The intermediate-term outcome of Chinese patients with anorexia nervosa in Hong Kong. *American Journal of Psychiatry, 160,* 967–972.

Lee, S., Ho, T. P., & Hsu, L. K. (1993). Fat phobic and non-fat phobic anorexia nervosa: a comparative study of 70 Chinese patients in Hong Kong. *Psychological Medicine, 23,* 999–1017.

Lee, S., & Lee, A. M. (2000). Disordered eating in three communities of China: A comparative study of female high school students in Hong Kong, Shenzhen, and rural Hunan. *International Journal of Eating Disorders, 27,* 317–327.

Le Grange, D. (1999). Family therapy for adolescent anorexia nervosa. *Journal of Clinical Psychology, 55,* 727–739.

Lewinsohn, P. M., Striegel-Moore, R. H., & Seeley, J. R. (2000). Epidemiology and natural course of eating disorders in young women from adolescence to young adulthood. *Journal of the American Academy of Child and Adolescent Psychiatry, 39,* 1284–1292.

Lilenfield, L. R., Kaye, W. H., Greeno, C. G., Merikangas, K. R., Plotnicov, K., Pollice, C., et al. (1998). A controlled family study of anorexia and bulimia. *Archives of General Psychiatry, 55,* 603–610.

Ma, J. L. C., Chow, M. Y. M., Lee, S., & Lai, Y. C. K. (2002). Family meaning of self-starvation: Themes discerned in family treatment in Hong Kong. *Journal of Family Therapy, 24,* 57–71.

Mangweth, B., Hudson, J. I., Pope, H. G., Hausmann, A., De Col, C., Laird, N. M., et al. (2003). Family study of the aggregation of eating disorders and mood disorders. *Psychological Medicine, 33,* 1319–1323.

Manley, R. S., Smye, V., & Srikameswaran, S. (2001). Addressing complex ethical issues in the treatment of children and adolescents with eating disorders: Application of a framework for ethical decision-making. *European Eating Disorders Review, 9,* 144–166.

Minuchin, S. (1978). *Families and family therapy.* London: Tavistock.

Nakamura, K., Yamamoto, M., Yamazaki, O., Kawashima, Y., Muto, K., Someya, T., et al. (2000). Prevalence of anorexia and bulimia nervosa in a geographically defined area in Japan. *International Journal of Eating Disorders, 28,* 173–180.

Nobakht, M., & Dezhkam, M. (2000). An epidemiological study of eating disorders in Iran. *International Journal of Eating Disorders, 28,* 265–271.

O'Brien, K. M., & Vincent, N. K. (2003). Psychiatric comorbidity in anorexia and bulimia nervosa: Nature, prevalence and causal relationships. *Clinical Psychological Review, 23,* 57–74.

Palazzoli, S. M. (1978). *Self-starvation: From individual to family therapy in the treatment of anorexia nervosa.* Northvale, NJ: Jason Aronson.

Pollice, C., Kaye, W. H., Greeno, C. G., & Weltzin, T. E. (1997). Relationship of depression, anxiety, and obsessionality to state of illness in anorexia nervosa. *International Journal of Eating Disorders, 21,* 367–376.

Rastam, M. (1992). Anorexia nervosa in 51 Swedish children and adolescents: Premorbid problems and comorbidity. *Journal of the American Academy of Child and Adolescent Psychiatry, 31,* 819–829.

Rastam, M., Gillberg, C., & Wentz, E. (2003). Outcome of teenage-onset anorexia nervosa in a Swedish community-based sample. *European Child & Adolescent Psychiatry, 12*(Suppl. 1), 78–90.

Reijonen, J. H., Pratt, H. D., Patel, D. R., & Greydanus, D. E. (2003). Eating disorders in the adolescent population: An overview. *Journal of Adolescent Research, 18,* 209–222.

Romans, S., Gendall, K. A., Martin, J. L., & Mullen, P. E. (2001). Child sexual abuse and later disordered eating: A New Zealand epidemiological study. *International Journal of Eating Disorders, 29,* 380–392.

Ruuska, J., Kaltiala-Heino, R., Rantanen, P., & Koivisto, A.-M. (2005). Psychopathological distress predicts suicidal ideation and self-harm in adolescent eating disorder outpatients. *European Child & Adolescent Psychiatry, 14*, 276–281.

Schmidt, U. (2003). Aetiology of eating disorders in the 21st century. New answers to old questions. *European Child & Adolescent Psychiatry, 12*(Suppl. 1), 30–37.

Smith, C., Feldman, S. S., Nasserbakht, A., & Steiner, H. (1993). Psychological characteristics and DSM-III-R diagnoses at 6-year follow-up of adolescent anorexia nervosa. *Journal of the American Academy of Child and Adolescent Psychiatry, 32*, 1237–1245.

Srinivasan, T. N., Suresh, T. R., & Jayaram, V. (1998). Emergence of eating disorders in India: Study of eating distress syndrome and development of a screening questionnaire. *International Journal of Social Psychiatry, 44*, 189–198.

Steiger, H. (2004). Eating disorders and the serotonin connection: State, trait and developmental effects. *Journal of Psychiatry Neuroscience, 29*, 20–29.

Steinhausen, H. C. (1997). Annotation: Outcome of anorexia nervosa in younger patient. *Journal of Child Psychological Psychiatry, 38*, 271–276.

Steinhausen, H. C., Boyadjieva, S., Griogoroiu-Serbanescu, M., & Neumärker, K. J. (2003). The outcome of adolescent eating disorders: Findings from an international collaborative study. *European Child & Adolescent Psychiatry, 12*, 91–98.

Strober, M., Freeman, R., Lampert, C., Diamond, J., & Kaye, W. (2000). Controlled family study of anorexia nervosa and bulimia nervosa: Evidence of shared liability and transmission of partial syndromes. *American Journal of Psychiatry, 157*, 393–401.

Strober, M., Freeman, R., & Morrell, W. (1997). The long-term course of severe anorexia nervosa in adolescents: Survival analysis of recovery, relapse and outcome predictors over 10–15 years in a prospective study. *International Journal of Eating Disorders, 22*, 339–360.

Surgenor, L. J., Horn, J., Plumridge, E. W., & Hudson, S. M. (2002). Anorexia nervosa and psychological control: A re-examination of selected theoretical accounts. *European Eating Disorders Review, 10*, 85–101.

Swenne, I., & Thurfjell, B. (2003). Clinical onset and diagnosis of eating disorders in premenarcheal girls preceded by inadequate weight gain and growth retardation. *Acta Paediatrica, 92*, 1133–1137.

Treasure, J. T., Wheeler, M., King, E. A., Gordon, P. A. L., & Russell, G. F. M. (1988). Weight gain and reproductive function: Ultrasonographic and endocrine features in anorexia nervosa. *Clinical Endocrinology, 29*, 607–616.

Wade, T. D., Bulik, C. M., Neale, M., & Kendler, K. S. (2000). Anorexia nervosa and major depression: Shared genetic and environmental risk factors. *American Journal of Psychiatry, 157*, 469–471.

Watson, T. L., Bowers, W. A., & Andersen, A. E. (2000). Involuntary treatment of eating disorders. *American Journal of Psychiatry, 157*, 1806–1810.

Wentz, E., Gillberg, C., Gillberg, I. C., & Rastam, M. (2001). Ten-year follow-up of adolescent-onset anorexia nervosa: psychiatric disorders and overall functioning scales. *Journal of Child Psychology and Psychiatry, 42*, 613–622.

Wong, S., Au, B., Lau, E., Lee, Y., Sham, A., & Sing, L. (2004). Osteoporosis in Chinese patients with anorexia nervosa. *International Journal of Eating Disorders, 36*, 104–108.

World Health Organization. (1993). *International classification of diseases* (10th ed.). Geneva: Author.

Zhu, A. J., & Walsh, B. T. (2002). In review: Pharmacological treatment of eating disorders. *Canadian Journal of Psychiatry, 47*, 227–234.

Zipfel, S., Lowe, B., & Herzog, W. (2003). Medical complications. In J. Treasure, U. Schmidt, & E. V. Furth (Eds.), *Handbook of eating disorders* (2nd ed., pp. 169–190). New York: John Wiley.

Chapter 3

Abrams, K. K., Allen, L. R., & Gray, J. J. (1998). Disordered eating attitudes and behaviors, psychological adjustment and ethnic identity—A comparison of black and white female college students. In R. J. Castillo (Ed.), *Meaning of madness* (pp. 138–144). Pacific Grove, CA: Brooks/Cole.

Andersson, M. (1995). Mother–daughter connection: The healing force in the treatment of eating disorders. *Journal of Feminist Family Therapy*, 6(4), 3–11.

Asen, E. (2002). Multiple family therapy: An overview. *Journal of Family Therapy*, 24, 3–16.

Becker, A. E. (2004). Television, disordered eating, and young women in Fiji: Negotiating body image and identity during rapid social change. *Culture, Medicine and Psychiatry*, 28, 533–559.

Beresin, E. V., Gordon, C., & Herzog, D. B. (1989). The process of recovering from anorexia nervosa. *American Academy of Psychoanalysis*, 17, 103–130.

Brown, L., Russell, J., Thornton, C., & Dunn, S. (1999). Dissociation, abuse and the eating disorders: Evidence from an Australian population. *Australian and New Zealand Journal of Psychiatry*, 33, 521–528.

Bruch, H. (1973). *Eating disorders*. New York: Basic Books.

Caritas-Hong Kong. (2004). *A survey of Hong Kong adolescents' attitude toward body shape*. Hong Kong: Author.

Chernin, K. (1986). *The hungry self*. London: Virago Press.

Chin, Y. K. 戚宜君 (1978). *Female beauty* 女性美譚. Taipei: Water Lily.

Churven, P. (2008). Hunger strike or medical disorder? Is anorexia caught in our flawed dichotomy between body and mind. *Australian and New Zealand Journal of Family Therapy*, 4, 184–190.

Dare, C., & Eisler, I. (1995). Family therapy. In G. Szmukler, C. Dare, & J. Treasure (Eds.), *Handbook of eating disorders: Theory, treatment and research* (pp. 333–349). London: John Wiley.

Dare, C., & Eisler, I. (2000). A multi-family group day treatment programme for adolescent eating disorder. *European Eating Disorders Review, 8,* 4–18.

Dare, C., Eisler, I., Russell, G. F. M., & Szmukler, G. (1990). Family therapy for anorexia nervosa: Implications from the results of a controlled trial of family and individual therapy. *Journal of Marital and Family Therapy, 16,* 39–57.

Eisler, I. (1995). Family models of eating disorders. In G. Szmukler, C. Dare, & J. Treasure (Eds.), *Handbook of eating disorders: Theory, treatment and research* (pp. 155–176). Chichester, UK: John Wiley.

Eisler, I. (2005). The empirical and theoretical base of family therapy and multiple family day therapy for adolescent anorexia nervosa. *Journal of Family Therapy, 27,* 104–131.

Gulik, R. H. V. (1961). *Sexual life in ancient China.* Leiden, Netherlands: Brill.

Graap, H., Bleich, S., Herbst, F., Trostmann, Y., Wancata, J., & de Zwaan, M. (2008). The needs of carers of patients with anorexia and bulimia nervosa. *European Eating Disorders Review, 16,* 21–29.

Herscovici, C. R., & Bay, L. (1996). Favourable outcome for anorexia nervosa patients treated in Argentina with a family approach. *Eating Disorders: The Journal of Treatment and Prevention, 4,* 59–66.

Hwang, J. L. 黃金麟 (2001). *History, body, nation: Modern formation of the Chinese body* 歷史、身體、國家：近代中國的身體形成. Taipei: LinKing.

Jackson, B. (2000). *Splendid slippers—A thousand years of an erotic tradition.* Berkeley, CA: Ten Speed Press.

Katzman, M. A., & Lee, S. (1997). Beyond body image: The integration of feminist and transcultural theories in the understanding of self-starvation. *International Journal of Eating Disorders, 22,* 385–394.

Ko, D. (2001). *Every step a lotus: Shoes for bound feet*. Berkeley: University of California Press.

Lawrence, M. (1984). *The anorexia experience*. London: Women's Press.

Lee, S. (1993). How abnormal is the desire for slimness? A survey of eating attitudes and behavior among Chinese undergraduates in Hong Kong. *Psychological Medicine, 23*, 437–451.

Lee, S. (1997). How lay is lay? Chinese students' perceptions of anorexia nervosa in Hong Kong. *Social Science and Medicine, 44*, 491–502.

Lee, S., & Lee, A. M. (2000). Disordered eating in three communities of China: A comparative study of female high school students in Hong Kong, Shenzhen, and rural Hunan. *International Journal of Eating Disorders, 27*, 317–327.

Leung, F., Lam, S., & Sze, S. (2001). Cultural expectations of thinness in Chinese women. *Eating Disorders, 9*, 339–350.

Leung, F., Lam, S., & Chan, I. (2001). Disordered eating attitudes and behaviors among adolescents in Hong Kong. *Journal of Youth Studies, 4*, 36–51.

Luepnitz, D. A. (1988). *The family interpreted*. New York: Basic Books.

Lock, J., Le Grange, D., Agras, W. S., & Dare, C. (2001). *Treatment manual for anorexia nervosa: A family-based approach*. New York: Guilford.

MacSween, M. (1993). *Anorexic bodies: A feminist and sociological perspective on anorexia nervosa*. New York: Routledge.

Maine, M. (1999). The gap in treatment. *Clinical Update, 1*(6), 1–3.

Martin, F. E. (1985). The treatment and outcome of anorexia nervosa in adolescents: A prospective study and five year follow-up. *Journal of Psychiatric Research, 19*, 509–514.

Micucci, J. A. (1998). *The adolescent in family therapy*. New York: Guilford.

Minuchin, S., Rosman, B. L., & Baker, L. (1978). *Psychosomatic families: Anorexia nervosa in context*. Cambridge, MA: Harvard University Press.

Nasser, M., & Katzman, M. (1999). Eating disorders: Transcultural perspectives inform prevention. In N. Piran, M. P. Levine, & C. Steiner-Adair (Eds.), *Preventing eating disorders* (pp. 26–43). New York: Brunner/Mazel.

Nasser, M., & Katzman, M. (2003). Sociocultural theories of eating disorders: An evolution in thought. In J. Treasure, U. Schmidt, & E. V. Furth (Eds.), *Handbook of eating disorders* (2nd ed., pp. 139–150). New York: John Wiley.

Neumark-Sztainer, D., Story, M., Hannan, P. J., Beuhring, T., & Resnick, M. D. (2000). Disordered eating among adolescents: Associations with sexual/physical abuse and other familial/psychosocial factors. *International Journal of Eating Disorders, 28*, 249–258.

Orbach, S. (1986). *Hunger strike*. London: Faber & Faber.

Ogden, J. (2003). *The psychology of eating: From healthy to disordered behavior*. Cambridge, MA: Blackwell.

Pak, Y. 柏楊 (1978). *Diet pornographic sex* 食色性也：柏楊縱談男女. Lanzhou: Lanzhou University Press.

Piran, N. (1999). One the move from tertiary to secondary and primary prevention: Working with an elite dance school. In N. Piran, M. P. Levine, & C. Steiner-Adair (Eds.), *Preventing eating disorders* (pp. 256–269). New York: Brunner/Mazel.

Ridley, M. (2003). *Nature via nurture*. New York: HarperCollins.

Russell, G. F. M., Dare, C., Eisler, I., & Le Grange, P. D. F. (1992). Controlled trials of family treatment in anorexia nervosa. In G. F. M. Russell, C. Dare, I. Eisler, & P. D. F. Le Grange (Eds.), *Psychobiology and treatment of anorexia nervosa and bulimia* (pp. 237–261). New York: American Psychiatric Press.

Selvini Palazzoli, M. (1985). *Self-starvation*. Northvale, NJ: Jason Aronson.

Scholz, M., Rix, M., Scholz, K., Gantchev, K., & Thomke, V. (2005). Multiple family therapy for anorexia nervosa: Concepts, experiences and results. *Journal of Family Therapy, 27*, 132–141.

Steiger, H., Stotland, S., Trottier, J., & Ghadirian, A. M. (1996). Familial eating concerns and psychopathological traits: Causal implications of transgenerational effects. *International Journal of Eating Disorders, 19*, 147–157.

Tozzi, F., Sullivan, P. F., Fear, J. L., McKenzie, J., & Bulik, C. M. (2003). Causes and recovery in anorexia nervosa: The patient's perspective. *International Journal of Eating Disorders, 33*, 143–154.

Treasure, J., Murphy, T., Szmukler, G., Todd, G., Gavan, K., & Joyce, J. (2001). The experience of caregiving for severe mental illness: A comparison between anorexia and psychosis. *Social Psychiatry Psychiatric Epidemiology, 36*, 343–347.

Wang, P. (2000). *Aching for beauty: Footbinding in China*. New York: Anchor Books.

White, M. (1983). Anorexia nervosa: A transgenerational system perspective. *Family Process, 22*, 255–273.

Whitney, J., Murray, J., Gavan, K., Todd, G., Whitaker, W., & Treasure, J. (2005). Experience of caring for someone with anorexia nervosa: Qualitative study. *British Journal of Psychiatry, 187*, 444–449.

Wong, T. 王家英, Ma, L. C. 馬麗莊, & Lau, Y. K. 劉玉琼 (2003). *Hong Kong people's work situations and perceptions of living under economic hardship: The predicament of vulnerable groups* 經濟困難下香港市民的家庭生活狀況及人生態度：社會工作介入的啓示. Hong Kong: Hong Kong Institute of Asia-Pacific Studies, The Chinese University of Hong Kong.

Chapter 4

Bronfenbrenner, U. (1989). Ecological systems theory. *Annals of Child Development, 6*, 187–249.

Bruch, H. (1973). *Eating disorders*. New York: Basic Books.

Chen, G. M. (2002). The impact of harmony on Chinese conflict management. In G. M. Chen & R. Ma (Eds.), *Chinese conflict management and resolution* (pp. 3–18). Westport, CT: Ablex.

Churven, P. (2008). Hunger strike or medical disorder? Is anorexia caught in our flawed dichotomy between body and mind. *Australian and New Zealand Journal of Family Therapy, 4*, 184–190.

Dare, C., & Eisler, I. (1995). Family therapy. In G. Szmukler, C. Dare, & J. Treasure (Eds.), *Handbook of eating disorders: Theory, treatment and research* (pp. 333–349). Chichester, UK: John Wiley.

Eisler, I. (2005). The empirical and theoretical base of family therapy and multiple family day therapy for adolescent anorexia nervosa. *Journal of Family Therapy, 27*, 104–131.

Fishman, H. C. (1996). Structural family therapy. In J. Werne & I. D. Yalom (Eds.), *Treating eating disorders* (pp. 187–215). San Francisco: Jossey-Bass.

Hoste, R. R., Zaitsoff, S., Hewell, K., & Le Grange, D. (2007). What can dropouts teach us about retention in eating disorder treatment studies? *International Journal of Eating Disorders, 40*, 668–671.

Le Grange, D., & Eisler, I. (2008). Family intervention in adolescent anorexia nervosa. *Child Adolescent Psychiatric Clinical Northern American, 18*, 159–173.

Lock, J., Le Grange, D., Agras, W. S., & Dare, C. (2001). *Treatment manual for anorexia nervosa: A family-based approach*. New York: Guilford.

Micucci, J. A. (1998). *The adolescent in family therapy*. New York: Guilford.

Minuchin, S., & Nichols, M. (1993). *Family healing*. New York: Free Press.

Minuchin, S., Nichols, M., & Lee, W. Y. (2007). *Assessing families and couples: From symptoms to system*. Upper Saddle River, NJ: Pearson.

Minuchin, S., Rosman, B. L., & Baker, L. (1978). *Psychosomatic families: Anorexia nervosa in context.* Cambridge, MA: Harvard University Press.

Rhodes, P. (2003). The Maudsley model of family therapy for children and adolescents with anorexia nervosa: Theory, clinical practice, and empirical support. *Australian and New Zealand Journal of Family Therapy, 24,* 191–198.

Schmidt, U., & Treasure, J. (2006). Anorexia nervosa: Valued and visible. A cognitive-interpersonal maintenance model and its implications for research and practice. *British Journal of Clinical Psychology, 45,* 343–366.

Selvini Palazzoli, M. (1981). *Self-starvation* (A. Pomerans, Trans.). Northvale, NJ: Jason Aronson.

Stierlin, H., & Weber, G. (1989). *Unlocking the family door: A systemic approach to the understanding and treatment of anorexia nervosa.* New York: Brunner/Mazel.

Wen, C. I., Chang, Y. H., Chang, L. Y., & Chu, C. (1989). Family structure and its related variables: A case of Taipei. In C. C. Yi & C. Chu (Eds.), *Social phenomena in Taiwan: An analysis* (pp. 1–24). Taipei: Institute of Social Science and Philosophy, Academia Sinica Press.

White, M. (1983). Anorexia nervosa: A transgenerational system perspective. *Family Process, 22,* 255–273.

Chapter 5

Diamond, G. S., & Liddle, H. A. (1999). Transforming negative parent-adolescent interactions: From impasse to dialogue. *Family Process, 38,* 5–26.

Eisler, I. (1995). Family models of eating disorders. In G. Szmukler, C. Dare, & J. Treasure (Eds.), *Handbook of eating disorders: Theory, treatment and research* (pp. 155–176). Chichester, UK: John Wiley.

Eisler, I. (1996). Combining individual and family therapy in adolescent anorexia nervosa: A family systems approach. In J. Werne & I. D. Yalom (Eds.), *Treating eating disorders* (pp. 217–257). San Francisco: Jossey-Bass.

Harden, J. (2005). "Uncharted waters": The experience of parents of young people with mental health problems. *Qualitative Health Research, 15,* 207–223.

Karp, D. A., & Tanarugsachock, V. (2000). Mental illness, caregiving, and emotional management. *Qualitative Health Research, 10,* 6–25.

Lock, J., Le Grange, D., Agras, W. S., & Dare, C. (2001). *Treatment manual for anorexia nervosa: A family-based approach.* New York: Guilford.

Ma, J. L. C., Lai, K., & Pun, S. H. (2002). Parenting distress and parental investment of Hong Kong Chinese parents with a child having an emotional or behavioral problem: A qualitative study. *Child and Family Social Work, 7,* 99–106.

Minuchin, S., & Fishman, H. C. (1981). *Family therapy techniques.* Cambridge, MA: Harvard University Press.

Minuchin, S., & Nichols, M. (1993). *Family healing.* New York: Free Press.

Minuchin, S., Nichols, M., & Lee, W. Y. (2007). *Assessing families and couples: From symptoms to system.* Upper Saddle River, NJ: Pearson.

Ng, M. L., & Ma, L. C. (2004). Hong Kong. In R. T. Francoeur & R. J. Noonan (Eds.), *Continuum complete international encyclopaedia of sexuality* (pp. 489–502). New York: Continuum.

Nichols, M. P., & Fellenberg, S. (2000). The effective use of enactments in family therapy: A discovery-oriented process study. *Journal of Marital and Family Therapy, 26,* 143–152.

Ogden, J. (2003). *The psychology of eating: From healthy to disordered behavior.* Cambridge, MA: Blackwell.

Stierlin, H., & Weber, G. (1989). *Unlocking the family door: A systemic approach to the understanding and treatment of anorexia nervosa.* New York: Brunner/Mazel.

Tomm, K. (1998). A question of perspective. *Journal of Marital and Family Therapy, 24,* 409–413.

Vitousek, K. M. (2005, April). *Alienating patients from the "anorexic self": Externalizing and related strategies.* Workshop presented at the Seventh International Conference on Eating Disorders, London.

Watzlawick, P., Weakland, J., & Fisch, R. (1974). *Change: Principles of problem formation and problem resolution.* New York: Norton.

White, M. (1983). Anorexia nervosa: A transgenerational system perspective. *Family Process, 22,* 255–273.

Xiao jing [Classic of filial piety]. (1960). In J. Legge (Trans.), *The Chinese classics* (Vols. 1–5). Hong Kong: Hong Kong University Press.

Chapter 6

Beumont, P. J. V., Russell, J. D., & Touyz, S. W. (1995). Psychological concerns in the maintenance of dieting disorders. In G. Szmukler, C. Dare, & J. Treasure (Eds.), *Handbook of eating disorders: Theory, treatment and research* (pp. 221–241). Chichester, UK: John Wiley.

Bowlby, J. (1969). *Attachment and loss, vol. 1: Attachment.* New York: Basic Books.

Brown, L., Russell, J., Thornton, C., & Dunn, S. (1999). Dissociation, abuse and the eating disorders: Evidence from an Australian population. *Australian and New Zealand Journal of Psychiatry, 33,* 521–528.

Bruch, H. (1973). *Eating disorders.* New York: Basic Books.

Cecchin, G. (1987). Hypothesizing, circularity, neutrality revisited: An invitation to curiosity. *Family Process, 26,* 405–413.

Dallos, R. (2004). Attachment narrative therapy: Integrating ideas from narrative and attachment theory in systemic family therapy with eating disorders. *Journal of Family Therapy, 26,* 40–65.

Dare, C., & Crowther, C. (1995). Living dangerously: Psychoanalytic psychotherapy of anorexia nervosa. In G. Szmukler, C. Dare, & J. Treasure

(Eds.), *Handbook of eating disorders: Theory, treatment and research* (pp. 293–308). Chichester, UK: John Wiley.

Eisler, I. (1996). Combining individual and family therapy in adolescent anorexia nervosa: A family systems approach. In J. Werne & I. D. Yalom (Eds.), *Treating eating disorders* (pp. 217–257). San Francisco: Jossey-Bass.

Faber, A. J. (2002). The role of hierarchy in parental nurturance. *American Journal of Family Therapy, 30,* 73–84.

Fishman, H. C. (1996). Structural family therapy. In J. Werne & I. D. Yalom (Eds.), *Treating eating disorders* (pp. 187–215). San Francisco: Jossey-Bass.

Geller, J., Williams, K. D., & Srikameswaran, S. (2001). Clinical stance in the treatment of chronic eating disorders. *European Eating Disorders Review, 9,* 365–373.

Gerrity, M. S., Earp, J. A. L., DeVellis, R. F., & Light, D. W. (1992). Uncertainty and professional work: Perception of physicians in clinical practice. *American Journal of Sociology, 97,* 1022–1051.

Hill, J., Fonagy, P., Safier, E., & Sargent, J. (2003). The ecology of attachment in the family. *Family Process, 42,* 205–221.

Hughes, P. (1997). The use of the countertransference in the therapy of patients with anorexia nervosa. *European Eating Disorders Review, 5,* 258–269.

Josephs, L. (1989). The world of the concrete: A comparative approach. *Contemporary Psychoanalysis, 75,* 477–500.

Krahn, D. D., Nairn, K., Gosnell, B. A., & Drewnowski, A. (1991). Stealing in eating disordered patients. *Journal of Clinical Psychiatry, 52,* 112–115.

LeVine, R. A. (1990). Infant environments in psychoanalysis—A cross cultural view. In J. W. Stigler, R. A. Shweder, & G. Herdt (Eds.), *Cultural psychology: Essays on comparative human development* (pp. 454–474). Cambridge, UK: Cambridge University Press.

Micucci, J. A. (1998). *The adolescent in family therapy.* New York: Guilford.

Miller, M. L. (1991). Understanding the eating-disordered patient: Engaging the concrete. *Bulletin of the Menninger Clinic, 55*(1), 85–91.

Selvini Palazzoli, M. (1985). *Self-starvation*. Northvale, NJ: Jason Aronson.

Shoebridge, P., & Gowers, S. G. (2000). Parental high concern and adolescent-onset anorexia nervosa: A case-control study to investigate direction of causality. *British Journal of Psychiatry, 176*, 132–137.

Stierlin, H., & Weber, G. (1989). *Unlocking the family door: A systemic approach to the understanding and treatment of anorexia nervosa*. New York: Brunner/Mazel.

Stone Fish, L. (2000). Hierarchical relationship development: Parent and children. *Journal of Marital and Family Therapy, 26*, 501–510.

Treasure, J. L., Schmidt, U. H., & Troop, N. A. (2000). Cognitive analytic therapy and the transtheoretical framework. In K. J. Miller & J. S. Mizes (Eds.), *Comparative treatments for eating disorders* (pp. 283–309). New York: Springer.

Chapter 7

Anderson, H., & Goolishian, H. (1992). The client is the expert: A not-knowing approach to therapy. In S. McNamee & K. J. Gergen (Eds.), *Therapy as social construction* (pp. 25–39). London: Sage.

Colton, A., & Pistrang, N. (2004). Adolescents' experiences of inpatient treatment for anorexia nervosa. *European Eating Disorders Review, 12*, 307–316.

Feld, R., Woodside, D. B., Kaplan, A. S., Olmsted, M. P., & Carter, J. C. (2001). Pretreatment motivational enhancement therapy for eating disorders: A pilot study. *International Journal of Eating Disorders, 29*, 393–400.

Gladding, S. T., Remley, T. P., & Huber, C. H. (2001). *Ethical, legal and professional issues in the practice of marriage and family therapy* (3rd ed.). Upper Saddle River, NJ: Merrill Prentice Hall.

Gowers, S. G., & Smyth, B. (2004). The impact of a motivational assessment interview on initial response to treatment in adolescent anorexia nervosa. *European Eating Disorders Review*, *12*, 87–93.

MacDonald, C. (2002). Treatment resistance in anorexia nervosa and the pervasiveness of ethics in clinical decision making. *Canadian Journal of Psychiatry*, *47*, 267–270.

McKenzie, J. M., & Joyce, P. R. (1992). Hospitalization for anorexia nervosa. *International Journal of Eating Disorders*, *11*, 235–241.

Prochaska, J. O., & DiClemente, C. C. (1983). Stages and processes of self-change in smoking: Toward an integrative model of change. *Journal of Consulting and Clinical Psychology*, *5*, 390–395.

Prochaska, J. O., DiClemente, C. C., & Norcross, J. C. (1992). In search of how people change: Applications to addictive behaviours. *American Psychologist*, *47*, 1102–1114.

Rathner, G. (1998). A plea against compulsory treatment of anorexia nervosa patients. In W. Vandereycken & P. J. V. Beumont (Eds.), *Treating eating disorders—Ethical, legal and personal issues* (pp.179–215). New York: New York University Press.

Tan, J., Hope, R. A., & Stewart, A. (2003a). Anorexia nervosa and personal identity: The accounts of patients and their parents. *International Journal of Law and Psychiatry*, *26*, 533–548.

Tan, J., Hope, R. A., & Stewart, A. (2003b). Competence to refuse treatment in anorexia nervosa. *International Journal of Law and Psychiatry*, *26*, 697–707.

Tan, J., Hope, R. A., Stewart, A., & Fitzpatrick, R. (2003). Control and compulsory treatment in anorexia nervosa: The views of patients and parents. *International Journal of Law and Psychiatry*, *26*, 627–645.

Treasure, J., & Ward, A. (1997). A practical guide to the use of motivational interviewing in anorexia nervosa. *European Eating Disorders Review*, *5*, 102–114.

Vitousek, K., Watson, S., & Wilson, G. T. (1998). Enhancing motivation for change in treatment-resistant eating disorders. *Clinical Psychology Review, 18*, 391–420.

Chapter 8

Andersson, M. (1995). Mother–daughter connection: The healing force in the treatment of eating disorders. *Journal of Feminist Family Therapy, 6*(4), 3–11.

Bowen, M. (1978). *Family therapy in clinical practice.* Northvale, NJ: Jason Aronson.

Hong Kong SAR Government. (2001). *Census report.* Hong Kong: Author.

Lau, Y. K. 劉玉琼, Ma, J. L. C. 馬麗莊, & Chan, Y. K. 陳膺強 (2002, October). *Women's concept of family in Hong Kong: A comparison of the objective and subjective definitions of family* 香港婦女的家庭觀念：客觀家庭結構與主觀家庭觀念比較. Paper presented at the Conference in Social Welfare Development of the Mainland, Hong Kong, Macau and Taiwan, Hong Kong.

Lau, Y. K. 劉玉琼, Ma, J. L. C. 馬麗莊, & Chan, Y. K. 陳膺強 (2006). The care of the elderly for Hong Kong families 香港家庭有關老人奉養的安排：養兒防老抑或自求多福？ In H. C. Yi 伊慶春 & Y. W. Chen 陳玉華 (Eds.), *The family status of Chinese women: Taiwan, Tianjin, Shanghai and Hong Kong compared* 華人婦女家庭地位：台灣、天津、上海、香港之比較 (pp. 269–306). Beijing: Social Sciences Academic Press.

Luepnitz, D. A. (1988). *The family interpreted.* New York: Basic Books.

Miller, R. B., Anderson, S., & Keala, D. K. (2004). Is Bowen theory valid? A review of basic research. *Journal of Marital and Family Therapy, 30*, 453–466.

Minuchin, S. (1978). *Families and family therapy.* London: Tavistock.

Wen, C. I., Chang, Y. H., Chang, L. Y., & Chu, C. (1989). Family structure and its related variables: A case of Taipei. In C. C. Yi & C. Chu (Eds.), *Social phenomena in Taiwan: An analysis* (pp. 1–24). Taipei: Institute of Social Science and Philosophy, Academia Sinica Press.

Wong, F. M. (1975). Industrialization and family structure in Hong Kong. *Journal of Marriage and Family, 37*, 985–1000.

Zhu, S. K 祝瑞開. (1999). *The history of marriage and families in China* 中國婚姻家庭史. Shanghai: Xue Lin.

Chapter 9

Bruch, H. (1973). *Eating disorders*. New York: Basic Books.

Eisler, I. (1995). Family models of eating disorders. In G. Szmukler, C. Dare, & J. Treasure (Eds.), *Handbook of eating disorders: Theory, treatment and research* (pp. 155–176). Chichester, UK: John Wiley.

Heaven, P. C. L. (1994). *Contemporary adolescence: A social psychological approach*. Melbourne: Macmillan.

Nichols, M. P., & Fellenberg, S. (2000). The effective use of enactments in family therapy: A discovery-oriented process study. *Journal of Marital and Family Therapy, 26*, 143–152.

Paxton, S. J. (1999). Peer relationships, body image, and disordered eating in adolescent girls: Implications for prevention. In N. Piran, M. P. Levine, & C. Steiner-Adair (Eds.), *Preventing eating disorders* (pp. 134–147). New York: Brunner/Mazel.

Sprenkle, D. H., & Blow, A. J. (2004). Common factors and our sacred models. *Journal of Marital and Family Therapy, 30*, 113–129.

Stierlin, H., & Weber, G. (1989). *Unlocking the family door: A systemic approach to the understanding and treatment of anorexia nervosa*. New York: Brunner/Mazel.

Treasure, J. (1997). *Anorexia nervosa: A survival guide for families, friends and sufferers*. Hove, UK: Psychology Press.

Chapter 10

Gard, M. C. E., & Freeman, C. P. (1996). The dismantling of a myth: A review of eating disorders and socioeconomic status. *International Journal of Eating Disorders, 20*, 1–12.

McClelland, L., & Crisp, A. (2001). Anorexia nervosa and social class. *International Journal of Eating Disorders, 29*, 150–156.

Micucci, J. A. (1998). *The adolescent in family therapy.* New York: Guilford.

Minuchin, P., Colapinto, J., & Minuchin, S. (1998). *Working with families of the poor.* New York: Guilford.

Nichols, M. P., & Fellenberg, S. (2000). The effective use of enactments in family therapy: A discovery-oriented process study. *Journal of Marital and Family Therapy, 26*, 143–152.

Sampson, R. J., & Laub, J. H. (1998). Urban poverty and the family context of delinquency. In R. F. Muuss & H. D. Porton (Eds.), *Adolescent behavior and society* (5th ed., pp. 118–135). New York: McGraw-Hill.

Chapter 11

Bruch, H. (1973). *Eating disorders.* New York: Basic Books.

Cole, C. L. (2005). Understanding qualitative research and ethnomethodology. *Forum Qualitative Sozialforschung/Forum: Qualitative Social Research, 6*(3), Article 12. Retrieved March 24, 2011, from http://www. Qualitative-research.net/fqs-exte/3-05-/05-3-12-e.htm/.

Krautter, T., & Lock, J. (2004). Is manualized family-based treatment for adolescent anorexia nervosa acceptable to patients? Patient satisfaction at the end of treatment. *Journal of Family Therapy, 26*, 66–82.

Krippendorff, K. (1980). *Content analysis: An introduction of its methodology.* Beverly Hills, CA: Sage.

Leung, S. S., Cole, T. J., Tse, L. Y., & Lau, J. T. (1998). Body mass index reference curves for Chinese children. *Annals of Human Biology, 25*, 169–174.

Ma, J. L. C., & Lai, K. (2006). Perceived treatment effectiveness of family therapy for Chinese patients suffering from anorexia nervosa: A qualitative inquiry. *Journal of Family Social Work, 10*(2), 59–74.

Ma, J. L. C., & Lai, K. (2009). Applicability of family therapy for Chinese children and adolescents suffering from anorexia nervosa in a Chinese context: A preliminary study. *Social Work in Mental Health, 7*, 402–423.

Miles, M. B., & Huberman, A. M. (1994). *An expanded sourcebook qualitative data analysis* (2nd ed.). London: Sage.

van Furth, E. F., van Strien, D. C., Martina, L. M. L., van Son, M. J. M., Hendrick, J. J. P., & van Engeland, H. (1996). Expressed emotion and the prediction of outcome in adolescent eating disorders. *International Journal of Eating Disorders, 20*, 19–31.

Yin, R. (1994). *Case study research design and methods* (2nd ed.). Thousand Oaks, CA: Sage.

Chapter 12

Cecchin, G. (1987). Hypothesizing, circularity, neutrality revisited: An invitation to curiosity. *Family Process, 26*, 405–413.

Feng, J. C 馮驥才. (2002). *Three-inch golden lotus* 三寸金蓮. Beijing: Author Publishers.

Fishman, H. C. (2006). Juvenile anorexia nervosa: Family therapy's natural niche. *Journal of Marital and Family Therapy, 32*, 405–514.

Ko, D. (2005). *Cinderella's sisters: A revisionist history of foot binding*. Berkeley: University of California Press.

Ma, J. L. C. (2008). Patients' perspective of family therapy in anorexia nervosa: A qualitative inquiry in a Chinese Context. *Australian and New Zealand Journal of Family Therapy, 29*, 10–16.

MacSween, M. (1993). *Anorexic bodies: A feminist and sociological perspective on anorexia nervosa*. New York: Routledge.

Minuchin, S., Nichols, M., & Lee, W. Y. (2007). *Assessing families and couples: From symptoms to system*. Upper Saddle River, NJ: Pearson.

Minuchin, S., Rosman, B. L., & Baker, L. (1978). *Psychosomatic families: Anorexia nervosa in context*. Cambridge, MA: Harvard University Press.

Moustakas, C. (1994). *Phenomenological research methods*. Thousand Oaks, CA: Sage.

Penn, P. (1982). Circular questioning. *Family Process, 21,* 267–280.

Stierlin, H., & Weber, G. (1989). *Unlocking the family door: A systemic approach to the understanding and treatment of anorexia nervosa*. New York: Brunner/Mazel.

Tseng, W. S., Lin, T. Y., & Yeh, E. K. (1995). Chinese societies and mental health. In T. Y. Lin, W. S. Tseng, & E. K. Yeh (Eds.), *Chinese societies and mental health* (pp. 3–18). Hong Kong: Oxford University Press.

Appendix 1

Beresin, E. V., Gordon, C., & Herzog, D. B. (1989). The process of recovering from anorexia nervosa. *American Academy of Psychoanalysis, 17,* 103–130.

Bruch, H. (1973). *Eating disorders*. New York: Basic Books.

Chen, G. M. (2002). The impact of harmony on Chinese conflict management. In G. M. Chen & R. Ma (Eds.), *Chinese conflict management and resolution* (pp. 3–18). Westport, CT: Ablex.

Devlin, M. J., & Walsh, T. (1995). Medication treatment for eating disorders. *Journal of Mental Health, 4,* 459–469.

Garrett, C. J. (1996). Recovery from anorexia nervosa: A Durkheimian interpretation. *Social Science and Medicine, 43,* 1489–1506.

Hong Kong SAR Government. (2001). *Census report*. Hong Kong: Author.

Hong Kong SAR Government. (2005). *Hong Kong statistics report.* Hong Kong: Author.

Hsu, L. K. G., Crisp, A. H., & Callender, J. S. (1992). Recovery in anorexia nervosa—The patient's perspective. *International Journal of Eating Disorders, 11,* 341–350.

Hung, O. L. 孔愛玲. (2001). Establishing a Chinese modernized indicators 關於建立有中國特色的現代化水評價指標體系的探索. In S. K. Lau 劉兆佳, P. S. Wan 尹寶珊, M. K. Lee 李明堃, & S. L. Wong 黃紹倫 (Eds.), *Social transformation and cultural change in Chinese societies* 社會轉型與文化變貌 (pp. 17–40). Hong Kong: The Chinese University Press.

Laird, J. (1995). Family-centered practice in the postmodern era. *Families in Societies, 76,* 150–162.

Lee, S. (1993). Gastric emptying and bloating in anorexia nervosa. *British Journal of Psychiatry, 163,* 128–129.

Lee, S. (1997). How lay is lay? Chinese students' perceptions of anorexia nervosa in Hong Kong. *Social Science and Medicine, 44,* 491–502.

Lee, S., Ho, T. P., & Hsu, L. K. G. (1993). Fat phobic and non-fat phobic anorexia nervosa—A comparative study of 70 Chinese patients in Hong Kong. *Psychological Medicine, 23,* 999–1017.

Lee, S., & Lee, A. M. (2000). Disordered eating in three communities of China: A comparative study of female high school students in Hong Kong, Shenzhen, and rural Hunan. *International Journal of Eating Disorders, 27,* 317–327.

Lee, S., Lee, A. M., Leung, T., & Yu, H. (1997). Psychometric properties of the Eating Disorder Inventory (EDI-1) in a non-clinical Chinese population in Hong Kong. *International Journal of Eating Disorders, 21,* 187–194.

Lee, S., Leung, T., Lee, A. M., Yu, H., & Leung, C. M. (1995). Body dissatisfaction among Chinese undergraduates and its implications for eating disorders in Hong Kong. *International Journal of Eating Disorders, 20,* 77–84.

Leung, F., Lam, S., & Chan, I. (2001). Disordered eating attitudes and behaviors among adolescents in Hong Kong. *Journal of Youth Studies, 4*, 36–51.

Lock, J., Le Grange, D., Agras, W. S., & Dare, C. (2001). *Treatment manual for anorexia nervosa: A family-based approach.* New York: Guilford.

Ma, L. C. J., & Chan, Z. C. Y. (2003). The different meanings of food in Chinese patients suffering from anorexia nervosa: Implications for clinical social work practice. *Social Work in Mental Health, 2*, 47–70.

Ma, L. C. J., Chow, M., Lee, S., & Lai, Y. C. K. (2002). Family meaning of self-starvation—Themes discerned in family treatment in Hong Kong. *Journal of Family Therapy, 24*, 57–71.

Miles, M. B., & Huberman, A. M. (1994). *An expanded sourcebook qualitative data analysis* (2nd ed.). London: Sage.

Palazzoli, M. S. (1985). *Self-starvation: From individual to family therapy in the treatment of anorexia nervosa.* Northvale, NJ: Jason Aronson.

Pearson, V., & Leung, B. K. P. (Eds.). (1995). *Women in Hong Kong.* Hong Kong: Oxford University Press.

Rorty, M., Yager, J., & Rossotto, E. (1993). Why and how do women recover from bulimia nervosa? The subjective appraisals of forty women recovered for a year or more. *International Journal of Eating Disorders, 14*, 249–260.

Salaff, J. W. (1998). *Working daughters of Hong Kong.* Cambridge, UK: Cambridge University Press.

Serpell, L., Treasure, P. F., Teasdale, J., & Sullivan, V. (1999). Anorexia nervosa: Friend or foe? *International Journal of Eating Disorders, 25*, 177–186.

Tozzi, F., Sullivan, P. F., Fear, J. L., McKenzie, J., & Bulik, C. M. (2003). Causes and recovery in anorexia nervosa: The patient's perspective. *International Journal of Eating Disorders, 33*, 143–154.

Westwood, R., Mehrain, T., & Cheung, F. (1995). *Gender and society in Hong Kong.* Hong Kong: Hong Kong Institute of Asia-Pacific Studies, The Chinese University of Hong Kong.

Appendix 2

Beresin, E. V., Gordon, C., & Herzog, D. B. (1989). The process of recovering from anorexia nervosa. *American Academy of Psychoanalysis, 17,* 103–130.

Cheung, F. M. (1995). Facts and myths about somatization among the Chinese. In T. Y. Lin, W. S. Tseng, & E. K. Yeh (Eds.), *Chinese societies and mental health* (pp. 156–166). Hong Kong: Oxford University Press.

Eisler, I. (1996). Combining individual and family therapy in adolescent anorexia nervosa: A family systems approach. In J. Werne & I. D. Yalom (Eds.), *Treating eating disorders* (pp. 217–257). San Francisco: Jossey-Bass.

Eisler, I. (2005). The empirical and theoretical base of family therapy and multiple family day therapy for adolescent anorexia nervosa. *Journal of Family Therapy, 27,* 104–131.

Ma, J. L. C. (2005). The diagnostic and therapeutic uses of family conflicts in a Chinese context: The case of anorexia nervosa. *Journal of Family Therapy, 27,* 24–42.

Scott, D. (1997). The researcher's personal responses as a source of insight in the research process. *Nursing Inquiry, 4,* 130–134.

Tozzi, F., Sullivan, P. F., Fear, J. L., McKenzie, J., & Bulik, C. M. (2003). Causes and recovery in anorexia nervosa: The patient's perspective. *International Journal of Eating Disorders, 33,* 143–154.

Index